John Calvin, Myth and Reality

John Calvin, Myth and Reality

IMAGES AND IMPACT
OF GENEVA'S REFORMER

Papers of the
2009 Calvin Studies
Society Colloquium

Edited by
AMY NELSON BURNETT

CASCADE *Books* • Eugene, Oregon

JOHN CALVIN, MYTH AND REALITY
Images and Impact of Geneva's Reformer
Papers of the 2009 Calvin Studies Society Colloquium

Copyright © 2011 Amy Nelson Burnett. All rights reserved. Except for brief quotations in critical publications or reviews, no part of this book may be reproduced in any manner without prior written permission from the publisher. Write: Permissions, Wipf and Stock Publishers, 199 W. 8th Ave., Suite 3, Eugene, OR 97401.

Cascade Books
A Division of Wipf and Stock Publishers
199 W. 8th Ave., Suite 3
Eugene, OR 97401
www.wipfandstock.com

ISBN 13: 978-1-60899-693-3

Cataloging-in-Publication data

John Calvin, Myth and Reality.

John Calvin, myth and reality : images and impact of Geneva's reformer ; papers of the 2009 Calvin Studies Society colloquium / edited by Amy Nelson Burnett.

xvi + 256 p.; 23 cm.—Includes bibliographical references and indexes.

ISBN 13: 978-1-60899-693-3

1. Calvin, Jean, 1509–1564. 2. Calvinism. I. Burnett, Amy Nelson. II. Calvin Studies Society. III. Title.

BX9422 .B87 2011

Manufactured in the USA.

In memory of Robert M. Kingdon (1927–2010)

Genevan 500
"With Weight and Majesty"

Contents

Abbreviations · ix

List of Contributors · xi

Introduction · xiii
   Amy Nelson Burnett

PART 1   Calvin: The Man and His Work

1. Demoting Calvin: The Issue of Calvin and the Reformed Tradition · 3
   Richard A. Muller

2. Calvin Never Changed His Mind—or Did He? Evidence from the Young Reformer's Teaching on Prayer · 18
   Elsie Anne McKee

3. The Good, the Bad, and the Indifferent: Myths, Realities, and Ambiguities in Calvin's Teaching about Women · 37
   John L. Thompson

4. Calvin and Church Discipline: Penance, Apology, and Reconciliation · 53
   Diane C. Margolf

PART 2   Appeal of and Responses to Calvinism

5. The Elders' Gaze: Women and Consistorial Discipline in Late Sixteenth-Century France · 69
   Graeme Murdock

Contents

6. Elements of Calvin's Theology and Practice in the Reformed Churches of Java in the Seventeenth Century · 91
   Yudha Thianto

7. A Devil's Siren or an Angel's Throat? The Pipe Organ Controversy among the Calvinists · 107
   Randall D. Engle

8. "Cruel, Cold and False": Calvin and the Calvinists through the Eyes of Their Dutch Opponents (1566–1619) · 126
   Mirjam G. K. van Veen

9. Calvinism at the Borders of the Empire: Johannes Wigand and the Lutheran Reaction to Calvinism · 139
   Irene Dingel

PART 3   The Impact of Calvin's Ideas

10. Respect for the Word: What Calvin and Wittgenstein Had against Images · 165
    Constantin Fasolt

11. God's Gracious Provision: Calvin and His Heirs on Political Order · 191
    David T. Koyzis

12. The Doctrine of Scripture in the Calvinist Churches in Korea · 207
    Jay J. Shim

Bibliography · 225

Index of Persons, Places, and Subjects · 249

Index of Scripture · 255

Abbreviations

Battles, *Institutes* John Calvin, *Institutes of the Christian Religion*, ed. John T. McNeill, trans. Ford Lewis Battles, 2 vols., Library of Christian Classics 20–21. Philadelphia: Westminster, 1960

CO *Joannis Calvini Opera quae supersunt omnia*. Edited by Wilhelm Baum et al. Corpus Reformatorum 29–87. Braunschweig: Schwetschke, 1863–1900

CR *Philippi Melanthonis Opera quae supersunt omnia*. Edited by Karl Bretschneider et al. Corpus Reformatorum 1–28. Halle, 1834–1860; New York: Johnson, 1963

CSEL *Corpus Scriptorum Ecclesiasticorum Latinorum*. Vienna: Österreichische Akademie der Wissenschaften, 1866–

LB *Desiderii Erasmi Roterodami Opera Omnia*. Edited by Jean Le Clerc. Leiden, 1703–6; repr. London: Gregg, 1962

LW Martin Luther. *Luther's Works*. Edited by Jaroslav Pelikan and Helmut T. Lehmann. St. Louis: Concordia, 1955–1986

MPG *Patrologiae cursus completus, Series Graeca*. Edited by J. P. Migne. Paris, 1857–1866

MPL *Patrologiae cursus completus, Series Latina*. Edited by J. P. Migne. Paris, 1844–1864

Abbreviations

OS	*Joannis Calvini Opera Selecta*. Edited by P. Barth et al. Munich: Kaiser, 1926–1959
PI	*Philosophical Investigations*. Translated by G. E. M. Anscombe. 3rd ed. New York: Macmillan, 1958
Selected Works	*Selected Works of John Calvin*. Edited by H. Beveridge and Jules Bonnet. Calvin Translation Society. Edinburgh: Calvin Translation Society, 1844–1858. Grand Rapids: Baker, 1983
TRE	*Theologische Realenzyklopädie*. Edited by Gerhard Müller. Berlin: de Gruyter, 1977–2004
WA	Martin Luther, *Werke: Kritische Gesamtausgabe*. Weimar: Böhlaus Nachfolger, 1883–1986
Z	*Huldreich Zwinglis sämtliche Werke*. Corpus Reformatorum 88–101. Leipzig: Heinsius, 1905–1991

List of Contributors

Amy Nelson Burnett, Professor of History at the University of Nebraska–Lincoln

Irene Dingel, Director of the Institute for European History, Division for Western Religious History, in Mainz and Professor of Church History at the University of Mainz (Germany)

Randall D. Engle, pastor of North Hills Christian Reformed Church, Troy, Michigan

Constantin Fasolt, Karl J. Weintraub Professor of History and the College at the University of Chicago, Chicago, Illinois

David T. Koyzis, Professor of Political Science at Redeemer University College, Ancaster, Ontario (Canada)

Diane C. Margolf, Professor of History at Colorado State University, Fort Collins, Colorado

Elsie Anne McKee, Archibald Alexander Professor of Reformation Studies and the History of Worship at Princeton Theological Seminary, Princeton, New Jersey

Richard A. Muller, P. J. Zondervan Professor of Historical Theology at Calvin Theological Seminary, Grand Rapids, Michigan

Graeme Murdock, Lecturer in History at Trinity College Dublin (Ireland)

Jay J. Shim, Professor of Theology at Dordt College, Sioux Center, Iowa

List of Contributors

Yudha Thianto, Professor of Theology at Trinity Christian College, Palos Heights, Illinois

John L. Thompson, Professor of Historical Theology and Gaylen and Susan Byker Professor of Reformed Theology at Fuller Theological Seminary, Pasadena, California

Mirjam G. K. van Veen, Professor of Church History and Dutch History at the Free University of Amsterdam (Netherlands)

Introduction

AMY NELSON BURNETT

Jean Calvin has long had an image problem. While modern audiences may have a positive attitude towards Martin Luther, their views of Calvin are more ambivalent. Geneva's reformer is recognized as one of the great religious thinkers of the early modern period and as a founding father of the Reformed branch of Protestantism and thus of those denominations that have had the greatest influence on American culture. At the same time, he is associated with the distasteful doctrine of double predestination, with the burning of Michael Servetus and religious intolerance more generally, and with strict self-discipline and the intrusive oversight of individual conduct.

These opposing evaluations of Calvin and his legacy are not new but stand in a long tradition of either glorifying or demonizing the reformer of Geneva.[1] The two views can in fact be found in the earliest biographies published after Calvin's death, one by his colleague and successor as leader of Geneva's church, Theodore Beza, and the other by his bitter opponent, Jerome Bolsec.[2] Complicating the picture further, the common use of the term *Calvinism* for the Reformed branch of Protestantism has caused many to credit or blame the Genevan reformer for ideas and practices that should more properly be attributed to his contemporaries and successors in Switzerland, Germany, the

---

1. Among Calvin's recent biographers, Gordon, *Calvin*, 336–39; McGrath, *A Life of John Calvin*, xiii–xv; and Strohm, *Johannes Calvin*, 6–10, discuss these contrasting views of Calvin.

2. Backus, *Life Writing*, 125–86.

Introduction

Netherlands, and the British Isles.[3] And as if that were not enough cause for confusion, at the beginning of the twentieth century the German sociologist Max Weber identified Calvinism with a specific mindset that encouraged capitalism and more rapid economic growth in those areas of Europe and North America most influenced by Reformed Christianity.[4] *Calvinism* thus became shorthand not only for a particular theological tradition but also for an entire set of cultural values and practices that owed as much to developments after Calvin's death as they did to Calvin himself. The result of all of these developments is a popular image of Calvin that has its roots in historical reality, but that has taken on a life of its own. The man is buried beneath the myth.

How does one begin to separate myth from reality? The 2009 Colloquium of the Calvin Studies Society, held to commemorate the five-hundredth anniversary of the reformer's birth, brought together thirteen scholars from a variety of disciplines to discuss the disparities between Calvin's real and his imagined impact. The results are collected in this volume.[5]

The chapters are divided into three sections. Those in part 1 all address popular modern images of Calvin, whether positive or negative. Richard Muller opens the discussion by challenging those theologians who have attributed to Calvin a timeless theology that transcends his own day. Muller's examination of references to Calvin in works by later Reformed theologians enables him to make a more accurate assessment of Calvin's role in the formation of the Reformed tradition. Elsie McKee takes on the view of Calvin as a static thinker whose theology remained unchanged over the course of his career. Her careful study of Calvin's use of 1 Tim 2:1-10 in his commentaries, sermons, and successive editions of the *Institutes* shows how his teaching on public prayer evolved in tandem with his pastoral experience and his growing knowledge of the exegetical tradition. John Thompson tackles the popular view of Calvin's teaching on women and shows how easily distortions in that view have arisen from failure to examine Calvin's own writings and

---

3. Benedict, *Christ's Churches*, xxii-iii.

4. Weber, *The Protestant Ethic*; Benedict, "Two Calvinisms," 208-28; Hamilton, "Max Weber's Protestant Ethic," 151-71.

5. The paper presented at the colloquium by Mark Valeri, "Calvin and the Social Order in Early America: Moral Ideals and Transatlantic Empire," is published in Davis, *John Calvin's American Legacy*, 19-41.

Introduction

to place them within their sixteenth-century context. Finally, Diane Margolf describes the workings of the Geneva Consistory not as an instrument of repression, as it has often been depicted, but as a means of promoting social reconciliation, with striking parallels to the Roman Catholic sacrament of confession and to the public apologies of politicians, preachers, and celebrities today.

In part 2, our attention moves from Calvin and Geneva to the spread of Calvinism more generally in the sixteenth and seventeenth centuries. The first two essays look at how institutions and practices developed by Calvin in Geneva were established in Reformed churches elsewhere. Graeme Murdock's case study describes efforts by the consistory of Nîmes to impose Reformed standards of dress and appearance on the female members of the congregation. Yudha Thianto compares church ordinances, confessions, and catechisms to show how practices and institutions moved from Geneva to the Netherlands to the Dutch East Indies. Randall Engle's essay shifts the focus slightly. While Murdoch and Thianto look particularly at continuities in Calvinist practices, Engle points to discontinuities between Calvin's attitude towards church music and the use of the organ in the Reformed churches of the Dutch Republic. The remaining two essays in this section look at negative reactions to Calvinism. Mirjam van Veen describes the negative stereotype of Calvin and the Reformed Church held in common by all of its Dutch opponents, whether Catholic, Anabaptist, Arminian, or Neutralist. Irene Dingel discusses the polemical works of the German theologian Johannes Wigand as a way to explain why Lutherans reacted with such hostility to the spread of Calvinism both within and on the borders of the Holy Roman Empire.

The final three chapters look especially at Calvin's ideas and their impact into the twentieth century. Constantin Fasolt finds intriguing parallels between Calvin and Ludwig Wittgenstein in their respective understanding of the relationship between self and reality. David Koyzis traces the impact of Calvin's political thought from Hugo Grotius and Johannes Althusius in the early modern period to modern interpreters of the nineteenth-century Dutch statesman and theologian Abraham Kuyper. Last but not least, Jay Shin examines the disagreement concerning Scripture between Hyungryong Park and Jaejoon Kim, two central figures in the Korean Presbyterian Church in the mid-twentieth century.

Introduction

Taken together, these essays both contribute to and reflect the current and ongoing re-evaluation of Calvin's importance and his impact in the five centuries since his birth. Their careful consideration of primary sources and historical context make it easier for us to separate myth from reality and to appreciate the genuine contribution of Geneva's reformer to the shaping of Reformed Christianity and culture.

The Calvin Studies Society would like to thank Calvin College and Calvin Theological Seminary in Grand Rapids, Michigan, which jointly hosted the 2009 colloquium, and the Calvin Center for Christian Scholarship and the Nagel Institute for the Study of World Christianity at Calvin College for providing additional financial support. Special thanks are due to Karin Maag and the staff of the H. Henry Meeter Center for Calvin Studies at Calvin College for taking care of local arrangements and ensuring that everything ran smoothly during the colloquium. Randall Engle contributed his arrangement of "Calvin's 500th," which added a note of levity to an otherwise staid academic gathering.

One familiar figure was missing from the scholars who were present for the 2009 Colloquium. Robert M. Kingdon was unable to attend due to health reasons, and he passed away in December 2010. Bob played a central role in advancing the study of Jean Calvin and Geneva not just in North America but also internationally, and the officers of the Calvin Studies Society would like to dedicate this volume to his memory in appreciation for his many years of scholarship and of service to the Society.

PART 1

Calvin: The Man and His Work

1

Demoting Calvin
The Issue of Calvin and the Reformed Tradition

RICHARD A. MULLER

2009 was the year of *promoting Calvin*. It therefore merits some attention that Calvin himself did not seek promotion. He yearned for the quiet life of a scholar and profoundly appreciated his few years of respite in Strasbourg between his sometimes-tumultuous years in Geneva. He did not choose a leadership role but had it thrust upon him. He was, despite his prominence, a retiring personality who attended nearly all Consistory meetings but seldom spoke. And he was buried, by his own wish, in an unmarked grave.[1] The year's celebrations, which included encomia on his theological greatness and his importance to education, political theory, philosophy, modern science, and a host of other fields to which his work was only tangentially related, would be less than pleasing to him—and, by the way, less than historically accurate. The title of this volume, *Calvin—Myth and Reality*, perhaps provides a mo-

---

1. Among the English-language biographies of Calvin, three are to be recommended: Cottret, *Calvin*, offers a fresh and insightful look at Calvin's life; Parker, *John Calvin*, offers significant analysis of the chronology of Calvin's early years, a careful and balanced survey of his life, and a sound reading of the *Institutes*; Walker, *John Calvin*, written at Calvin's four-hundredth centenary, remains notable for its grasp of the sources and its detail.

ment of salutary caution, if the myth and the reality are not confused, and as long as it is not the myth that is promoted.

Mythology and the Need for a Demotion

There is perhaps no better way to begin a presentation of this theme than with the following characterization of Calvin's work by a noted writer of the twentieth century: "It belongs to the great merit of John Calvin that he worked out the difficult transition from the medieval mode of thinking in theology to the modern mode, and placed the theology of Reform on a scientific basis . . . Calvin made such a forward advance in theological thinking that he outstripped his contemporaries by centuries, with the result that they tended to fall back upon an old Aristotelian framework, modified by Renaissance humanism, in order to interpret him. Thus there was produced what history has called 'Calvinism.'"[2]

In short, Calvin's contemporaries and successors simply could not grasp his insight. When he used the same words and phrases, the same technical terms and distinctions that other thinkers of the sixteenth and seventeenth centuries used, indeed, when he entered into dialogue and debate with them, he clearly filled his words with utterly different meanings, leaving their proper interpretation to the twentieth century! Add to this a comment such as,

> history is at least as much subject as object, at least as much here in my eyes as there in the sources. The historical Calvin is not a fixed, finished, dead entity imprisoned in the years 1509–64 and unable to leave them. The fifty-nine volumes of the *Corpus Reformatorum* that contain his works are not secretly his coffin. In Calvin studies, we cannot keep to what he once said as though he had nothing more or new to say today! His work did not simply occur then; it still occurs today. In what he once said he still speaks, saying what he once wanted to say. We may not speak merely of Calvin's historical impact; Calvin himself has an ongoing history into which we insert ourselves when we deal with him.[3]

2. Torrance, "Knowledge of God," 76.
3. Barth, *The Theology of John Calvin*, 6–7.

Why study Calvin as a thinker of the past when we can experience the *event* of Calvin today?

Some, to be sure, have reveled in such language. And that is quite unfortunate, as is a good deal of the theological literature on Calvin that either explicitly or implicitly takes such an approach: Calvin's theology is presented as if, from early on in his career, he knew intimately and in detail the whole body of Christian doctrine, as if he had mastered (prior to rejecting it) the medieval Scholastic tradition in philosophy as well as theology, as if he began writing with a profound knowledge of the fathers of the early church, as if his thought was in no way dependent on the work of predecessors and contemporaries—and, indeed, as if he utterly transcended his time. His patterns of expression, his theological arguments, and his exegetical conclusions are read out into dialogue with modern theology and philosophy as if they fit easily into modern modes of thought.

As if Calvin did not live, think, and learn within an early sixteenth-century context . . . As if he were not a product of his own education, its breadth and its limitations . . . As if the Reformed tradition, which had its beginnings before Calvin and that was developed in Calvin's own day not only by Calvin but by a goodly number of other reformers, somewhere, somehow, decided that Calvin was its only normative thinker for the space of approximately three centuries. Sadly, this ahistorical approach has not simply collapsed under the weight of its own mythology. It has become its own self-sustaining trajectory in what we somewhat facetiously call Calvin studies.

By way of example, a very recent study presents Calvin's theology, seldom citing anything other than the *Institutes*. It labors at ignoring Calvin's predecessors and contemporaries, denies the notion that Calvin ought to be considered as one major codifier of the Reformed tradition among others, identifies Calvin as "the greatest systematic thinker" of his era whose theology is a "complete and sufficient subject" for investigation, characterizes the 1559 *Institutes* as "a single text to study by which every exposition can be judged," and, without having examined any of the texts of later Reformed theologians, reiterates the old "Calvin against the Calvinists" theme. The author concludes his set of undocumented assertions with the comment that "Calvin is not a Calvinist because union with Christ is at the heart of his theology—

not theirs."[4] What our author might have found out had he researched other sixteenth- and seventeenth-century sources is that union with Christ was not the sole property of Calvin in his own time, remained a rather significant focus of later Reformed theology and piety, and was developed by seventeenth-century writers often in a fullness not found in Calvin.[5] And, of course, had he not so thoroughly decontextualized and dogmatized Calvin, he might not have tried to contort union with Christ into a new central dogma or structural principle for the *Institutes*.[6]

The Calvin presented by these three authors is a mythological being: Calvin abstracted from and elevated out of his context, speaking not to his contemporaries but to the twentieth or twenty-first century, and doing so without reference to the very tradition that somewhat unwillingly permitted the name *Calvinist* to replace its chosen title, *Reformed* or, indeed, as many sixteenth- and seventeenth-century sources would have it, *Reformed Catholic*. As for the method of such studies, it is perhaps best described by a modified form of George Tyrrell's comment about Harnack's *Essence of Christianity*—the authors of this view of Calvin have stared down the well of history and have seen a pious modern Protestant face reflected back at them.

Some Contextual Premises

The Calvin encountered in sixteenth-century documents thought like his sixteenth-century contemporaries: he framed his work in terms of an Aristotelianism modified both by centuries of Christian meditation and by developments in Renaissance philosophy and method, notably some Stoic and Platonic strains. He was trained, not as a theologian, but after a basic bachelor's-degree training in logic, rhetoric, and philosophy, as a lawyer. He began his theological work not as a trained expert but—as his own account clearly indicates—as an amateur who needed

---

4. Partee, *The Theology of John Calvin*, 3, 4, 25, 27.

5. Cf. Farthing, "*De coniugio spirituali*," 621–52; Jones, "Union With Christ," 186–208; Kapic, *Communion with God*; Yuille, *The Inner Sanctum*.

6. Partee, *The Theology of John Calvin*, 40–41, et passim; the approach followed here by Partee is well described as a "mythology of coherence" in Skinner, "Meaning and Understanding," 3–53.

to learn theology as he preached, lectured, and wrote.[7] In his career as an organizer of the Reformation in Geneva, he learned theology in the process of preaching and lecturing through the Bible, augmenting his *Institutes* as he preached and lectured, and defending the Reformation and his own theology in long series of tracts and treatises, mostly polemical. Much of that learning process rested on Calvin's engagement with the thought of other reformers, most notably, Luther, Bucer, Melanchthon, and Bullinger,[8] as can be illustrated not only by a comparison of their works but by the character of their correspondence. Calvin, to make the point simply, was a lot more learned in theology in 1559 as he published the final edition of the *Institutes* than he was in 1536 when he published the first edition.

In the process of this career, he certainly came to know the church fathers quite well, albeit not at the level of fluency of various contemporaries or later Reformed writers—among contemporaries, certainly Wolfgang Musculus and John Jewel;[9] among the later writers, Amandus Polanus von Polansdorf, whose *Syntagma theologiae* evidences a deep and careful reading of the Fathers; or Abraham Scultetus and Andreas Rivetus, both of whom wrote patrologies.[10]

It is unclear how much medieval theology and philosophy Calvin ever mastered—and again, various contemporaries and successors were certainly more adept in these matters as well. Calvin certainly did not have a mastery of the tradition of commentaries on Lombard's *Sentences*, and it is unlikely that he ever read either the *Sentence* commentary or either of the *Summas* of Thomas Aquinas. His later writings contain some accents of Scotus or Scotism, but their source is as yet undetermined. He probably never read the works of Ockham or of John Major as has been sometimes alleged, nor is there any indication (also alleged) that he had an acquaintance with the writings of Richard of Saint Victor. His attacks on "Scholastic" doctrine often do not apply to

---

7. Calvin, *Commentary on the Book of Psalms*, 1: xli.

8. Cf. e.g., Wendel, *Calvin*, 122–44; with Spijker, "Calvin's Friendship," 169–86; Zachman, "Restoring Access," 205–28; Muller, *The Unaccommodated Calvin*, 118–30; Rorem, "Calvin and Bullinger," 155–84, 357–89.

9. Basil, *Opera D. Basilii*; cf. Backus, *Lectures humanistes de Basile de Césarée*, 35–42; and see Jewel, *Defence of the Apologie of the Church of England*, for the full text.

10. Polanus von Polansdorf, *Syntagma theologiae christianae*; Scultetus, *Medulla theologiae patrum*; Rivetus, *Critici sacri libri IV*; on which see Backus, "The Fathers in Calvinist Orthodoxy," 2:839–66.

the major theologians of the medieval period.¹¹ On this issue as well, several of his contemporaries, perhaps most notably Vermigli, were more adept at the tradition than Calvin and more precise both in their critiques and in their appropriations of the medieval Scholastics. The same can be said of many of the Reformed writers in the next several generations.

Calvin's *Institutes*, although the most famous, is but one of several major theological surveys produced in what can be called the second phase of the Reformation: it stands beside the large-scale works of Heinrich Bullinger, Wolfgang Musculus, Peter Martyr Vermigli, and Andreas Hyperius and in a clear and strong relation to the structure and method of Philipp Melanchthon's *Loci communes theologici*.¹² Indeed, comparison of Calvin's *Institutes* with the works of these thinkers reveals that in many ways they were more learned theologically than Calvin, and that on quite a few issues it is they, not Calvin, who set the patterns of argument taken up in the broader Reformed tradition. This influence of Calvin's contemporaries did not arise, moreover, because Calvin was misunderstood in his own time, but because he was rather well understood and, on various issues (free will being one of them) his Reformed contemporaries offered clearer, more stable formulations, more aware both of the traditional arguments and of the actual shape of the question, and therefore not nearly as subject either to misunderstanding or to easy critique as Calvin's.

The *Institutes* and the commentaries were fairly frequently referenced in the seventeenth century, often in tandem with the works of other Reformers of the mid-sixteenth century like Vermigli, Musculus, and Beza—the latter being referenced primarily as a commentator.¹³ A good case can be made, moreover, from an examination of theological works of the later sixteenth and of the seventeenth century, that Calvin's most significant contribution to the Reformed tradition actually came by way of his commentaries—which continued to be cited with regularity throughout the seventeenth century.¹⁴ The point is simply that

11. See Muller, *The Unaccommodated Calvin*, 39–61, on Calvin's approach to "scholasticism."

12. See Muller, "*Ordo docendi*," 123–40.

13. E.g., Turretin, *Institutio theologiae elencticae*, VI.vii.7; viii.5, 8; IX.ix.17, 40, 42; XII.viii.6; x.18.

14. Cf. Leigh, *A Systeme or Body of Divinity*, I.iii (41–51); iv (55); ix (138); Witsius,

Calvin, when properly set into his context, can be seen to have belonged to a group of major formulators or codifiers of the doctrine and practice of the Reformation and to have been a major contributor to the confessions and church orders that served to structure the process of confessionalization evidenced in the latter part of the sixteenth century. He was one among several significant thinkers of his generation, a codifier and framer of the Reformation, sometimes but not always *primus inter pares*, and consistently a voice in the broader conversations of the Reformers with one another.

Calvin in the Conversation

A rather significant index to this issue of Calvin's place among his contemporaries lies in his correspondence. This correspondence, the scope of which cannot even be fully inferred from the *Calvini Opera*, evidences a network of Reformers writing to one another concerning the conduct of the Reformation on theological, political, and organizational issues, in which Calvin appeared quite clearly as a central figure, but not as an authority to whom the others appeal. Bucer consistently appears as the elder statesman of reform, deeply respected by Calvin, often offering advice in theological matters. Melanchthon's letters present a picture sometimes of proximity of views (as in the case of the Lord's Supper), sometimes of disagreement and worry or annoyance on both sides (as in the case of predestination). Bullinger's letters evidence mutual respect but also can assume a tone of superiority and occasionally condescension. Laski's letters indicate a sense of parity and a genuine unwillingness to adjust eucharistic language merely to please Calvin. What is more, the nature of the Reformation correspondence is mistaken if the letters are read as a series of fellow Reformers in correspondence with Calvin: there are letters from Bullinger to Laski, Laski to Hardenburg, Hardenburg to Melanchthon, Melanchthon to Cranmer, Cranmer to Bucer and Vermigli, Vermigli to Bucer, and so forth, all related to the issues raised by and with Calvin in his letters to these same leaders of the Reformation—but never with Calvin as the focus. In other words, no single theologian is the center of this correspondence, and focus on a single writer as the center obscures the nature of the whole.

De oeconomia foederum Dei, I.vii.8, 12; III.iii.2; iv.19; viii.26; xi.10; IV.iv.24, 34, 48, 50, 52; vi.68; vii.2; xii.33, 34, 44; xiii.4, 15; xv.32; xvi.50; xvii.33.

John Calvin, Myth and Reality

This extensive circle of correspondence points us also to the issue of vocabulary raised briefly with reference to the decontextualizing approach of the several modern writers noted at the outset. The letters of the Reformers point toward a common context of Reform, a continued mutual updating on a broad series of common concerns, the beginnings of confessionalization, and debate over and development of a shared theological vocabulary. Calvin's correspondence with Vermigli and Laski, for example, concerns the establishment of a common eucharistic terminology and, within the boundaries of a general agreement that language concerning "substance, or transfusion, or commingling of parts" was to be ruled out, a significant disagreement over Laski's concentration on language of "communion" and "participation," and adds a note of annoyance over unwillingness to agree fully with Calvin's (and presumably Vermigli's) understanding of predestination.[15] Vermigli also had noted to Bucer the need to establish a suitable language of Christ's presence in the Lord's Supper,[16] and Laski had corresponded with Bucer on communion with Christ in the sacrament, and with Bullinger expressing common ground on the limitation of "reception of the Supper" in private homes.[17]

Another example, as analyzed by Venema, is the correspondence that went on among Calvin, Traheron, and Bullinger concerning the doctrine of predestination.[18] Bullinger worried over the tendency of Calvin's doctrine to set aside an understanding of the universal offer of salvation, and he viewed Calvin as highly incautious in identifying the fall of Adam as divinely decreed, indeed, divinely administered—while to Traheron he stood apart from Melanchthon's more synergistic formulations without being led closer to Calvin by Traheron's advocacy of the Genevan position. Calvin, of course, did not set aside his views but did plead for unity on the doctrine in general. The problem of

---

15. Cf. Laski to Calvin (24 April 1551), in CO 14: 107-8; Laski to Calvin (13 March 1554), in CO 15: 81-84; Calvin to Vermigli (18 Jan. 1555), in CO 15:388 (*Selected Works*, 6:124); and note Laski, *Catechismus ecclesiae Emdanae*, Q & R, 67, in *Joannis a Lasco Opera*, 2:530, with Laski, *Catechismus ecclesiae Londini*, Q. 240, in ibid., 2:468, on the Lord's Supper.

16. Vermigli to Bucer (26 Dec. 1548), in *The Zurich Letters*, 2:470.

17. Laski to Bucer (23 June 1545), in *The Zurich Letters*, 2:591-92; Laski to Bullinger (7 June 1551), in *Opera*, 2:653-55.

18. Venema, *Heinrich Bullinger*, 57-69.

inclusion of the fall in the eternal decree, moreover, was not resolved between Calvin and Bullinger but left as a problem for later generations of Reformed thinkers. They, whether infra- or supralapsarian, would indicate quite consistently that, although the fall must be understood as belonging to the divine decree (given that nothing can exist unless God wills it), it belonged in such a way that its contingency and Adam's freedom were not merely respected but established. In the state of integrity Adam was able to stand or fall, refrain from sinning or sin, and specifically that, *in sensu diviso*, the fall was not necessary: "it was possible for [Adam] to fall or not to fall."[19] The language does not come from Calvin, nor, indeed, from Bullinger. It is rooted in a long-standing tradition of logic and philosophy concerning necessities of the consequence and could be drawn from Vermigli.[20]

Calvin and the Complex of Formulation: Some Reflections

This is not to say that Calvin was without considerable influence both as a commentator and as formulator of doctrine, but it does offer a starting point for taking a suitably historical or contextualized approach to his influence. First, a few words about Calvin as commentator. It is perhaps here that his influence was the greatest in the two centuries after his time. When responding to the accusation that he had depreciated Calvin's theology while recommending Aquinas, Suarez, and Molina, Jacob Arminius affirmed quite strongly his admiration for Calvin, specifically for Calvin the commentator while noting the *Institutes* must be read "with discrimination, as the writings of all men ought to be read."[21] The late sixteenth-century composite commentaries of Augustin Marlorat regularly identify Calvin as one of the primary sources of interpretive opinion.[22] The English commentator John Mayer, whose annotations on the Old and New Testaments focused on texts of difficult or debated

---

19. Maccovius, *Distinctiones et regulae*, viii.2; ix.2; cf. Turretin, *Institutio*, IV.iv.2.

20. Vermigli, *Common Places*, I.xvi.4; cf. ibid., I.xvii on the question of the authorship of sin.

21. Arminius to Sebastian Egberts, 3 May 1607, in van Limborch and Hartsoeker, *Praestantium ac eruditorum virorum epistolae*, Epist. 101; also cited in Brandt, *The Life of James Arminius*, 299-300.

22. E.g., Marlorat, *A Catholike. . . exposition of the Holy Gospell*; and Marlorat, *A Catholike. . . exposition of St. Marke and Luke*.

interpretation, consistently cited Calvin's interpretations as significant and almost as consistently agreed with Calvin.[23] The examples can easily be multiplied. But there is also a need to ask a bit more closely the implication of this fairly consistent valuation of Calvin as a commentator by Protestants of the sixteenth and seventeenth centuries, given that one can also cite exegetical works of the developing Reformed tradition that do not reference Calvin, such as Matthew Poole's *Synopsis Criticorum*—which cites such sixteenth-century scholars as Sebastian Münster and Peter Martyr Vermigli.[24] The reason for use of Calvin in the first mentioned commentaries and for his absence from Poole's work is that Calvin was treasured as a theological commentator, who did not leave a major legacy in biblical philology. Other Reformers of his day wrote the technical commentaries, among the Reformed, most notably Vermigli and Musculus. Calvin did, arguably, set the standard for Reformed theological meditation on Scripture.

In short, Calvin was recognized by contemporaries and successors alike as a major interpreter of the Bible. Recent scholarship has largely set aside the simplistic claims of moderns that Calvin's methods are harbingers of the literal approaches of higher criticism and that Calvin's sense of the narrative line of the biblical history is somehow allied to what is presently thought of as the reconstructed historical context of a text.[25] What can now be seen is that Calvin's methods and results stand in closer relationship with those of predecessors and contemporaries like Bucer, Bullinger, and Melanchthon, and that although in many cases he stands firmly in a particular trajectory of interpretation, his conclusions are not exclusively followed by later Reformed exegetes—including those who stated their admiration for his commentaries. By way of example, Calvin's restraint in christologizing the Psalter stood in continuity with Bucer, but was not invariably followed by later Reformed commentators. Even Calvin's famous distancing of his method from those of Bucer, Bullinger, and Melanchthon stands in a good deal of continuity with their methods inasmuch as he did assume, like Bucer and Bullinger, the need to comment on each verse,

---

23. Mayer, *Commentarie upon the New Testament*; and Mayer, *A Commentary upon the Whole Old Testament*.

24. Poole, *Synopsis criticorum aliorumque sacrae*.

25. Cf. e.g., Steinmetz, *Calvin in Context*; Thompson, *John Calvin*; and Zachman, *John Calvin as Teacher*, 103–30.

and like all three that the exegesis was productive of topical materials to be gathered into theological *loci*: he simply chose not to set these *loci* into his commentaries.

A similarly cautious approach needs to be taken with regard to Calvin's doctrinal influences on later Reformed theology. A fair amount of ink has been spilled in the last thirty or forty years over the relationship of Calvin's thought to later Reformed covenant-theology: writers who have taken covenant to be either a form of legalism or alternatively an antidote to predestinarianism have, for nearly opposite reasons, distanced Calvin from the development of federalism; writers who have identified covenant theology as offering a sense of the unity of the testaments in the proclamation of salvation by grace alone as well as those who have recognized strongly bilateral emphases in Calvin's thought have credited him with an influence on the development of covenant theology. It is probably fair to say, however, that no careful reader of sixteenth- and seventeenth-century texts would view Calvin as the sole progenitor or even the primary inspiration of later federalism.

Calvin's wonderfully clear definition of a covenant of grace, one in substance but several in its administrations, was hardly original to him: nearly identical language can be found in works by Zwingli and Bullinger.[26] He certainly stands as a significant transmitter of the basic definition as also of a rather clear definition of how the covenant has both unilateral and bilateral aspects. As to other issues, Calvin hints briefly at the existence of a prelapsarian covenant and he indicates prelapsarian sacraments, but he never elaborates on these points—that was certainly left to later Reformed writers. He offers an identification of Sinai and the gospel as the legal and evangelical covenants but does not fully work out how a legal covenant can stand within the boundaries of the one covenant of grace in its several administrations—that, again was left to others. Certainly, among his contemporaries Bullinger and Musculus offered more impetus toward the development of covenantal thought than Calvin, and among the later writers, Ursinus, Olevianus, Fenner, Perkins, Cameron, and Rollock (just to mention a few) contributed far more to the flowering of covenantal thought. As in the case of other doctrinal topics, much of Calvin's impact on later argumentation,

---

26. Cf. Calvin, *Institutio*, II.x.2, CO 2:313–14, with Huldrych Zwingli, *Refutation of the Tricks of the Catabaptists*, *Ulrich Zwingli*, 234; and Bullinger, *De testamento seu foedere Dei*, fol. 2r–3r, 28r.

including argumentation found in theological systems, can be traced to the continuing use of his commentaries as offering sound readings of particular texts—and the full impact of Calvin's work on later covenantal thought will be missed by those who read only his *Institutes*.[27]

Certainly Calvin's christological formulations set a pattern for developing Reformed theology. But even here assessment must exercise caution. Calvin gave to the Reformed (and arguably even the Lutheran) tradition an impetus to develop Christology in terms emphasizing the shape of Christ's work, namely, the language of the threefold mediatorial office: prophet, king and priest. As much scholarship has recognized, the idea itself was not new—emphases on various offices of Christ had appeared earlier in the tradition. Eusebius of Caesarea had, in fact, begun his *Ecclesiastical History* with a full reference to Christ's threefold office, and there were references to Christ as prophet, priest, and king in medieval theology.[28] Calvin was, however, the first major writer to draw the full formula into a formal christological exposition—and the model had an enormous impact.[29]

There are, however, several cautionary notes to be sounded concerning the influence of Calvin's Christology. First, the formula, as it became the norm in Reformed circles, moved away from Calvin's ordering—prophet, king, and priest—to an ordering that in the view of later Reformed thinkers better observed the order of Christ's earthly ministry in the revelation of the offices, namely, prophet, priest and king. Second, Calvin's emphasis on the person of the mediator as precisely suited to the office, namely, as necessarily both divine and human, has clear parallels in the work of later Reformed writers. One only need mention Lord's Day Six (qq. 16–17) of the Heidelberg Catechism. But here Calvin's influence is not to be measured in the development of new formulae but in the transmission of old formulae and in the common ground he occupied with his predecessors, contemporaries, and successors. Third, other aspects of Calvin's Christology, notably his way of formulating the language of two natures in one essence or substance, left much to desire from a technical perspective, having a nearly-Nestorian accent at the very point that Calvin is attempting to

27. As, e.g., Baker, *Heinrich Bullinger*, 193–98.

28. Eusebius of Caesarea, *Church History*, I.iii.9, 19; cf. Thomas Aquinas, *Summa theologiae*, III, q. 7, a. 8 (prophet); q. 22, a. 1, ad 3 (lawgiver, priest and king).

29. See the discussion in Franks, *Work of Christ*, 348–51.

avoid the Lutheran charge of Nestorianism, namely, in his initial language of how the two natures effect a person ("Quomodo duae naturae Mediatoria efficiant personam")—although his statements that Christ's person is "constituted" from two natures probably reflect, whether directly or indirectly, John of Damascus's use of *sunthetikos* in the specific context of arguing the anhypostatic character of Christ's humanity.[30] Still, it was left to later Reformed theologians to argue more clearly the standard post-Chalcedonian orthodoxy of the anhypostatic and enhypostatic character of Christ's humanity.[31]

Similar reflections are also called for concerning Calvin's formulation of free choice. Both as an exegete of the relevant biblical passages and as a definer or defender of the doctrine in the *Institutes* and in his various treatises touching the subject, Calvin took his place in an older line of thought and defended its understandings: specifically, he took up the argument for the bondage or servitude of human choice almost precisely where Luther's famous treatise against Erasmus had left it and carried the argument forward against Pighius and others.[32] What is clear here, however, is that neither Luther nor Calvin produced the balanced statement that would become normative for later Protestant thought. Both directed their aim toward the very restricted topic of the inability of human beings freely to choose a meritorious or saving good, and that both made their point so restrictively and hyperbolically that a reading of their works apart from the broader context of definition and conversation on the issue of free choice could lead to the conclusion that human beings can do no good whatsoever. Contemporaries of Calvin, like Musculus and Vermigli, offered more nuanced discussion, stating specifically that there was no debate over the issue of whether human beings have free choice in matters of daily existence, civil conduct, and moral decisions—all but a few philosophers were agreed that the will is free and has both freedom of contradiction and freedom of contrariety.[33] The narrow and debated question was the issue of freedom to choose meritoriously or fully righteously before God—and this

---

30. Calvin, *Institutio*, II.xiv, title and section 5; cf. John of Damascus, *De fide orthodoxa*, III.iv, vi.

31. See the selections in Heppe, *Reformed Dogmatics*, 427–35.

32. Cf. Calvin, *The Bondage and Liberation of the Will*, with Heckel, "'His Spear through My Side.'"

33. Cf. Vermigli, *Common Places*, II.ii; Musculus, *Loci communes*, ix.

the Reformers denied. It was, by he way, Vermigli's and Musculus' understanding that passed over into Reformed orthodoxy.[34]

Some Conclusions

By way of conclusion, I would like to pose and briefly answer the question, Why demote Calvin? Were Calvin not the victim of a kind of dogmatic Peter Principle—namely that he has so often been promoted far beyond the level of his competence—, the demotion would hardly be necessary. The issue is to return to reality (if one is permitted to speak of reality these days) or, at least, to offer a historically situated picture of Calvin and his accomplishments. From the perspective of the three theologians noted earlier, clearly, a historically situated, suitably contextualized approach to Calvin is undesirable. It removes the mythological but (dogmatically speaking) incredibly useful Calvin from their systematic toolkit.

Calvin scholarship, in the incredibly dangerous year of celebration, evidences a series of sometimes mutually exclusive trajectories, at least two of which examine his thought. Among these, there is a historical or intellectual-history trajectory and a dogmatic or theologistic trajectory. From the perspective of the theologistic trajectory, the historical approach involves a significant demotion of Calvin as a thinker because it insists on placing him among his contemporaries as an exegete, organizer, and theologian who came to his task after fundamental directions of the Reform had been established by others, and because it refrains from bestowing on him an absolutely iconic place at the foundation of the Reformed tradition. From the perspective of the historical trajectory, the dogmatic approach involves a rather extreme distortion by way of promotion of Calvin because it insists on abstracting him from his context and examining his thought as if its issues, debates, and very language need not be understood as belonging to a conversation among contemporaries leading toward the formulation of a fairly diverse tradition.

The irony of the theologistic exercise is that in promoting Calvin to the status of sole normative figure for the Reformed tradition, it rather

---

34. E.g., Perkins, "A Treatise of Gods Grace and Mans Free-Will," in *Whole Works*, 1: 704, col. 1; Gomarus, *Disputationem theologicarum decima-quarta*, i; Turretin, *Institutio*, X.iii.4.

effectively *removes* the Reformed tradition. If we create a Calvin who looks incredibly like Schleiermacher or Hodge or Barth or Berkouwer, and remove his theology from the world of Zwingli, Bucer, Bullinger, Vermigli, Beza, Ursinus, Olevianus, Zanchi, and the rest; or if we claim that Calvin was christocentric or focused on union with Christ and that other Reformed theologians were not or did not (without, of course, ever examining them to ascertain their thoughts on the matter or, indeed, without ever examining Calvin himself contextually); or if we focus on *Calvinus solus* and leap over a host of Reformed writers who lived between 1564 and 1800, we have identified a tradition of one, which isn't a tradition at all.

Thus the reason for demoting Calvin—demoting him, in other words, in order to accord him his rightful place in the Reformation of the sixteenth century and in the larger Reformed tradition.

2

Calvin Never Changed His Mind—or Did He?
Evidence from the Young Reformer's Teaching on Prayer

ELSIE ANNE MCKEE

Among the common legends about Calvin is that he never changed his mind. This is not the place to discuss at length the bases for this assumption, but it can be said that one important grounds for such a claim is the way that the reformer has most often been read: as the man of one book, the 1559 *Institutes of the Christian Religion*. In the latter part of the twentieth century it has been recognized that the reformer of Geneva was much more than the author of one book, and that there is development over time as well as variation in the different genres of his writing.[1] It was not simply rhetoric when he said that he was one who wrote as he learned and learned as he wrote.[2] Still, it is uncommon to be able to point to real changes in Calvin's thought. However, that is what this essay would like to propose: to point out one or two small but significant and lasting changes in the teaching of the *Institutes* itself be-

---

1. The expanded use of Calvin's commentaries in teaching and research, and especially the new interest in his sermons, are among the more notable factors, although it is important to recognize that his catechisms and other ecclesiastical and pastoral writings have also received more attention.

2. In 1543 Calvin adds this quotation from Augustine's letters (143, 2) to his letter to the reader in the Latin *Institutes*; OS 3:7. See Augustine, *Letters 100-155*, 302.

tween 1536 and 1539. These are changes brought about by what appears to be a changing perspective on several biblical texts related to prayer.

The first and more important text is 1 Tim 2:1–2, which Calvin quotes in full in the 1536 *Institutes*. The context is chapter six, the topic civil magistrates, and the question whether it is appropriate to pray for rulers: "Paul says: 'I exhort that supplications, prayers, intercessions, and thanksgivings be made for all people; for kings and all who are set in authority, that we may lead a peaceable and quiet life in all piety and honorableness.'"[3]

Praying for kings and others in authority was not itself novel, but it was important in a new way for sixteenth-century Protestants. The primary focus here, however, is verse 1, and especially the issue of whether the prayers in question are liturgical and/or clerical, or nonliturgical and therefore also the practice of laity and/or used in private contexts. These two verses are part of a passage that influences their interpretation for most exegetes. Verses 3 through 7, which indicate that such prayers are pleasing to God, who desires all to be saved, and add a confession of Christ as the sole mediator, are less directly related to the present purpose, but sometimes they play a part. (For example, the phrase about God's desiring all to be saved raises the problem of predestination for at least some writers, Calvin among them. Naturally, the christological confession is much more important in the wider Christian use of these verses than the matter of public or private prayer, but it is not the focus at present.[4]) Verses 8 and 9, however, which describe instructions about men lifting holy hands in prayer, and women covering their heads, are linked more closely to the beginning of the chapter and play a minor role in the present investigation.

---

3. *Institutio* 1536, chap. 6; OS 1:274. Margin has 1 Tim. 2. See Calvin, *Institution 1536*, 235–36. In 1553 and 1559 margin has 1 Tim. 2.a.1.

4. Some notes on how these verses are related to the present text in the commentary: "*God willeth that all men should be saved*. For what could be more reasonable than that all our prayers should be conformed to this decree of God? . . . There is a duty of love to care a great deal for the salvation of all those to whom God extends His call and to testify to this by godly prayers," *The First and Second Epistles . . . to Timothy*, 208–9 = CO 29:268–69. The relative importance of the different parts of the pericope is evident in the fact that the two sermons on 1 Tim. 2:5–6 were published by Girard in 1555, shortly after they were preached and years before the rest of the sermons appeared in print; cf. Peter and Gilmont, *Bibliotheca Calviniana* 2:584, item 55/8.

John Calvin, Myth and Reality

This essay is divided into three main parts. First is an examination of Calvin's use of 1 Tim 2:1–2, 8, in the *Institutes* from 1536 to 1559. The second part is a summary of the relevant exegetical history that Calvin inherited and a brief examination of what he says in the commentary published in 1548 and the sermons from the mid-1550s (1554–1555, published 1561). The third short section examines Calvin's use of 1 Sam 1:13 (Hannah's prayer before the ark of the covenant) as it is used in the *Institutes* and sermons, and places this also in the context of exegetical history. A fuller exegetical study of this material will be presented elsewhere.

Calvin's Teaching on 1 Timothy 2:1–2, 8

Calvin cites or alludes to 1 Tim 2:1 five times in the 1536 *Institutes*. Three of these are marked in sixteenth-century editions, one more is added by modern editors, the fifth is my own contribution. In two cases these are citations of verses 1–2, once of verse 1 with 8, and twice verse 1 appears alone. There is one additional reference each to verse 2 and verse 8. Most citations of verse 1 are found in the chapter on prayer, and those of verse 2 appear in chapter six on civil government.

Several references are fairly general. Calvin cites 1 Tim 2[:1] to identify Paul's way of defining the major categories of prayer, which he understands as two: petition and thanksgiving.[5] A joint reference to 1 Tim 2[:1–2] and James 5[:16] serves as the basis for (living) Christians praying for each other, an act of love.[6] The one previously unnoticed allusion to verse 1 is found in the discussion of the Lord's Prayer where Calvin says that Christians are to pray for all people on

---

5. *Institutio* 1536, chap. 3; OS 1:101: "Orationis (ut hoc nomen nunc accipimus) duae sunt partes: petitio et gratiarum actio. Petitione cordis nostri desideria apud Deum deponimus, petentes ab ipsius bonitate, primum quae ipsius duntaxat gloriae serviunt, deinde quae usibus etiam nostris conducunt (1 Tim. 2). Gratiarum actione ..." Margin has 1 Tim. 2. In 1553 and 1559 margin has 1 Tim. 2.a.1.

6. *Institutio* 1536, chap. 3; OS 1:100: "vicissim alter alterius precibus commendare se possunt (1 Tim 2, James 5)." Margin has 1 Tim. 2, James 5. Calvin, *Institution 1536*, 96, identifies this as 1 Tim 2:1–7, which seems unduly loose. In fact, this is the only 1536 marginal citation of 1 Tim 2 which, along with James 5, disappears from all later editions. Since both texts are dropped from the margin but the language remains, it appears that Calvin decided that the connection between this verse and 1 Tim 2[1–2] and James 5[16] was unnecessary. See below at n. 11 *et passim.* for more on marginal references and their significance.

earth, not just believers or those whom they know.⁷ Naturally, verse 2 is used to emphasize the biblical warrant for praying for kings and other rulers. This topic is very important in the Reformation, but it will be treated more fully in another place.⁸ The ironic reference to verse 8 occurs in Calvin's discussion of false sacraments, where he argues that not all biblical instructions are intended as sacraments. "Paul wishes men to lift up pure hands in every place, and the saints praying with raised hands is often mentioned; and [so] lifting up hands also should be made a sacrament."⁹

The most interesting citation of 1 Tim 2:1 and 8 in 1536 is paired with 1 Thess 5:17 and outlines Calvin's clear distinction between public or liturgical prayer and individual or private prayer.

> This is the reason why Paul elsewhere enjoins us to pray without ceasing (1 Thess. 5, 1 Tim. 2); he wants everyone in every season, every hour, every place, every matter, to raise every prayer to God, to expect all things from Him and to give Him praise for all things, since He constantly provides us with reasons for praising and praying to Him. However, this constancy in praying has regard to each one's own, private prayers; it does not pertain to the public prayers of the church which can neither be constant nor should they be done otherwise than in the way agreed upon in the common polity by all. For it is necessary for human use that certain hours, indifferent to God, are agreed upon and set out so that all may be accommodated and all things

---

7. *Institutio* 1536, chap. 3; OS 1:107: "Ad hanc igitur legem christiani hominis orationem exigi oportet, ut communis sit, ac omnes complectatur, qui illi sunt in Christo fratres. Neque solum quos tales ad praesens videt atque cognoscit, sed omnes qui super terram agunt homines."

8. Besides the quotation of verse 1–2 above at n. 3, there is a second allusion to verse 2 in chapter six on civil rulers about the fruit of praying for magistrates, i.e., a quiet and peaceable life. *Institutio* 1536; OS 1: 270: "ut eius manu ac praesidiis adversus flagitiosorum hominum improbitatem et iniurias defensi, quietam ac securam vitam agamus." This text has no marginal reference, either in 1536 or later, probably because it was considered unnecessary. For a fuller exploration of this, see McKee, "Calvin and Praying," 130–40.

9. *Institutio* 1536, chap. 5; OS 1:218 "Paulus vult in omni loco viros tollere puras manus, et elevatis manibus oratio saepius a sanctis facta memoratur (1 Tim. 2, Psal. 63, 88, 141, 143), et manuum quoque extensio sacramentum fiat." Margin has 1 Tim. 2, Ps. 63, 88, 141, 143. See Battles, *Institution 1536*, 234. In 1553 and 1559 margin has 1 Tim. 2.c.8 but none of the Psalms which are found in 1536 and 1539.

may be done decently and in order in the church (according to Paul's instruction, 1 Cor. 14).[10]

Before analyzing this further, it is important to demonstrate that Calvin was in fact referring to 1 Tim 2:1 (and 8) here. In 1536 there were of course no verse numbers marked, and the marginal note "1 Tim. 2" could be intended simply to mean verse 8 with the reference to "all places." The answer is found in the later editions of the *Institutes* where letters and numbers are assigned to the verses. It is not surprising that Robert Stephanus, who created the verse divisions that became standard, was the first to apply them to Calvin's *Institutes*. Within two years of his introducing the divisions, Stephanus's printing of the 1553 *Institutes* gives this marginal citation: "1 Tim. a. 1 & c. 8."[11] As will be demonstrated below, Calvin's commentary makes it clear that the issue of public or private prayer is associated with 1 Tim 2:1. Plainly, then, in 1536 Calvin considered both 1 Thess 5:17 and 1 Tim 2:1 and 8 as Paul's commands about nonliturgical prayer, i.e., private and individual practice.

---

10. *Institutio* 1536, chap. 3; OS 1:102: "Haec ratio est, cur alibi Paulus sine intermissione orare iubeat (1. Thess. 5, 1 Tim. 2), volens omni tempore, omni hora, omni loco, omnibus in rebus, erecta esse ad Deum omnium vota, quae et omnia ab eo expectent et omnium laudem illi referant, ut perpetua laudandi orandique argumenta nobis proponuntur. Haec autem orandi assiduitas, proprias ac privatas cuiusque respicit, nihil ad publicas ecclesiae orationes pertinet, quae nec assiduae esse possunt, nec aliter etiam fieri debunt, quam ex politia quae communi inter omnes consensu convenerit. Ideo et certae horae condicuntur ac praestituuntur, ut apud Deum indifferentes, ita hominum usibus necessariae, ut omnium commoditati prospectum sit et omnia decenter et composite (iuxta Pauli sententiam) (1 Cor. 14) in ecclesia administrentur." Margin has 1 Thess. 5, 1 Tim. 2 (*omni tempore* refers to seasons or time of year, not every hour in the day, but Battles omits *omni hora* as if the two phrases were identical; Calvin, *Institution* 1536, 99). For development, see below.

11. There are several reasons to note carefully what is put in the margins. One is simply that Calvin's citations are often made from memory (and especially in the case of the Psalms sometimes influenced by the Vulgate) and thus the marginalia give an indication of what the author intended. When the later editions—Stephanus 1553 appears to be the first—cite the medieval letter and the new verse number, they make explicit what was sometimes previously educated guesswork. Even if it was the publisher–printer who added verses to the marginal notes, in this case it was a scholar who knew the reformer's work well; also, it is quite unlikely that Calvin would have failed to correct Stephanus if there had been serious disagreement. Thus the marginalia also can serve to show what Calvin thought was necessary or significant, since he quite often gives recognizable quotations which are not emphasized by any marginal reference. Therefore here in each citation the marginal references are noted.

Calvin Never Changed His Mind

As is well known, the 1539 *Institutes* is a much larger book than the first edition, going from six to seventeen chapters; much is added and many original parts receive new nuances or sometimes expansion. However, in at least a few places there are also actual changes, and one of these places is the interpretation of 1 Tim 2:1. In this edition there are three new citations of verse 1 and one each of verse 2 and 8.[12] The one that joins verses 1 and 2 has a liturgical connotation: "He told Timothy to make solemn prayers in church for kings and princes."[13] (The 1541 French omits "in the church" but retains "prieres solennelles" to indicate liturgical prayers.[14])

The longer 1536 passage quoted above undergoes some significant changes in 1539, however. Additions are marked by underlining; omissions are struck out.

---

12. *Institutes* 1539, chap. 9 on prayer; 9:9:60–64 in Wevers, *Institutes*, I: "Ita unus statuitur mediator Christus, cuius intercessione propritius et exorabilis nobis reddatur pater. Quanquam interim et sua sanctis intercessione relinquuntur, quibus alii aliorum salutem mutuo inter se Deo commendent. De quibus meminit Apostolus: sed tales, quae ab unica illa dependeant." Margin has 1 Tim. 2. In 1553 and 1559 the margin has 1 Tim. 2.a.1. *Institutes* 1539, 9:10:11–12 in Wevers, *Institutes*: "Quum vero alibi unicum Dei et hominum Mediatorem illus nuncupat, an non ad precationes respicit, quorum ante paulo meminerat?" Margin has 1 Tim. 2. In 1553 and 1559 margin has 1 Tim. 2.b.5. Verse 8: *Institutes* 1539, chap. 9; 9:17:22–28 in Wevers, *Institutes*: "Interim vero quemadmodum neque in media hominum turba, si quando ita tulerat occasio, a precando abstinebat: si nos in locis omnibus, quoties opus fuerit, tollamus puras manus. Quin etiam ut communes fidelibus preces Dei verbo edicuntur: sic et templa publica iis peragendis destinata esse oportet. Ubi qui orationem cum dei populo communicare respuunt, non est, quod isto praetextu abutantur: cubiculum se ingredi, quo domini mandato pareant." Margin has [1] Tim. 2. In 1553 and 1559 margin has 1 Tim. 2.c.8.

13. *Institutes* 1539, chap. 8; 8:15:82–88 in Wevers, *Institutes*: "Proferunt eas Apostoli sententias, quod velit Dominus omnes salvos fieri, et ad veritatis agnitionem pervenire. Omnes etiam sub incredulitate concluserit, ut omnium misereatur. Quod item per prophetam Dominus ipse denunciat, se nolle mortem peccatoris, sed magis ut convertatur, et vivat, primus Apostoli locus importune huc adducitur. De singulis enim, non hominibus, sed hominum ordinibus, illic eum loqui facillime ex contextu evincitur. Praeceperat Timotheo, solemnes in ecclesia precationes, pro regibus et principibus, concipere." Margin has 1 Tim. 2 [beside verse 4 but context means verse 1–2]. In 1553 and 1559 margin has 1 Tim. 2.a.4.

14. *Institutes* 1541, chap. 8, *Jean Calvin: Institution* 2:35: "Il avoit commandé à Timothée de faire prieres solennelles pour les Roys et Princes." Margin has 1 Tim. 2 in same place as 1539 Latin.

John Calvin, Myth and Reality

This is the reason why Paul elsewhere enjoins us to pray without ceasing (1 Thess. 5, 1 Tim. 2). To be sure, he wants everyone with as much constancy as possible, in every season, every hour, every place, every matter, to raise every prayer to God, to expect all things from Him and to give Him praise for all things, since He constantly provides us with reasons for praising and praying to Him. However, although this constancy in praying especially has regard to each one's own, private prayers, nevertheless it does not pertains somewhat to the public prayers of the church which can neither be constant nor should they be done otherwise than in the way agreed upon in the common polity by all.[15]

Quite clearly Calvin has shifted the application of 1 Tim 2:1-2 to include the context of public prayers, the liturgy of the church. Not only is "although... especially" (etsi prasertim) added, but also the language is changed from "not" (nihil) to "nevertheless... somewhat" (nonnihil ... tamen). Also in Latin the reference to every hour (omni hora) is dropped although the 1541 French retains it: "à toute heure." Calvin also adds the pastoral note of a conditional phrase: "with as much constancy as possible" (Nempe... quanta fieri potest assiduitate), as if recognizing that praying without ceasing is an ideal even for private prayers.

There are no additional references to this pericope in the *Institutes* until 1559. In that year's major revisions, this section of 1536 revised in 1539 is divided between two paragraphs (3.20.28, 3.20.29). More significantly, the reference to 1 Tim 2:1—but not 1 Thess 5—is definitively dropped.[16] By this point, after commenting on and preaching through

---

15. *Institutes* 1539, chap. 9; 9:16:12–24 in Wevers, *Institutes*: "Haec ratio est, cur alibi Paulus sine intermissione orare iubeat (1. Thess. 5[17], 1 Tim. 2[1,8]). Nempe volens, quanta fieri potest assiduitate, omni tempore, omni hora, omni loco, omnibus in rebus, erecta esse ad Deum omnium vota, quae et omnia ab eo expectent et omnium laudem illi referant, ut perpetua laudandi orandique argumenta nobis proponuntur. Haec autem orandi assiduitas, etsi praesertim proprias ac privatas cuiusque respicit, nonnihil tamen ad publicas ecclesiae orationes pertinet. Atqui nec assiduae esse possunt, nec aliter etiam fieri debunt, quam ex politia quae communi inter omnes consensu convenerit. Fateor sane. Ideo enim et certae horae condicuntur ac praestituuntur, ut apud Deum indifferentes, ita homium usibus necessariae, *quo sit* omnium commoditati prospectum sit et omnia decenter et composite (iuxta Pauli sententiam) (1 Cor. 14) in ecclesia administrentur. Sed enim istud nihil obstat, quo minus unaquaeque ecclesia, cum subinde ad frequentiorem precationum usum se extimulare, tum maiore aliqua necessitate admonita, acriore studio flagrare debeat." Margin has 1 Thess. 5, 2 [typo for 1] Tim. 2.

16. *Institutes* 1559, 3.20.28; OS 4:337–338: "Haec ratio est cur praecipiat Paulus

the pastoral epistles, Calvin apparently had decided that this particular verse did not apply to his argument about praying without ceasing. Confirmation of this shift from private to public is evident in the addition of another allusion to verse 1 and citation of verse 2 with an explicit liturgical meaning in the context of defending the rule of civil authorities: "The best illustration of all [for the rightness of civil government among Christians] is the place in Paul where, when he exhorts Timothy to make prayers for kings in the public assembly, he immediately adds the reason: 'That under them we may lead a quiet life, with all piety and honorableness' (1 Tim. 2:2)."[17] The two new references to verse 8 in 1559 do not alter the picture in the *Institutes*.[18]

Before examining Calvin's exegetical works on these verses, it is appropriate to give a summary of the history of relevant verses in this passage to see what might have led the reformer to change his mind.

---

sine intermissione et orare et gratias agere (1. Thess. 5[17], 1 Tim.2[1,8]). Nempe volens scilicet, quanta fieri potest assiduitate, omni tempore, omni hora, omni loco, omnibus in rebus, erecta esse ad Deum omnium vota, quae et omnia ab eo expectent et omnium ei laudem illi referant, ut perpetua laudandi orandique argumenta nobis *offert*.

3.20.29 "Haec autem orandi assiduitas, etsi praesertim proprias ac privatas cuiusque respicit, nonnihil tamen ad publicas ecclesiae orationes pertinet. Atqui nec assiduae esse possunt, nec aliter etiam fieri debunt quam ex politia, quae communi inter omnes consensu convenerit. Fateor sane. Ideo enim et certae horae condicuntur ac praestituuntur, ut apud Deum indifferentes, ita hominum usibus necessariae, quo sit omnium commoditati prospectum sit et omnia decenter et composite (iuxta Pauli sententiam) (1 Cor. 14) in ecclesia administrentur. Sed enim istud nihil obstat, quo minus unaquaeque ecclesia, cum subinde ad frequentiorem precationum usum se extimulare, tum maiore aliqua necessitate admonita, acriore studio flagrare debeat." Margin has only 1 Thess. 5.c.17. (In 1553 margin was 1 Thess. 5.c.17, 1 Tim. 2.a.1 & c.8.)

17. *Institutes* 1559, 4.20.5; OS 5:476: "Omnium vero maxime illustris est locus Pauli, ubi Timotheum admonens, in coetu publico concipiendas esse preces pro Regibus, rationem mox subiicit, Ut tranquillam vitam sub ipsis agamus cum omni pietate et honestate [1. Tim. 2.a.2]." Margin has 1 Tim. 2.a.2.

18. *Institutes* 1559, 3.20.39; OS 4:349: "Huc referre licet quod Paulus suae aetatis fideles hortatur ut puras manus ubique tollant absque contentione: qui dissidium precibus ianuam claudere admonens, unanimes vota sua in commune vult conferre." Margin has 1 Tim. 2.c.8. 3.25.7; OS 4:446: "Quid quod singulas eorum partes sibi Deus sanctificari praecipit? Quod vult linguis nomen suum celebrari, tolli ad se puras manus (1 Tim. 2.c.8), sacrificia offerri?" Margin has 1 Tim. 2.c.8.

John Calvin, Myth and Reality

1 Timothy 2:1–2, 8 in Exegetical History

The exegetical history of 1 Tim 2:1–2, 8–9 sheds an interesting light on the world in which Calvin thought about the passage.[19] In fact, the majority of patristic and medieval writers considered this verse a reference to public or liturgical prayers, usually led by clergy. The motivation for such identification is the fact that Apostle Paul is addressing bishop Timothy and the need to explain why the apostle uses so many names for prayer.

Early voices in East and West make this interpretation clear. Ambrosiaster says that this instruction is followed by our priests (*sacerdotes nostri*).[20] Chrysostom, followed by Theophylactus, refers to daily morning and evening prayer led by clergy. Hugh of St. Cher repeatedly quotes Chrysostom, but his position on this point is Augustinian.[21] It is no surprise that the single most important voice for the Western tradition was that of Augustine, who discusses this text at some length in his response to a question from Paulinus of Nola about how the four words for *prayer* in verse 1 differed. In the midst of a long explanation of the Greek meanings of the different words for *prayer*, Augustine identifies these words with specific parts of the Mass.

> But I choose to understand in these words what the whole or almost the whole Church usually understands, and thus we take <u>precationes</u> as those prayers which we make in the celebration of the sacraments before we begin to bless the offerings on the Lord's table. We take <u>orationes</u> to be those prayers said when the offerings are blessed and broken for distribution, and almost every Church concludes this whole prayer with the Lord's Prayer . . . "<u>Intercessions</u>," however, or "petitions," . . . are made when the people are blessed. For then the bishops, like defense lawyers, offer to God's most merciful power those under their protection by the imposition of hands. After they have done this and have partaken of the sacrament, everything is ended with

---

19. In the interests of space, only references are provided here; the full notes for the exegetical history will be presented elsewhere.

20. *Ambrosiaster . . . in Epistulas Paulinas*, CSEL 81, 259. He is cited by Erasmus on this passage, though not this particular point; cf. n. 26.

21. Chrysostom, Homily 6 on 1 Tim. 2:1–4, MPG 62:530; Theophylactus, MPG 125: 28, 30 is a virtual abbreviated quotation. For Hugh of St. Cher, see n. 23.

the thanksgiving, which the apostle also emphasized with these last words.²²

In fact, following Augustine there is a strong tradition in the West of emphasizing the liturgical and clerical character of 1 Tim 2:1-2 by identifying the four words for *prayer* with specific prayers of the Mass. Hugh of St. Cher is the most elaborate,²³ but most medieval exegetes, including the *glossa ordinaria*,²⁴ make this clerical or liturgical interpretation even when (as often happens) they also offer a variety of other meanings for each of the four words (e.g., as prayer for the dead or intercessions through the saints) or use them to identify appropriate acts of those who pray.²⁵

Some changes in the interpretation of this pericope come into view with the humanist and religious reforms of Calvin's immediate predecessors or contemporaries. There are several different directions: along with the traditional liturgical reading of verses 1-2 there is a reaction against the identification of these prayers as public worship, but the introduction of a liturgical reading of verse 8 or 9. Erasmus's *Annotations* were a key source of the new ideas. For example, one indication of the new perspective is in the description in verse 2 about the life under a good ruler; Erasmus challenges the Vulgate's use of *castitate* in favor of *honestate* with its wider application among lay Christians.²⁶ The most important change, however, is the humanist's comment on the word *omnium* in 1 Tim 2:1, which he indicates is grammatically ambiguous. "It is uncertain whether it refers to 'first' or to 'prayers' and both meanings are allowable. If it is referred to the former, this will be the sense: that prayer should be done first, that is, before all things, and Chrysostom and Ambrose [Ambrosiaster] explain it in this way. If it is referred to the latter [prayers], the sense will be that prayers should be made by all."²⁷

---

22. Augustine, Letter 149, 16, in *Letters 100-155*, 368 (italics added).

23. Hugh of St. Cher: Introduction, *Opera omnia. Tomus Septimus: In Epistolas omnes* . . . , F210v (Dd2v).

24. Gloss: *Biblia Latina*, vol. 4.

25. Gloss: *Biblia Latina*. Nicolas of Lyra on 1 Tim 2:1, *Postilla*, vol. 4. Denis the Carthusian, *Opera Omnia*, 13:415.

26. Erasmus, *Annotationes*, LB 6:932.

27. Ibid., 931.

John Calvin, Myth and Reality

It is notable here that Erasmus does not identify verse 1 with public worship but opens the door to several other interpretations. The reading "by all" was not apparently taken up explicitly by exegetes, although it is possible or even probable that this helped shape Calvin's initial reading of I Tim 2:1 as referring to prayer by all Christians, i.e., private prayer. However, there is evidence that Erasmus's alternative reading, "first," was picked up by theologians for whom Scripture was an authoritative guide to practice for the life of the church. Some in the Zwinglian tradition interpreted 1 Tim 2:1 as not only a reference to public worship but also as a rubric about the order of the service. The title of the liturgical form published in Zurich in 1526 uses this passage as its warrant for beginning worship with prayers: "A form of prayers according to the teaching of Paul, 1 Tim. 2[:1–7], which is now used in Zurich at the beginning of the sermon (preaching service)."[28] A similar but slightly different literal application is later followed by some Puritans.[29]

The traditional idea of 1 Tim 2:1–2 as a reference to public worship was common to some reformers in different communities, both Lutheran and Reformed. Although he does not focus on liturgical order in the same way as Zwingli, Heinrich Bullinger's commentary on the passage is in effect a mini-treatise on public worship. Under the heading: "the ecclesiastical assembly is instructed," he describes right and wrong worship, contrasting the New Testament (Acts 2:42) and patristic teaching with the degeneration under the papacy and the "abuses" of the Mass.[30] Caspar Cruciger and Alexander Alesius also interpret 1 Tim 2:1ff. as liturgical or public prayer. It is evident from other remarks that these two are following Philipp Melanchthon's commentary, although the latter is less explicit about the precise meaning of verse 1, speaking of prayers "in the church" without specific reference to "public."[31]

28. "Ein kurtze gmeine form, kinder ze touffenn, die ee ze bestäten, die predig anzefahen und zuo enden, wie es zuo Zürich gebrucht wirdt." The third section: "Ein form des bittens nach der leer Pauli, 1. Timoth. 2 [:1–7], die man yetz Zürich brucht im anfang der predigen" [different printing has Predigtgottesdienstes]; this appeared in 1526 and several later printings; Z 6/5:431.

29. Davies, *Worship and Theology*, 259.

30. Bullinger, *In omnes apostolicas epistolas*, fol. 561–63 [562–63 misnumbered]; fol. 561, "Instruitur Coetus Ecclesiasticus."

31. Cruciger, *In Epistolae Pauli ad Timotheum*, 58. Alesius, *Expositio Prioris Epistolae ad Timotheum*, C2v. Melanchthon, *Scripta Exegetica*, CR 15:1316. (He is one of the few who make no mention of women's dress; verse 9 was not important enough for comment.)

The new, probably Erasmian-influenced perspective on 1 Tim 2:1–2, which becomes notable in the sixteenth century, understood this passage in a more general, nonliturgical sense, without explicit reference to public worship or clergy. However, Erasmus does retain the more traditional liturgical connotation of women's dress in verse 9. The larger context of verse 9 is public worship, but the medieval exegetical tradition does not refer specifically to public worship in regard to women's dress, probably because the common view of this whole pericope was public worship. For those like Erasmus, who did not share the liturgical reading of verses 1–2, the introduction of a reference to public worship in verse 9 is noteworthy. The *Annotations* contribute to this interpretation by their silence on liturgy in verses 1–2. However, it is the *Paraphrases* that express Erasmus's typical ethical "philosophy of Christ" orientation by placing the moral exhortation about women's dress in verse 9 in the context of public worship.[32] Conrad Pellican, Johannes Bugenhagen, and, as might be expected, the "maverick" Catholic commentator Thomas de Vio Cardinal Cajetan are among those who resist the clerical-liturgical interpretation of 1 Tim 2:1–2. They and others, however, follow Erasmus in referring to public worship when discussing women's dress.[33]

More intriguing is the way some Lutherans associate verse 8 with public prayer. For Thomas Venatorius this follows lengthy polemic in verse 1 against the traditional (Mass) liturgy.[34] Luther's 1528 lecture on this passage gives a more interesting exposition. First he indicates that

---

32. Erasmus, *Paraphrases*, 1 Tim. 2:1, LB 7:1039.

33. Bugenhagen on verse 1 says Paul is instructing bishops how to teach their hearers and gives simple definitions of different words for prayer; on verse 5 he rejects prayer for the dead; on verse 9 he follows Erasmus in seeing that prayer refers to women as well as men but also women's dress should not distract men "ad orationem publicam;" *Annotationes. . . In Epistolas Pauli*, 203-4, 206, 207. Pellican follows Erasmus' *Paraphrases* in his introduction and then gives extensive, more Protestant explanations of the four words. *In omnes apostolicas epistolas. . . commentarii*, 479–80, 485–86. Cajetan, *Epistolae Pauli et aliorum*, 141r, cf. 141v.

34. Thomas Venatorius, *In Divi Pauli . . . distributiones*, on verse 1-2 is essentially a polemical rejection of the traditional liturgical practice of those who read this verse as "orationes, quae fiunt in publicis congregationibus" ("32r" = 40r) with language about cutting off the pious members from the mystical body and against superstitions and magic and emphasis on the spirit of prayer. On verse 8 he indicates that this discussion of prayer "maxime vero ubi tota se confert orationem ecclesia: qua de re hanc Apostoli sententiam audire libet" (51v). On 9 he refers to women's dress "in coetu sacro" (52r).

it is not certain whether Paul is speaking of public or private prayer, but "chiefly it seems to speak of public prayer" in 1 Tim. 2:1–10 because of the references to physical movements, "vestiges of which remain" in the Lutheran practice of the Lord's Prayer. Luther adds a second somewhat unexpected argument for identifying verse 8 as public prayer by the fact that here men are separated from women, according to Jewish practice, which is continued in "public prayer" of the academic world.[35]

Here is a brief summary: The exegetical history of 1 Tim 2:1–2 is not univocal in identifying these prayers as liturgical, and the text itself (as is evident in Erasmus's *Annotations*) might be said to favor a nonliturgical context. This makes Calvin's use of the verse all the more interesting. It appears that the reformer first follows the new pattern of Erasmus when in 1536 he reads these verses as referring to private prayer, over against the traditional liturgical idea. By 1539, however, he has found reason to change the identification of this passage to include or even give primary weight to an interpretation as public worship.

Whether Calvin's reasoning was exegetical or pastoral or more likely both, it appears that he continued to reflect on the complexity of these verses in his exegetical works: commentaries and sermons. As with the *Institutes*, a considerable part of the exposition is devoted to practical matters such as the attitude toward rulers, prayer for all people, and the central confession of Christ as sole mediator. With regard to verses 1–2, however, the commentary and sermons offer similar views but visible differences of emphasis. This does refer to public worship, but with his congregation he can also give attention to private prayer.

The commentary's academic exposition of 1 Timothy is clearly intended to instruct. Its treatment of verse 1 is succinct: "[f]irst [Paul] deals with public prayer and orders that it should be made not only for believers but for all people."[36] Here Calvin means public worship, the liturgy (which he names "La forme des prieres") and not specific individual prayers, for he goes on to reject explicitly Augustine's view of the four words for *prayer* as related to specific liturgical prayers.[37] The com-

---

35. Luther, "Vorlesung über den 1. Timotheusbrief" (1528), WA 26:42. In fact, in explaining Matt 6:6 he indicates that in the closet one can use "words and gestures that he could not use if he were in human company"; LW 21:139.

36. Calvin, commentary on 1 Tim 2:1, CO 52:265: "Ac initio quidem de publicis orationibus disserit: quae jubet non pro fidelibus modo concipi, sed pro universo genere humano."

37. Calvin, commentary on 1 Tim 2:1, CO 52:265: "Porro quid inter se differant tres

Calvin Never Changed His Mind

mentary thus reflects the same position as is seen in the additions to the *Institutes* from 1539 to the end, i.e., a liturgical locus for the prayers. (Only the 1536 passage that was changed retains a dual interpretation until the association of 1 Tim 2:1-2 with individual prayers is apparently dropped in 1559.) On the other hand, the commentary notes on verse 8 slightly change the emphasis found in the *Institutes* citations, but not in the way that Erasmus and various Lutherans do. Calvin explains "every place" in verse 8 much as he does God's will for "all people to be saved" in verse 4. Thus "every place" refers to every kind of human group, i.e., Gentiles as well as Jews, and so means prayer offered up everywhere on earth. However, with regard to the issue of public/private, the view of verse 8 appears to be the same as in the *Institutes*; there is no particular liturgical or public connotation,[38] and as will be evident below, Calvin does not agree with the idea that lifting hands is a gesture particularly for public worship.

The discussion of 1 Tim 2:1 and 8 in the sermons preached in 1554 offers a more intriguing dimension to Calvin's interpretation of this passage. The explicit identification for the prayers is a public or liturgical context. After insisting that prayer is the first duty of Christians, the preacher rebukes those who are lax: "But look now what our 'Christianity' is: for we see that few devote themselves to praying to God, or if they do it, it is like a ritual and then they have done their duty. In short, it is only like a show without power or any zeal; and if one is so cold in making public prayers, consider what it is like when each one prays at home and in private."[39]

Here as in the *Institutes* passage that is changed in 1539, there is the link between public and private, although in reverse order.

However, the far greater weight of the homily treats prayer in a much more general and hortatory fashion; the subject could be understood as private or individual prayer as much as—or more than—li-

---

species ex quatuor quas Paulus enumerat, fateor me non penitus tenere. Puerile quidem enim est, quod Pauli verba Augustinus ad ritus suo tempore usitatos detorquet."

38. Calvin, commentary on 1 Tim 2:8, CO 52:273-75.

39. Sermon on 1 Tim 1:1-2; CO 53:126: "Mais regardons maintenant quelle est nostre Chrestienté: car nous voyons que bien peu s'addonnent à prier Dieu: ou si on le fait, c'est comme par ceremonie et acquit. Brief, ce n'est sinon comme une monstre sans vertu, ne zele aucun: et si on est bien froid à faire prieres publiques, regardons que ce sera d'un chacun en sa maison et en son privé."

turgical. The several references to praying in the morning and at night are the only explicit designations of time or place.[40] This may represent the influence of Chrysostom or an adaptation, although Calvin does not cite this favorite exegete, and the application is not absolutely clear. Although Geneva had daily morning services that of course included prayers, and both the printed texts and Calvin's own formulations followed the general pattern given in 1 Tim 2:1, it is equally or more likely that the morning and evening prayers to which he refers in the sermon are individual ones like those models given in his catechism (especially since only on Sunday was there an afternoon service, and it was not really "evening").[41] Whatever the judgment on this point, it is plain that in preaching on the text Calvin was more concerned to teach and exhort the congregation to pray than to instruct them about whether 1 Tim 2:1 dealt with public or private prayers. The homiletic exposition of lifting hands (verse 8) clearly does not follow Erasmus or Luther. Here Calvin combines both the idea of all groups or communities of people (from the commentary) with the interpretation of this as private prayer found in the 1536 *Institutes*, and reads this as an expression of human feeling in prayer. Further, he explicitly says that the instructions about praying everywhere apply to women as well as men.[42] (Although he certainly agreed with Luther about separating men and women in the academic sphere, he does not consider that context here.)

Calvin's exegetical treatment of 1 Tim 2:1–2 confirmed the changed interpretation made in 1539 but also weighted it differently in commentary and sermon, and situated his thought in relationship to the

---

40. Calvin, sermon on 1 Tim. 2:1–2; CO 53:126: "Maintenant nous voyons quelle est l'intention de S. Paul en ce passage: c'est asçavoir de monstrer à quoy les enfans de Dieu se doyvent employer: c'est à ne point travailler en vain, et sans aucun profit: c'est à invoquer Dieu, et en le priant avoir le soin du salut de tout le monde: et que soir et matin ils s'appliquent à cela... Voilà (di-je) le vray examen pour sçavoir comment nous aurons profité en l'Evangile: c'est si nous sommes ardens à prier Dieu, que nous ayons ceste affection-là qui nous solicite iour et nuict." For Chrysosom see below at n. 44.

41. For all prayers collected in one place, see McKee, *John Calvin*, 111–12, 126–31, 134, 151–52, 155–56, 172–77, 211–19, 221–39.

42. Calvin, sermon on 1 Tim. 2:8; CO 53:183–87. Among the points: contrast of certainty that God hears because we pray through Christ with uncertainty of traditional papal prayers (which try to reach God by other routes: "circuits obliques") because they do not trust in God, 53:185; or the differences between Jewish and Christian prayer (Jews prayed at home but held their liturgy in the temple, while Christians now pray to God everywhere because Christ is the temple, 53:186–87).

exegetical heritage, both positively and negatively. His interpretation of these verses as public worship was reaffirmed in the 1559 addition to the *Institutes* (after the homilies were preached), but the pastor's voice in the sermons is noteworthy. Calvin wanted his hearers to pray both in the gathered community and at home; 1 Tim 2:1 does not explicitly bind prayer to any time or place, so Calvin's exposition also ranges freely according to what he thinks is most edifying. He could assume that those who heard his sermons knew the liturgy, which prayed at some length for rulers and all sorts of people, so the relevance of this text to public worship did not need to be emphasized from the pulpit.

The clearly nonliturgical interpretation in 1536—which is the minority voice in the exegetical tradition—is clearly modified in 1539, and that change is fully supported by the 1548 commentary and the 1559 addition to the *Institutes*, and expressed though not emphasized in the sermons. Without attempting to assign a cause, it may be noted that Calvin's rethinking of the public/private point may have been partly the result of a critical appropriation of the tradition. While he explicitly rejects Augustine's identification of verse 1 with the liturgy of his day, and although he does not mention Chrysostom, it seems that Calvin is following his favorite patristic exegete. He certainly did not follow the Erasmian-Zwinglian proof-text idea of making 1 Tim 2:1 a rubric for beginning worship with prayers, but he did change his mind about the (primary) context of the prayers. The change from an individual or private application to a public or liturgical one also coincides with Calvin's own move from young scholar to pastor, and this experiential influence cannot be discounted.

Calvin's Use of 1 Samuel 1:13

As a kind of evidence for this last hypothesis it is interesting to examine briefly one other similar change made between the first and second editions of the *Institutes*. In 1536 Calvin's discussion of prayer included a reference to 1 Sam 1:13 in the context of intelligible prayer and the essential requirement for the heart to be engaged in praying. "'Finally, in private prayer the tongue is not even necessary, if the inward sense were enough by itself to incite itself, so that sometimes the best prayers

John Calvin, Myth and Reality

are not spoken, as is seen in the examples of Moses and Hannah' (Exod. 14 [:15], 1 Sam. 1[:13])."[43]

This association of Exod 14:15 and 1 Sam 1:13 is almost certainly dependent on Chrysostom's sermons on this passage. In fact, Exodus 14 does not mention Moses praying to God, but Chrysostom reads verse 15 ("Why are you calling out to me?") as God's response to a silent prayer by Moses. Calvin's commentary (published in 1563) on Exod 14:15 follows this interpretation.[44]

In 1539 this passage of the *Institutes* undergoes considerable change. First, the reference to Moses drops out entirely, although the commentary shows that Calvin's understanding of Exod 14:15 has not changed. What is different is the point the reformer wants to make about prayer. The revised passage of 1539 is no longer focused on praying without voice, and Calvin appears to have changed his understanding of Hannah's prayer. It is not silent, but it is also certainly not scripted; her intense feelings, coming from her heart, tumble out without premeditation, and her physical movement is the unconscious expression of her prayer.

> Finally, in private prayer the tongue is not even necessary, except when the inward feeling either is not enough of itself to incite itself or when it is so vehemently aroused by itself that it causes the tongue to act. For even if the best prayers are sometimes not spoken, it often nevertheless happens that, when the feelings of the mind are aroused both the tongue and other members of the body break forth into gestures, without ostentation. From this came Hannah's uncertain murmur (1 Sam. 1[:13]); all the saints constantly experience something like it when they burst out in broken and disconnected speech. However the gestures of the body usually observed in praying, such as kneeling and uncovering the head, these are exercises by which we seek to increase our veneration of God's majesty.[45]

---

43. *Institutio* 1536, chap. 3, OS 1:104: "Postremo, ne esse quidem orationi privatae necessariam linguam, si interior sensus sibi ipse ad incitationem satis esset, ut optimae interdum orationes voce careant quo modo in exemplo Mosis et Hannae spectatu (Exod. 14, 1 Sam. 1)."

44. CO 24:151–52. Chrysostom, *Old Testament Homilies*, homily 2 on Hannah, 1:86.

45. *Institutes* 1539, chap. 9; 9:19:21—20 in Wevers, *Institutes*: "Postremo, ne esse quidem orationi privatae necessariam linguam, nisi quo ad [si] interior sensus, vel sibi ipse ad incitationem sufficere non valet vel incitationis vehementia linguae actionem

Calvin Never Changed His Mind

Note that not only has the interpretation of Hannah's prayer changed, but Calvin also considers this a positive thing and, more surprisingly, adds that "all the saints constantly experience" it! This reading remains unchanged through to the last edition of 1559. Calvin's sermons on I Samuel effectively give this same view, with a number of references to this as a frequent experience of the faithful.[46]

A limited survey of the exegetical history of 1 Sam. 1:13 does not reveal any discussion of Hannah comparable to Calvin's. For most writers the key issue is the importance of inward prayer of the heart, not external show,[47] a point that some Protestants develop in polemic against the traditional church (along with explanations for how Hannah's vows are different from traditional Catholic ones).[48] In view of his reading of

---

secum rapit. Nam etsi [satis esset, ut] optimae interdum orationes voce *carent* saepe tamen usu venit, ut affectu mentis exultante, et lingua in vocem, et membra alia in gesticulationem, sine ambitione erumpant. Inde scilicet incertum illud Hannae murmur [1 Reg. 1], cuius simile quiddam sancti omnes perpetuo in se experiuntur; dum in abruptas et concisas voces prosiliunt. Corporis autem gestus in praecatione observari soliti: quales sunt geniculatio, et capitis detectio, exercitia sunt, quibus ad maiorem Dei venerationem assurgere conamur." Quo modo in exemplo Mosis et Hannae spectatu [Exod. 14, 1 Sam. 1])." Margin has 1 Sam. 1 [NO Exod. 14]

46. Third sermon, on 1 Sam. 1:11-17; comment on verse 13, CO 29:270-71: "Verum tamen et hoc observandum, saepe inter precandum etiam os et labia esse adhibenda, quod nimirum tanta sit nostrae mentis levitas, ut subende variis cogitationibus preces nostrae veluti quibusdam fluctibus frangantur, quas pura mente concipi oportuit. Quam infirmatem superaturi ardenter Deum orare, et non tantum labiorum sed linguarum etiam motu nos ipsos excitari, torporemque discutere debemus." This does not apply to public prayers. Continues with application and importance of heart, then returns to Hannah's example, David's roaring like a lion, Ezekiel's groaning and sobbing; Isaiah's teaching on the necessity of the heart. "Saepe veri venit ut precandum coram hominibus stulti fatuique appareamus, quod incautis nescio qui oris et manuum gestus excitant insolentiores: verum Deo cor nostrum approbari satis est: quae pars est orationem maxima, dummodo sine fuco et simulatione ad Deum accedamus."

47. Interlinear gloss; Glossa ordinaria, *Biblia Latina*, vol. 2. Nicolas of Lyra, *Postilla*, vol. 1. Hugh of St. Cher quotes the ordinary gloss, *Opera omnia. Tomus Primus. In libros Genesis*, 220r. Denis, the Carthusian, *Opera omnia*, vol. 3.

48. Bugenhagen, *Annotationes . . . in Deuteronomium*, 186-88. Pellican, *Commentaria Bibliorum . . . Tomus Secundus in quo continetur. . . Samuelis*, f61v. Borrhaus, *In sacram Josuae*, 303. Vermigli, *In duos libros Samuelis . . . commentarii*, 8r. Martyr's positive exposition has much in common with Calvin's: This passage refers to private prayer, not public; words are not necessary but can be useful to excite us to pray; God does not care about the physical movement provided it is not hypocritical but comes from faith, 8v. Cajetan goes his own way, *In . . . historiales libros commentarii*, 377r-v.

Hannah's prayer it may be significant that Calvin, unlike Luther, did not think that the physical motions in 1 Tim 2:8 pointed to the context of public prayer. Even if the New Testament passage was instruction about lifting the hands in prayer, such gestures could also be spontaneous.

The importance of this experiential view of prayer is evident elsewhere in Calvin's public writings. Although no biblical text is cited there, Calvin's reflection on the depth of emotion in prayer and how it may manifest itself actually reappears in his Geneva Catechism in the question about using the tongue in prayer. Having answered positively about the use of the voice, the student adds, "Further, the ardor and vehemence of the heart's zeal sometimes constrains the tongue to speak without the person's having thought about it."[49] This is a rather remarkable fact, given how short the catechism is by comparison with the *Institutes*. Even a summary of instruction on praying should include this point about the devout movement of the heart in spontaneous prayer, clear evidence that Calvin thought this was important for everyone to know.

One might speculate that in 1539 Calvin changed his interpretation of 1 Sam 1:13 because he had experienced Hannah's kind of prayer either in himself or—if that is too far-fetched a speculation—in his pastoral work. And that may be an even more surprising challenge to the legend of the man who never changed his mind than the alterations in 1 Tim 2:1 and 1 Sam 1:13 between 1536 and 1539!

---

49. Calvin, Geneva Catechism, OC 6:87: "et aussi le zele du cueur, par son ardeur et vehemence, contraint souvent la langue à parler sans que on y pense." 6:88: "Ad haec, hominem interdum studii vehementia huc impellit, ut praeter consilium lingua in vocem prorumpat."

3

The Good, the Bad, and the Indifferent
Myths, Realities, and Ambiguities in Calvin's Teachings about Women

JOHN L. THOMPSON

Despite a career cut short by what today would be regarded as an early death, John Calvin is remembered for doing and saying many things. But Calvin was and remains a controversial figure, and anyone who applies the basic rules of evidence and fair play will discover that he is also remembered for many things that he never did or said. Just as news today is often reduced to sound bites, it is all too common for Calvin's legacy to be reduced to a single provocative feature, often misrepresented. Sometimes that sole feature pertains to predestination, or to the roots of capitalism, or to Calvin as the hunter of heretics. At other times, the scandal may be Calvin's sumptuary laws and social control. And occasionally the focus falls on Calvin and the place of women in family, church, and society.

It is the last of these topics that I will consider here. In seeking to separate the myths about Calvin from the realities, I've divided my considerations into three categories: the good, the bad, and the indifferent. The first two represent the tendency to turn Calvin into an archetype—

either to cast him as a timeless role model, or to uncover him as a villain and archenemy. Let me begin with the second of these.

"Bad Calvin"

More than ten years ago Tom Davis observed that "in the American cultural consciousness," at least, "[t]he word 'Calvin' seems to be shorthand for a range of negative thoughts and feelings."[1] Indeed, in a pair of innovative studies, Davis examined how Calvin and Calvinism came to be regarded as virtually un-American and as symbols of intolerance, largely as a result of the way in which nineteenth-century history textbooks and popular fiction vilified Calvin for his lethal judgmentalism against Servetus and for his gloomy doctrine of predestination. Davis's conclusions are illuminating but not encouraging, insofar as he documents the tendentious distortion of Calvin and Calvinism not only in these nineteenth-century sources, but also in the supposedly critical studies of this literature in our own day. The dour stereotype still thrives.

What Davis found in his sources is part of a larger pattern, one that extends also to the contested field of women's studies. Here, too, Calvin has often garnered a reputation that is less than deserved. Let me report on two myths in particular.

Myth #1: Calvin Invented Patriarchy and the Subordination of Women

My depiction of this first myth about Calvin may seem overly dramatic, but it is not far from the mark in describing how in many modern feminist works, Calvin appears only in cameo, as a whipping boy for the ills of patriarchy. The "best" scenario here is when Calvin's teachings about the nature and role of women are simply profiled as bad ideas. A classic representative of this approach would be Rosemary Radford Reuther, whose many books often include historical surveys that present writers such as Luther and Calvin in fair detail and with respectable nuance. Granted, Reuther thinks Luther and Calvin were substantially wrong, but their historical contexts are not necessarily belittled or dissolved.[2]

---

1. Davis, "Images of Intolerance," 234–48; Davis, "Rhetorical War and Reflex," 443–56.

2. See, for instance, Reuther, *Introducing Redemption*, 44–47, where she fairly presents the complexity of Luther and Calvin in a chapter titled "Conflicting Paradigms of

More problematic, however, are studies or surveys that introduce Calvin's views only within a highly prejudicial framework. Alison Findlay, for example, correctly reports Calvin's doctrine of women's subordination as based on the deception of Eve, but she begins her account by introducing Calvin as simply one of the Renaissance's "anti-feminist writers," as if Calvin would recognize himself in that description.[3] More tendentious still is the survey of the subordination of women in Western theology offered by Pamela Cooper-White in the space of a page and a half, beginning with Augustine, Aquinas, Luther, Calvin, and Knox, and ending with Bishop Pike and Karl Barth. It is not her haste that astonishes, it is rather her setup: the section heading for this survey is "Woman as Subhuman," in a chapter titled "Images of Women: Pornography and the Connection to Violence."[4] Is Calvin really to be treated under such headings as these?

Calvin comes off poorly in other ways, too, because patriarchy brings other sins in its wake. Yet another work announces that Calvin "was a particularly severe commentator on women," whose accounts of the fall "emphasize Eve's guilt and the blame and iniquity that all women have inherited from her." There is no indication that Calvin also has much to say about Adam's guilt, but there is an assertion, later on, that Calvin was among those Protestants who regarded sex as "defiling."[5] Calvin's patriarchy has also been the target of deconstruction. Describing the subversive effects of the Puritans' appropriation of feminine imagery, Ivy Schweitzer identifies Calvin's account of the nature of faith in Christ as "phallogocentric," insofar as *faith* (to use the words of John 1:12, as Calvin does) grants one the privilege to become a *son* of God—thereby ungendering if not erasing women altogether.[6]

Redemption and Gender in the Reformation Era." For Calvin in her other works, see *Sexism and God-Talk*, 98–99; *Women and Redemption*, 122–26.

3. Findlay, *A Feminist Perspective*, 12–13, 33, 44. Findlay repeatedly cites an excerpt from Calvin's sermon on Ephesians 5—not directly, to be sure, but as excerpted from another work, Aughterson, *Renaissance Woman*, which furnishes an excerpt from two of Calvin's sermons that comprise slightly more than two pages.

4. Cooper-White, *The Cry of Tamar*, 50–51; her account of Calvin is derived from the work of Joy Bussert (n. 13, below).

5. Brown and McBride, *Women's Roles*, 21–22, 64; the account of Calvin here is also derived from Aughterson's sourcebook (n. 3, above).

6. Schweitzer, "Puritan Legacies," 125–41, here citing 130.

Many of these distorted and mythic accounts of Calvin stem from a sheer lack of scholarship. One writer begins a survey of women in the Bible by alluding to the tragedy of a Scottish woman burned alive in 1591 "for seeking pain relief when she gave birth." This tragic death stemmed from a horrific misinterpretation of Genesis 3—and one is surprised suddenly to see, alone on stage, John Calvin, who "added to the problems this text created for women" when he expounded it in terms of male rule and women's obedience.[7] Another writer, seeking to expose the blind spots of modern historians, says Calvin "maintained that political equality for women would be a 'deviation from the original and proper order of nature.'"[8] The notion of "political equality" simply stands in here as a general denigration of Calvin's patriarchy, and the quotation is not explored—nor could it be, since this author lifted it from yet another writer's uncredited quotation, in a passage that goes on to report that Calvin also "spoke favorably of polygamy, suggesting that it would help to keep women from being unwed and childless."[9] The most poignant example, however, comes from a book written for girls, titled *Girls Are Equal Too: The Teenage Girl's How-to-Survive Book*. Not surprisingly, Calvin plays a marginal role in this work, but about halfway through, in a chapter on the history of the women's movement, the authors report how "John Calvin said woman's only useful function was to bear children, and he spoke out against political equality for women."[10] Once again, it is clear that no primary sources were harmed in the making of this book.

Myth #2: Calvin's Theology Encourages Violence against Women

The first myth I've described here, that Calvin bears a significant amount of blame for the dissemination of patriarchy, leads to a more focused

---

7. Parales, *Hidden Voices*, 1. Curiously, Parales furnishes no reference to Calvin, only to Reuther, *Sexism and God-Talk*, 98.

8. Parenti, *History as Mystery*, 88.

9. Stone, *When God Was a Woman*, 226. In fact, Calvin may have been more hostile to polygamy than any of his contemporaries; see Thompson, "Patriarchs, Polygamy, and Private Resistance," 3–27.

10. Carlson and Carlson, *Girls Are Equal Too*, 109. The subtitle on the cover, quoted in the text, differs from that of the book's title page: *Girls Are Equal Too: How to Survive For Teenage Girls*.

charge. I want to introduce this as a second myth before responding also to the first. Earlier I mentioned the unending fallout from the Servetus affair. In the field of women's studies, another incident from Calvin's life has likewise led to enduring scandal. It all stems from a letter he wrote to an unnamed woman in 1559. Here is how Calvin's letter is framed by James Leehan in his book on pastoral care for victims of domestic violence.

> All too often, Jesus as the suffering servant is held up as a model for a person suffering family violence. *The most famous example of this is John Calvin.* His admonition to a battered woman is well known among religious persons working in the domestic violence field. Although Calvin had "special sympathy for women who are evilly and roughly treated by their husbands," he could not find himself "permitted by the Word of God ... to advise a woman to leave her husband." Instead, he exhorted her to "bear with patience the cross which God has seen fit to place upon her; and meanwhile not to deviate from the duty which she has before God to please her husband, but to be faithful whatever happens." Such advice is not helpful; it is dangerous.[11]

Several questions might be raised here. First, is it true that Calvin has become a byword among those who work in the field of domestic abuse? Judging from recent books in the field, it might seem that he has. But that question leads immediately to another, namely, how does one go about becoming a byword like this? The process may be nominally rooted in history, but it proceeds more like gossip. Calvin's letter is critiqued not only in Leehan's work and in Pamela Cooper-White's influential book on violence against women, *The Cry of Tamar*, but also by yet another book in this genre, *Women and the Value of Suffering*, and by the more recent *Sourcebook on Violence against Women*.[12] However, not one of these sources ever claims to have read Calvin; instead, they all derive from Joy Bussert's 1986 work, *Battered Women*, which also did not cite Calvin directly but drew key lines from a classic article by

---

11. Leehan, *Pastoral Care for Survivors*, 110 (italics mine). The quotation of Calvin is derived from the work of Joy Bussert, n. 13, below.

12. Cooper-White, *The Cry of Tamar*, 50–51; Rankka, *Women and the Value of Suffering*, 64; Fortune, "Religious Issues," 375.

Jane Dempsey Douglass, who excerpted about half of Calvin's short letter from an earlier full translation.[13]

Clearly, these otherwise well-intentioned studies have levied a serious charge against Calvin on the basis of a single text, examined partially, at a distance, and without regard for context. So another question arises: Is this a fair judgment against Calvin? Does this anecdote self-evidently represent the sum of Calvin's demeanor and disposition towards women? In fact, the big picture here has been unfairly cropped. No one among these counselors and therapists seems to wonder what the unnamed woman originally wrote or whether Calvin knew more about her than appears from these excerpted lines. To be sure, this woman's letter does not survive, but there is another pair of exchanges involving a Protestant woman mistreated by her Roman Catholic husband where we *can* hear both sides, Calvin's and the woman's. Jane Douglass called attention also to this earlier case, but because Bussert did not cite it, none of Bussert's many copyists knew of it.[14]

Reading this earlier letter of 1552 (also sent by an unnamed woman) alongside Calvin's reply to her and his reply to the other woman in 1559, one can see that Calvin takes their "perplexity and anguish" seriously and attempts to respond with pastoral compassion. He also regards the women in these harsh circumstances as God's agents, called on to bear an open witness to the gospel. Calvin's letters to women have been studied by Charmarie Jenkins Blaisedell, who does not disguise the apparent offense of Calvin's call to suffer an abusive husband in hopes of his conversion. But she also characterizes Calvin as egalitarian in such matters: "Calvin seems to have reserved no more sympathy for women than for men. While he may have thought of woman as the weaker ves-

---

13. Bussert, *Battered Women*, 11–12; Douglass, "Women and the Continental Reformation," 300–301. The full text of Calvin's letter is translated in Hughes, *Register*, 344–45; the original text of Calvin's letter, sent in the name of the Company of Pastors, is found in CO 17:539 (no. 3064, 4 June 1559). Bussert's footnote is defective, but a study of her excerpt suggests that she has simply further reduced Douglass's earlier excerpt—a deduction corroborated both by the presence of *Religion and Sexism* (but not Hughes's *Register*) in her bibliography and by the peculiarities of her citation. Not all are dependent on Bussert, however. At least one other writer went directly to Douglass's article and perhaps to Hughes; see Clarke, *Pastoral Care*, 75.

14. Both the woman's and Calvin's letters are translated in Hughes, *Register*, 193–98; original texts may be found in CO 14:337–40 (no. 1634, 24 June 1552) and 10a: 239–41 (22 July 1552).

sel, in spiritual matters he treated her as if she were equal to man."[15] In his replies to these particular women, Calvin does allow that they might well flee their husbands, but only (he adds) after they have "done their duty" by bearing witness. Indeed, he urges both women not only to please their husbands but also to stand up to them and "show that it is not her intention to change her position."[16] In other words, Calvin has approvingly revisited two classic loci in Christian theology: the *clausula Petri* of Acts 5:29, whereby, ultimately, Protestant wives must obey God rather than Roman Catholic husbands; and the patristic tradition of warranting flight in times of persecution. It is especially striking that in advising these women, Calvin has stepped well beyond the "silent submission" that 1 Peter 3:1–6 enjoins upon any woman married to an unbelieving husband.

It ought to be obvious, then, that Calvin was no friend of domestic violence. As Douglass notes, despite his traditionalism, Calvin still stressed mutuality in marriage and worked to end the double standard in divorce.[17] The Consistory of Geneva typically excommunicated men who beat their wives, and handed them over to the city council for various harsher penalties, including fines and jail time. In 1557 one father who refused to support his own child was thus imprisoned, and his wages were garnished.[18] Nonetheless, selecting quotes and anecdotes that favor Calvin from the perspective of our own day seems as preposterous as perpetuating the myth that Calvin hated women, because still other quotes and anecdotes will remind us that the sensitivities of sixteenth-century Geneva are not our own. William Monter chronicled the shifting fortunes of women in Geneva over the course of two and a half centuries; Jeffrey Watt has also underscored that gains in one area were often matched by losses elsewhere.[19] Even more pointedly, Mary Potter Engel has argued that it is easy to misinterpret changes in the

---

15. Blaisdell, "Calvin's Letters," 74; Blaisdell, "Calvin's and Loyola's Letters," 235–53.

16. Translation from Hughes, *Register*, 345; CO 17:539: "Mais tenir bon quoy quil en soit et monstrer qu'elle n'a point deliberé de changer de propos."

17. Douglass, "Women and the Continental Reformation," 299, 303–4.

18. See Monter, "Consistory of Geneva," 63–84, esp. nn. 34–36 there; Monter, "Women in Calvinist Geneva," 189–209, esp. 194; Watt, "Women and the Consistory," 429–39. For the case of Thibault Gaultier, who refused to support a child he fathered with a servant, see Spierling, "Father, Son, and Pious Christian," 101.

19. For Monter and Watt, see the previous note.

rhetoric surrounding marriage and family life as signaling *ideological* changes that we would like to see in the past, as we read our values into their behavior.[20]

To these warnings we ought to add, once more, that restraint is crucial in the practice of history. Calvin's letter to the persecuted noblewoman in 1552 is a case in point: the letter he received was hand-delivered, and the letter itself speaks of "other reasons . . . which you may learn from the carrier of this letter," but which could not be written down. Calvin was just as secretive: he sent his reply by a gentlemen "who . . . will inform her of what we have said by word of mouth."[21] Geneva's position here was a complicated one. As Robert Kingdon has observed, Catholics commonly complained that the self-styled "persecuted" spouses whom the Consistory welcomed to Geneva were, to the contrary, simple cases of partners deserting their marriages.[22] Which side had the whole truth? In at least some of these vexed cases, Calvin may well have known more than he put into writing.

Myths about "bad Calvin" have taken other forms, too, some of which I have described elsewhere,[23] but let me add just one remark before moving on. It seems to me that what Tom Davis said about nineteenth-century history textbooks also applies here: Calvin has become a symbol in the minds of many feminists for the worst that Christianity has to offer with respect to women; but the Calvin who is vilified in this way is, unfairly, a scapegoat, a figure of straw.

"Good Calvin"

We turn now to the "good" Calvin. Here there are really two mutually opposed myths, insofar as there is an active dispute over how to interpret Calvin on certain points pertaining to women in their private

---

20. Engel, "Historical Theology and Violence," 59.
21. Translations from Hughes, *Register*, 196, 198 (CO 14:340, 10a:241).
22. Kingdon, *Adultery and Divorce*, 143–44, 155–56.
23. For example, Calvin is treated especially poorly by Gerda Lerner in her influential work, *The Creation of Patriarchy*. For my critique of how she selectively quotes Calvin as hardly bothered by Lot's willingness to offer his daughters to the men of Sodom, see Thompson, *Writing the Wrongs*, 216–17. As in the case of Bussert's selective citation of Calvin, so also has Lerner's misrepresentation of Calvin misled other writers.

The Good, the Bad, and the Indifferent

and public roles. My procedure here will be to set forth both sides as concisely as possible, then reflect on the two perspectives together.

Myth #3: Calvin Perfectly Expounds the Biblical View of the Hierarchical, Patriarchal Family

What I'm calling a third myth requires careful parsing. I'm not suggesting that the Bible cannot be read as teaching patriarchy: certainly, Calvin reads it that way. Instead, what I'm interacting with here is more the way Calvin is elevated to canonical status by some present-day advocates of patriarchy as the only legitimate or authentically biblical worldview. Granted, it can be hard to draw the line between commending Calvin as a solid interpreter of biblical passages that address gender roles, on the one hand, and treating his exposition as virtually flawless, on the other.

Unsurprisingly, the loftiest treatments of Calvin as theoretician of women and the family are often found online, though not always there. One common manifestation of this view of Calvin is simply the posting of excerpts from Calvin's works, often his sermons, with a suitable headline suggesting that beyond the framework provided by the headline, Calvin's words present a self-evident case. For example, the website of Vision Forum Ministries, in addition to furnishing a thoughtful exposition of "The Tenets of Biblical Patriarchy," also excerpts Calvin's sermon on 1 Tim 2:13–15 with the headline, "John Calvin on Women Rejoicing in Their Role as Homemakers." Another page quotes the same sermon alongside Knox's *First Blast of the Trumpet against the Monstrous Regiment of Women* as defenses of "the doctrine of male headship" and as twin antidotes to "the radical egalitarianism that has become the rage in Evangelical circles in our day," insofar as both Calvin and Knox "rather affirmed the doctrine of male headship and female submission as taught in the Scriptures."[24] There are other sites that post Calvin in similar ways, such as excerpting the letter to Bullinger in which Calvin asserts that "women rulers are God's judgment" as clear proof that Calvin would not support women politicians today.[25]

24. These three pages are found at Vision Forum Ministries, "Calvin and Knox," "John Calvin," and "Biblical Tenets."

25. "Here Calvin removes any doubt concerning the view he and the other reformers would take of complementarians who lately have taken to denying that the creation

There are also, of course, print publications that style Calvin as a spokesman on behalf of biblical patriarchy. Not all that long ago, Calvin's little-known trio of sermons on 1 Cor 11:3–16 appeared in English under the title, *Men, Women, and Order in the Church*. Calvin is mostly allowed to speak for himself, but the short introduction makes clear that the booklet intends to alert readers as to "how far we have moved from the heritage of the Reformers and their Puritan disciples" and to invoke Calvin to testify that "within the divine order, men are appointed to rule over women."[26]

Obviously, all these sources share a commitment to honor the Christian past, and commendably so. So, on the one hand, these would-be Calvinist bloggers urge their readers "to fall in love with our fathers and mothers who are long gone, feeding from their generous hands as they lead us back to the precious truths of Scripture—back to God and His Word." But there is also a tendency to brook no opposition to a reading of the past that is explicitly designed "to escape the suppressive egalitarian and feminist ethos permeating the Church today," and to that end, Calvin helps prove there is really only one way to read the Bible on the topic of the "order of the sexes," and that way has been "boringly normal throughout all Church history."[27] However, I would not characterize these views as perpetrating a myth about Calvin if I truly felt that they had captured the whole truth about the past, as if Calvin harbored no secrets or second thoughts. In general, the problem with these chauvinistic readings of Calvin, just like the other myths I have described, is that they read Calvin too selectively—as we'll see.

Myth #4: Calvin Was Genuinely Open to Change in Gender Roles, and Possibly a Proto-Feminist

Our third myth is only half of an equation, for there is a fourth myth that offers the opposing point of view. I've already mentioned Jane Douglass's fine essay on women in the Reformation, but she also authored a longer and more focused study titled *Women, Freedom, and*

---

order of the sexes applies outside the church and home." See Bayly, "Calvin: Woman rulers are God's judgment."

26. Skolnitsky, *Men, Women, and Order*, 4, back cover.

27. All quotations in this paragraph are taken from Bayly, "John Calvin on Deborah," which also excerpts Calvin's commentary on 1 Tim 2:11–13.

Calvin. That book does a good job of extrapolating significant themes in Calvin's thought—especially his understanding of Christian freedom—and probing the implications for Calvin's understanding of women in leadership roles. Moreover, she does this with a particular sensitivity to the historical ferment of Renaissance humanism that surrounded Calvin and the historical personages—especially key sixteenth-century women—whom Calvin surely knew and interacted with. But Douglass's greatest contribution, I think, was to call attention to two statements where Calvin declares that the prohibition against women speaking in church in 1 Cor 14:34–35 is not a "fixed, unchangeable decree" but rather a matter of polity and therefore among the *adiaphora*, those "middle things" that are neither good nor evil, neither commanded nor forbidden, in which the church and those who make up its congregations have an undeniable measure of freedom. For Douglass, the clear implication of what one might call the "demotion" of Paul's prohibition against women's speaking and even proclaiming the gospel in public is to suggest that Calvin granted a measure of *approval* to such activities, and even that Calvin was "open to future change" in the direction of women's ordination "on theological grounds."[28]

Douglass makes a few unguarded or (perhaps) optimistic statements in her provocative study, but on the whole she is quite sober, reminding us that it would be a mistake "to make Calvin a hero in the matter of women's ordination."[29] By and large, only the occasional writer has taken her optimistic statements about Calvin's openness to change and allowed them to stand as apparently the whole truth, or the most important truth.[30] Usually, even those later studies with explicit feminist interests have presented Douglass's revisionist picture of Calvin as only part of a bigger picture.[31]

What has prevented later feminist and other historians from embracing Douglass's account of Calvin's teachings about women is the

28. Douglass, *Women, Freedom, and Calvin*, 10; cf. 62, 104–5, 121.

29. Ibid., 10.

30. See, for example, the qualified endorsement of Douglass in Anderson, "Reading Tabitha," 32 n. 59. See also the conclusion drawn by van Huyssteen, *Alone in the World?* 131.

31. See the considerable but skeptical appreciation for Douglass's portrait of Calvin in Tucker and Liefeld, *Daughters of the Church*, 175–76; and Kvam et al., *Eve & Adam*, 254–55.

mass of his other, more usual statements that not only reiterate traditional hierarchical views but also lapse occasionally into what strikes us as patriarchal *excess*—such as Calvin's declaration that God is more glorified in the birth of a boy than a girl, or his parroting of Jerome's view that God shames men by raising up women, whom Calvin then likens to God's using stones, fools, or the mute.[32] Clearly, Calvin is not the man of feminist dreams. But Calvin is also a dubious ally for twenty-first-century patriarchs, not only because of excesses like those just mentioned, which also exceed their exegetical warrants, but also on account of the *exceptions* that Calvin did, in fact, accommodate, just as Douglass asserted, even if he was ill at ease to speak of them. Curious and surprising as it is to find Calvin ceding any degree of approval to women's proclaiming the gospel in public, that approval cannot be denied either in Calvin's theory or in his actual experience. Moreover, Calvin's clear if uncomfortable approval of women's public proclamation of the gospel is not unique to him: it is an opinion shared by others in his day, including Jacques Lefèvre d'Étaples, Martin Luther, François Lambert, and Peter Martyr Vermigli.[33]

In short, Calvin cannot be reduced only to his most traditional views, nor can he be purified of those traditions so as to leave only his most progressive or egalitarian asides, however much both extremes have their advocates today. Instead, a holistic reading of Calvin forces us to integrate the patriarchal Calvin with the Calvin who could accommodate exceptions. Any other "good" Calvin would be merely a creature of our myth making.

---

32. Calvin, *Sermon 11 on Job* 3:3 (CO 33:146–47): "Il est vray que l'image de Dieu est bien inprimee par tout: mais si est-ce que la femme est inferieure à l'homme; il faut que nous allions par ces degrez-là que Dieu a instituez en l'ordre de nature. Ainsi donc c'est raison que Dieu soit glorifié et aux masles, et aux femelles: toutesfois il doit estre principalement glorifié, quand un homme, c'est à dire un masle sera nay." Jerome's dismissal of women as leaders is found in *Contra Jovinianum* 1.25; Calvin makes the same point in *Serm. 1 Tim.* 2:13–15 (CO 53:221–22) and *Comm. Ezek.* 13:17–18 (CO 40:288).

33. I have written at length on this issue elsewhere, including "Rules Proved by Exceptions"; "Patriarchy and Prophetesses"; *Daughters of Sarah*.

Calvin in the Middle

Is there a resolution to these partisan readings of Calvin on the topic of women's public roles? As I have hinted, if there is, it would entail not an either/or but a both/and. One source of confusion in reading Calvin surely stems from an ambiguity, if not a contradiction, that must be laid on Calvin's desk and not on our own. In brief, Calvin is caught between two competing views of polity, two understandings of the church's external arrangements, two notions of *adiaphora* or indifferent matters, and it is difficult to conclude that he was aware of his own emerging self-contradiction.

What we have in Calvin is thus a series of blurred definitions, all of which reveal his grappling with the Bible's authority as something that is *layered*, so to speak. It is easy to lose track of Calvin on this point. For example, Calvin often speaks of *polity*—the external arrangements by which the church governs itself—as an indifferent matter, something that is by no means fixed by Scripture or by divine authority, but which can be adjusted by churches and congregations to suit their own sense of what is useful, beneficial, and appropriate. Calvin makes this point in many contexts, including in his 1543 appeal to Charles V, a treatise that the English-speaking world knows as *On the Necessity of Reforming the Church*. There Calvin argues that the essentials of the Christian religion consist, broadly speaking, in worship and salvation, alongside which sacraments and polity are strictly secondary concerns.[34] Calvin's argument that some biblical teachings and practices are more central than others was by no means a new idea, but it obviously had to affect how he would rule on all kinds of practical matters as well as his estimate of many of the received traditions of the Roman Catholic Church. Consequently, Calvin often had to enunciate his working principle here, as in the 1543 *Institutes*, where he says the practice of kneeling in church for prayer is by no means a divine commandment, yet it *is* an expression of decorum—and while decorum may be a rather general category, flexible if not vague, decorum is also something Paul sets forth as "a command of the Lord."[35]

---

34. Calvin, "The Necessity of Reforming the Church," in *Selected Works* 1:123–234. Actually, Calvin illustrates his point by describing worship and salvation as the *soul* of Christianity, while sacraments and polity constitute its *body*. See my essay, "John Calvin's Understanding."

35. Calvin, *Institutes* IV.x.30, OS 5:192, Battles, *Institutes*, 1207–8.

Calvin's discussion of decorum, of course, always stems from an implicit conversation with 1 Cor 14:40. There, after some very specific directions about prophecy and other spiritual gifts (and also following his insistence that women not speak in church!), Paul suggests that his real concern is not these specific recommendations but the general principle of decency and order. And that is where we find Calvin insisting that even Paul's rule about women's silence is merely an expression or application of the general principle, as if keeping women from speaking or teaching were merely one way among many others by which decorum might be expressed. From the first edition of the *Institutes* through the last, Calvin let stand these provocative phrases: "These are no fixed and permanent sanctions by which we are bound, but outward rudiments for human weakness ... What? ... Is that decree of Paul's concerning [women's] silence so holy that it cannot be broken without great offense? ... Not at all. ... And there is a place where it is no less proper for her to speak than elsewhere to remain silent."[36]

These lines were supplemented in Calvin's 1546 commentary on 1 Cor 14:34–40, where he again identified Paul's restrictions on women as merely an application of the more general principle of decorum: "Because he is arguing here about external arrangements (*externa politia*), he regards it as sufficient just to point out what is unseemly so that the Corinthians might avoid it. Likewise, a discerning reader should recognize here that [Paul] is dealing with things neither good nor bad, indifferent matters (*medias et indifferentes*), in which nothing should be forbidden except what works against decorum and edification."[37]

So far, everything Calvin has said looks as if he is indeed arguing for flexibility in polity. But, having given these things with his right hand, Calvin then seems to take them away with his left. What he says in the *Institutes* about this elusive place where it is proper for a woman to speak (and, presumably, teach) appears alongside three other examples of common church practices that Calvin also regards as "indifferent," that is, as matters of polity that exist largely for the sake of decorum. These three are the propriety of women keeping their heads covered in public, kneeling for prayer in church, and giving corpses a decent burial.

---

36. In 1543, Calvin rewrote the passage, splitting it between what would finally become IV.x.29 and 31, so that women's head coverings illustrated *decorum* while the command against women teaching illustrated *order*.

37. Calvin, *Comm. 1 Cor.* 14:34, CO 49:533.

Calvin has other examples too, but these are the ones he returns to after some intervening remarks—and what arrests the attention of the truly discerning reader is that in none of these instances does Calvin actually envision any *enduring* changes in any of the four practices, even though he has plainly implied that changed contexts do require changed practices. Instead, Calvin affirms that there is no shame in a woman's having a bare head—*if* she has rushed out to help a neighbor without a scarf. There is nothing unholy about burying a corpse without a shroud—*if* one cannot be found. And there is no offense when a man does not kneel for prayer—*if* his knees are stiff from disease.

What Calvin's illustrations reveal is that despite the supposed lesser status and lesser authority of such supposedly indifferent matters as women's head coverings and women's silence, Calvin himself cannot really imagine genuine and enduring changes in these arrangements. Instead, he can at most imagine their temporary suspension, a position that is precisely mirrored in the allowance he shared with Luther, Vermigli, and others that women may serve as teachers or preachers in emergencies, but only for a limited time.

What we also see at work in Calvin is something else that was common among the Reformers, namely, multiple understandings of what constituted truly indifferent matters. Sometimes matters were regarded as indifferent if they were neither morally good nor morally evil; sometimes, if they were neither commanded nor forbidden by Scripture; and sometimes, if they had no bearing on either gaining or losing salvation.[38] Calvin is perfectly capable of silently switching from the second definition to the third and back again, all in the same paragraph. In other words, when Calvin insists that the prohibition against women's teaching in church is an external arrangement, a matter of polity and thus indifferent, he really means only that it is indifferent to *salvation*: a woman might, therefore, be drawn by necessity to share the gospel in public, and no one should think her salvation is thereby endangered. But Calvin also thinks the rule against women's teaching in public is not just one possible application of the principle of decorum, decency, and order: it is also an application that appears in the Bible itself as bearing apostolic approval, and it may even be the Lord's own command.

---

38. For a more detailed introduction to *adiaphora* in the sixteenth century, as well as more on Calvin's use of the concept, see Thompson, *Daughters of Sarah*, 229–67, and the other studies cited there.

Consequently, as a practice, it is not absolutely indifferent, because it is discouraged by God's word, even if it remains a matter of polity. A good way to clarify Calvin's working distinction might be to contrast *human* polity with *divine* polity—except that this is a distinction that Calvin himself does not articulate or always observe, neither in his theory nor in his practice.

It is fair to conclude, then, that on the subject of women's roles in public and private, Calvin remained firmly fixed in the middle, and in more ways than one. Living in an era of religious turmoil, a time of ecclesiastical renewal and social change, Calvin learned by experience that his ideals for the reformation of the church were unlikely to be implemented in full any time soon, however well defined they may have been. Thus, while his theology is steeped in traditionalism and patriarchy, his practice reveals him as acutely aware that the theories of patriarchal exegesis cannot—indeed, *should* not—always be applied. Sometimes a woman must speak up on behalf of the gospel against a belligerent husband, and even against 1 Peter 3. In some circumstances, a woman may be better suited than any man to proclaim the gospel even in public, and for her this may amount to a divine, if temporary, calling. So if Calvin was no feminist, neither was his patriarchy unaccommodated to the needs of his day. Moreover, to the extent that Calvin manifested even a qualified openness to the ministry of women, he indicates his middle stance in yet another way: namely, as a discerning reader not only of how Christian women were being called and used by God in his day but also of how the lesser teachings of Scripture must not be confused with the central doctrines that bear on salvation itself. If Calvin's account of such matters of polity as properly belonging among the *adiaphora* or "middle things" strikes us as a bit muddled or (more charitably) as unfinished, it remains to his credit that he read the Bible well enough to see the extremes of legalism and libertinism and to take his stance between.

4

Calvin and Church Discipline
Penance, Apology, and Reconciliation

DIANE C. MARGOLF

On Thursday, 27 April 1542, two brothers named Jehan and Claude Curtet were summoned to appear before Geneva's consistory, the institution responsible for implementing church discipline in the city-state. When asked why he and his brother "do not live together in peace," Jehan Curtet, a butcher, replied, "He wants to live like respectable people and does not want to do otherwise."[1] His brother Claude, a cutler, was asked why he had not appeared in church to partake of communion on the Sunday before Easter. Claude responded that "he does not love his said brother and that they are at law . . . he did not receive Holy Communion last Easter and does not say his Pater because he wishes harm to his brother and when he sees his brother he thinks he sees his hostility."[2] The consistory urged the two men to be reconciled to each other but especially aimed its admonitions at Claude Curtet: "And they declare him to be outside the union of the faithful, and considering this the preachers do not hold him as belonging to religion, and in view of his bad heart that he be proceeded against more rigorously by the

---

1. Kingdon et al., *Registers*, 52.
2. Ibid., 53.

Seigneurie [i.e., the secular government of Geneva]. And that men be assigned to reconcile them, as otherwise there would be great scandal. And [Claude] was admonished to expel all rage from his heart."[3]

Claude Curtet believed that his brother blamed him for the loss of Vétraz, a village where he had been a tenant farmer, and that had been seized by the king of France two years earlier. As noted above, the two brothers were engaged in a lawsuit, but the personal enmity between them had also led Claude to withdraw from participation in communion, thus jeopardizing his membership in the Reformed community of Geneva and creating a potential scandal within that community. A month later, in May 1542, the consistory again admonished Claude Curtet to mend his relationship with Jehan, and Claude assured the consistory that "he would be pleased to pardon his brother."[4]

Hostilities between the Curtets continued, however, and Claude had been imprisoned as part of the judicial proceedings when the consistory managed to achieve its goal of reconciling the two men nearly a year later, in March 1543. At that time, Jehan and Claude were again summoned and urged to set aside their differences: " Jehan said he is ready to do all that respectable people would do. Claude said that he would leave vengeance to God after having heard the admonitions of the lord [syndic]. They were exhorted to pardon each other. Claude having heard the holy doctrine, they pardoned each other, made peace and pardoned each other and shook hands in the sign of peace."[5]

The resolution of the Curtets' dispute contains the classic elements of such incidents: the cooperation of secular and church authorities in admonishing the brothers to reconcile, the invocation of "holy doctrine" as part of the exhortation to pardon, and a physical gesture (the handshake) to conclude and perhaps reinforce the reconciliation accomplished by verbal forgiveness.

The consistory's role in attempting to resolve disputes like the one between the Curtets reveals much about "myths and realities" concerning church discipline in Calvin's Geneva and elsewhere in sixteenth-century Europe. In keeping with the theme of this volume, I will focus on the relationship between Calvin, church discipline, and three areas where myth and historical reality collide: first, the purposes of church

3. Ibid.
4. Ibid., 57.
5. Ibid., 217.

discipline in Geneva and other areas that adopted Calvinist reform; second, the relationship between Calvinist church discipline and penance in early modern Catholicism; and third, the connections between sixteenth-century reconciliations and modern practices of public apology. I should add that by *myths* I do not mean falsehoods or fictions but rather interpretations that seek to explain practices and developments, and that have been widely accepted and disseminated. There are certainly elements of truth in each of the myths I will mention, but in recent years both archival scholarship and trends in the historiography of the Reformation more generally have brought new "realities" to the fore, thus challenging and enriching our understanding of Calvinist church discipline. The last of these three topics will be the most speculative.

Calvin and the Purposes of Church Discipline

Like the doctrine of predestination, church discipline is often associated specifically with John Calvin and his particular contributions to the Protestant Reformation in sixteenth-century Europe. The association stems in part from Calvin's own writings, including the *Institutes of the Christian Religion*. In this work, Calvin argued that church discipline—including the power to excommunicate and reconcile offenders—was essential to unite the members of a Christian community, and to keep each in his or her proper place.[6] Discipline for Calvin accompanied the marks of a true Christian church, which were the correct preaching of doctrine and administration of the sacraments. Its purpose was not merely to punish, but to provoke a personal sense of shame and a desire for forgiveness among offenders. In the case of minor faults, Calvin argued that verbal rebukes should be used to "bring [the sinner] back to himself, that he may rejoice rather than be sad that he has been corrected."[7] Those who refused or defied such mild correction, or who committed more public offenses that caused scandal to the church and community, merited harsher treatment; indeed, they could be denied participation in communion until they demonstrated true repentance and were publicly reconciled with the church.[8]

---

6. Calvin, *Institutes*, IV.xii.1, quoted in Kingdon, et al., *Registers*, xvii.
7. Battles, *Institutes*, 1234 (IV.xii).
8. Ibid., 1230–35.

With the historian's gift of hindsight, we know that Calvin's views on church discipline prevailed in Geneva. Yet Calvin's initial attempt to establish church discipline there in 1537 resulted in his being banished from the city-state. When he returned four years later, he insisted that the Genevan government approve the Ecclesiastical Ordinances of 1541, which established a new institution, the consistory, to administer church discipline.[9] Composed of about a dozen city councilors and all of the city's Reformed ministers, the consistory was led by a syndic (one of four elected magistrates who were at the top of Geneva's political hierarchy), who interrogated the men and women summoned before the group. The consistory could deliver admonishments and decree excommunications; it could also send offenders to Geneva's secular court, which could impose more serious corporal or monetary penalties. The minutes of consistory sessions, including summaries of interrogations, orders for further investigation, and judgments, provide insight into the workings of church discipline in Geneva, as well as a treasure trove of information about daily life, family relations, and religious beliefs and practices among ordinary citizens.

In Geneva and elsewhere, the consistory clearly functioned as an instrument of morals control; its purpose was to identify and reform behaviors that threatened the establishment of a godly community, ranging from gambling and immodest dress to sexual misconduct and violence. Historians have emphasized that the consistories' power of excommunication (that is, the power to forbid community members' participation in Communion) could be a meaningful threat in sixteenth-century towns and villages. The consistories' ability to impose public humiliation as a penalty for certain types of sinful behavior, and sometimes as a necessary demonstration of repentance prior to readmission to the sacrament, has also been viewed as an important part of their role in disciplining members of Reformed communities. Studies of church discipline in such communities across Europe abound with accounts of men and women who were required to stand at church doors, in marketplaces or before congregations, to sit on repentance stools or kneel before their kin and neighbors, to wear distinctive

---

9. A good summary of these developments is Naphy, "Calvin and Geneva," 309-22. See also Naphy, *Calvin and the Consolidation*; Kingdon, *Adultery and Divorce*, 7-30; Kingdon, "Social Control and Political Control," 521-32; and Grosse, *L'Excommunication*.

clothing and verbally express their remorse and regret.[10] The "myth" of Calvinist church discipline in early modern Europe, then, includes the notion that it was essentially punitive and repressive.

Yet this is only part of the story. While Reformed church discipline could certainly involve public humiliation and both social and spiritual exclusion, Calvin himself emphasized that the goal of such discipline was to bring about the individual's repentance and reconciliation with God and the church, rather than simply to punish external behavior. Mildness and restraint were therefore preferable to harshness in administering discipline: "Unless this gentleness is maintained in both private and public censures," he wrote, "there is danger lest we soon slide down from discipline to butchery."[11]

Consistory records from Geneva during the early 1540s reflect Calvin's emphasis on reconciliation as an important part of church discipline. This was the period when Geneva's inhabitants had to give up many traditional religious practices, adopt the tenets of the Reformed faith, and accept the authority of the newly created consistory to implement church discipline for those who struggled with or resisted these changes. The consistory records reveal many instances in which this panel of lay and clerical authorities (which included Calvin himself until his death in 1564) sought to resolve disputes and reconcile feuding parties as part of the larger task of reforming society. In doing so, the consistory urged people to replace ignorance and sin with proper beliefs and behaviors, and to put aside divisive emotions, such as anger, in favor of peace and forgiveness.[12] The consistory looked for signs of repentance as well as changed behavior; such signs included verbal admissions of wrongdoing (apologies) and emotions that were appropriate to the occasion.

For example, in November 1543 two widows were summoned before the consistory because they had allegedly made vows to St. Claude—something that was inconsistent with the Reformed rejection of the cult of saints. One woman denied the charge, but the other, Tevene

---

10. For examples, see Chareyre, "'The Great Difficulties,'" 63–96; Mentzer, "Marking the Taboo," 97–128; Graham, Social Disciplining," 129–57; Murdock, "Church Building and Discipline," 136–54; and Parker, "The Rituals of Reconciliation," 101–15.

11. Battles, *Institutes*, 1238.

12. Kingdon, "Efforts to Control Hate," 113–22.

Peronet, acknowledged the act and apologized: "It was because of her husband who was ill," the record states, "and she was badly advised and repents from her heart and begs mercy of God and the Seigneurie and the Company . . . And now she knows well the fault she committed and is very unhappy about it." For its part, the consistory, "having heard some repentance," admonished her to return in two weeks to demonstrate a better knowledge of prayer and confession, and to make sure that her son was similarly instructed.[13] Not all of those summoned before the consistory acknowledged their offenses and expressed repentance, however. A mason named Claude Morel appeared before the consistory in June 1544. Accused of blasphemy, Morel claimed that he attended sermons regularly and had heard Calvin preach the previous Sunday. But he could not recall the content of the sermon and said all of his prayers in Latin, so the consistory gave him a month "to learn to pray to the Lord" (presumably in French) and ordered him to have his son do the same.[14] Unlike Tevene Peronet, he gave no indication that he saw his actions as erroneous or repented them.

As in the case of the Curtet brothers noted above, the consistory often intervened in disputes among family members. On 23 March 1542 Philipaz Costel was summoned to explain the conflict among herself, her mother, and her husband, Pierre; her mother's appearance before the consistory a week earlier apparently had not satisfied their concerns. Philipaz claimed that she found herself caught in the middle of a dispute about her younger brother's marriage. The register entry suggests that her husband's imprisonment (possibly on a murder charge) was also a source of tension in the family. The consistory decided that "the mother and daughter should not be in discord from now on, but live in peace with each other" and ordered "that a respectable man be provided who will report on how they have made peace."[15] Jacquemaz Renault was brought before the consistory in April 1543 due to "anger against her husband and household," which in turn had led her to blasphemy and absenting herself from Communion. "She confesses having been very wrong and begs mercy of God and of justice," according to the register

---

13. Kingdon et al., *Registers*, 295. She returned on December 18 but still "said the prayer and the confession very poorly"; ibid., 302.

14. Ibid., 404–5.

15. Ibid., 23 (for Philipaz Costel) and 19–20 (for Dominique de Ulmodaz, her mother).

entry, and so the consistory remanded her before Geneva's council for further admonitions to amend her behavior.[16] When the consistory interrogated Guigoz Veilliard about rudeness and insults toward his father, Jehan, and mother-in-law, Reniere, in May 1542, Guigoz argued that he was the injured party, claiming that "he [was] persecuted more by his father than by anyone else." The consistory urged Jehan to take the lead in reconciling his quarrelsome family (assisted by three members of the consistory), noting that otherwise they would be forbidden to participate in Communion. Guigoz was also ordered "to honor his father and mother-in-law."[17] The tensions in this family carried over into other relationships as well. Six months later, the consistory sought to resolve a dispute between Reniere and Jane Guyone. The two women had exchanged insults, and though they had received Communion and attended sermons, their conflict had persisted. Urged by the consistory, they "made friendly, perpetual, durable peace, all their enmity being put in the past."[18]

As the last case suggests, the consistory exhorted all members of Geneva's Reformed community to pardon their offenses against each other, not just family members. In 1543 Antoine Checand, a syndic, and John Calvin presided over the reconciliation of goldsmith Ypolite Revit and Bartholomie Achard, a widow who had remarried. Achard denied having called Revit a traitor, though she admitted reproaching him for "wicked" behavior in a financial transaction. Exhorted to resolve their differences, "they pardoned each other and shook hands in sign of peace from now on." Bartholomie agreed "to hold him for a respectable man and would never again say anything like the aforesaid words," while Revit asked that their reconciliation be recorded in writing for future reference.[19] At the same consistory session, four women "put into suspension all words and reproaches" that they had exchanged about a sale of wheat, having been admonished to reconcile by Checand and Calvin.[20] A year later, the consistory investigated a quarrel between Aymoz Pilliod and Loys Franch. Pilliod claimed that Franch "bears him

16. Ibid., 226–27.
17. Ibid., 78–79.
18. Ibid., 151–52.
19. Ibid., 270.
20. Ibid., 271.

a grudge, and if he comes across him he means to be revenged on him," but the consistory urged him to wait until Franch could be summoned and the two men "brought to good accord and peace."[21] Two weeks later, Franch appeared before the consistory and made the following statements about the dispute between them: "The said Pilliod made him crippled and ill, and may God pardon him. And he did nothing to him, and let him mind his own business and he will mind his own, and he has no hatred against him and no grudge against him and does not look for him and leaves vengeance to God."[22]

After conferring with two members of the consistory, however, Franch repeated that "the thing is very serious for him, but he is content to pardon him [i.e., Pilliod] for the honor of God and justice." After being severely admonished, Pilliod responded in kind: he "begged mercy and pardon of him, throwing himself on the ground," and was pardoned by Franch.[23]

Cases such as these indicate that Geneva's consistory engaged in peacemaking as well as penalizing; it actively promoted the reconciliation of quarrels and disputes within families and the Reformed community at large as an important element of church discipline. Of course, this activity occurred in the context of a broader tradition in medieval and early modern Christianity that required individuals to have clear consciences and good relations with their neighbors and kinfolk before participating in Communion. Although Calvin did not persuade Genevan authorities to celebrate Communion as often as he wished, the fact that it was offered four times per year meant that the consistory's task of promoting repentance and reconciliation in relation to participating in Communion would be an ongoing endeavor.[24] In addition, it appears that the Geneva consistory's implementation of church discipline was well supported by both secular authorities and citizens, which may help to explain its exceptional level of activity in this area.[25]

---

21. Ibid., 405.

22. Ibid., 411.

23. Ibid., 412.

24. Wandel, *The Eucharist in the Reformation*, 168-78. The four times were Easter, Pentecost, mid-September, and Christmas. See also Burnett, *The Yoke of Christ*.

25. Benedict, *Christ's Churches*, 461-89. For an alternative view of conflict and opposition among Geneva's lay elites and Reformed ministers, see Naphy, "Baptisms, Church Riots, and Social Unrest," 87-97.

While some men and women questioned, mocked, or resisted the consistory's authority, its version of church discipline became part of Calvin's legacy in Geneva and was transported to other parts of Europe that adopted Reformed religion.

According to historian Philip Benedict, the Reformed consistory thus functioned as "the essential agency for effecting the communal moral regeneration that appeared so attractive to so many amid the initial excitement of the Reformation."[26] Perhaps because it was a communal institution (i.e., situated in a community) the consistory also adapted to local and regional circumstances and applied church discipline accordingly. In the past thirty years, research among the archives of consistorial records in France, England, Scotland, and the Netherlands has revealed much about the continuities of Calvinist church discipline in sixteenth-century Europe, as well as divergences. In general, church discipline depended for its success upon the efforts of lay elites as well as Reformed clergy. The elders who visited church members, and who sometimes were actively on the lookout for truants from worship, blasphemers, fornicators, and other miscreants, were usually from the middling or upper levels of society and were often responsible for reporting offenses to be investigated. Neighbors and family members might report misconduct or resist doing so, and those who were summoned to appear before a consistory might ignore the order. The nature and extent of consistorial activity, and the successful implementation of church discipline, thus depended on the support and cooperation of the faithful. In many early modern European Reformed communities, church discipline influenced standards of behavior related to marriage, sexual conduct, and violence, while efforts to control or abolish other activities traditionally associated with sociability (such as dancing) were often less successful.[27] In contrast to the "myth" that Calvinist church discipline was a uniform and largely repressive system of morals control, those who lived under such discipline may have seen themselves as "participating in a community of believers who felt a measure of responsibility for each other's behavior."[28]

---

26. Benedict, *Christ's Churches*, 460.

27. See Mentzer, *Sin and the Calvinists*; Todd, "Profane Pastimes," 123–56; and Mentzer, "Sociability and Culpability," 45–57.

28. Benedict, *Christ's Churches*, 489.

Calvinist Church Discipline and Roman Catholic Penance

The second myth that I wish to explore concerns the relationship between Calvin's view of church discipline and the Roman Catholic tradition of penance in the sixteenth century. Calvin argued that while church discipline was necessary and salutary for Christian believers and communities, penance as preached and practiced by the Roman Catholics of his day was a human invention, and a corrupt one at that. Drawing upon his study of the Christian Scriptures and patristic sources, Calvin claimed that penance in the early Christian church had involved a public ritual of reconciliation. Sinners who demonstrated appropriate and sincere repentance were encouraged to have faith in divine pardon for their misdeed, and the church (that is, the community of Christian believers) was enjoined to readmit the offenders to its fellowship. The ritual was fundamentally collective and not dependent on the bishop's authority alone for its meaning or effectiveness. Although it was not a sacrament, it promoted good order and peace among the faithful.

In Calvin's view, however, the Roman Catholic Church had replaced the "true and holy discipline" of the ancient church with auricular confession, thus enhancing the clergy's power over the laity in an illegitimate manner. Calvin thus used his considerable training in law, humanist scholarship, and theology to mount a polemical attack on Catholic penance, which he viewed as an abuse of authentic church discipline.[29] In a treatise titled *La vraie façon de réformer l'Eglise chrétienne et d'apaiser les différents qui sont en elle*, first published in Latin and French in 1549, Calvin emphasized that the Roman Catholic interpretation and practice of penance diverted a power to clerics that rightly belonged only to God:

"These great mediators [*moyenneurs*] promise us the remission of our sins, on the condition that we have confessed them into the ear of a priest. And what is that, I ask you, if not to subject to the law of men the absolution which is given to us by the grace of God? . . . Besides, those

---

29. The quotation comes from "Calvin's Reply to Sadoleto," in Olin, *A Reformation Debate*, 57. On Calvin's use of patristic sources to critique contemporary Catholic views of penance, see Lane, *John Calvin*; Van Oort, "John Calvin and the Church Fathers," 661–700; and Zachmann, *John Calvin and Roman Catholicism*.

who attribute so much to men, that sins may not be pardoned except according to their taste, commit too great an offense against God." [30]

Of course, to Roman Catholics at the time it seemed that Calvin's views were misguided and dangerous. To take just one example, in his dedicatory epistle for an English translation of Luis de Granada's *Memoriall of a Christian Life*, published in 1599, Richard Hopkins criticized the "calvinisticall Ministers" in Scotland, Holland, England, and the Low Countries for their notions of church governance: "And so every light headed Minister, joyned with a few ignorant Sineors [seigneurs] ... would rule as it were a Pope and so many Kinges, or rather tirants, in every severall parish church, that thereby they may have free liberty of theyr loose consciences... And therefore let no man marvaile [marvel], that these new Preachers doe never preach to the people, to doe pennance for their sins."[31]

The distinctions between Calvinist and Roman Catholic interpretations of church discipline and penance that were so clear (and so hotly contested) in the sixteenth century, however, have been reassessed in recent years. Social and cultural historians of the early modern period have emphasized the value of comparative rather than confessional approaches to analyzing the reform efforts of Calvinists and Roman Catholics.[32] According to one such study, Calvin's views on church discipline, the proper treatment of public and private sins, and the need to reform society and morals in Geneva were mirrored in the efforts of Carlo Borromeo, archbishop of Milan. Responding to the decrees and mandates of the Council of Trent, Borromeo "instructed his confessors to make their penitents renounce concubines, taverns, brothels, and the gaming table," in much the same way that Calvin insisted on the consistory's legitimate authority to admonish and possibly excommunicate Genevans who engaged in exactly the same types of public

---

30. Calvin, *La Vraie façon*, 22: "Ces beaux moyenneurs nous promettent bien la rémission de nos péchés, à condition que nous les avons confessés à l'oreille d'un prêtre. Et qu'est-ce, je vous prie, que cela, sinon assujettir à la loi des homes l'absolution qui nous est donnée par la grace de Dieu? ... Davantage, ceux qui attribuent tant aux homes, que les péchés ne soient point pardonnés, sinon à leur appétit, font un trop grand outrage à Dieu."

31. Luis, de Granada, *Memoriall*, 7, 11.

32. Holt, "The Social History of the Reformation," 133–44; Karant-Nunn, "Changing One's Mind," 1101–27; Laven, "Encountering the Counter-Reformation," 706–26.

immorality.[33] Both men also encountered and overcame opposition to their reform policies from lay elites.[34] The myth of opposing and mutually hostile Calvinist and Catholic views on church discipline, confession, and penance is certainly grounded in historical reality. But to the extent that historians study these topics as elements of a widespread concern to instill piety and to reform public morals in early modern Europe that transcended confessional boundaries, we will likely appreciate the distinctiveness of Calvin's contributions in the context of what he shared with his opponents.

Sixteenth-Century Reconciliations and Modern Public Apologies

As noted above, current approaches to the study of church discipline and the activities of Calvinist consistories tend to emphasize their specific connections to time and place—that is, to particular communities and to sixteenth-century people's beliefs about social order, hierarchy, honor, and privilege. All of this helps to explain the consistories' role in disciplining those who offended church and communal norms, as well as in reconciling those whose quarrels, conflicts, and emotions threatened the community's stability and morals. At the same time, it has been argued that the spread of Calvinist church discipline in the sixteenth century laid the foundation for a modern mentality regarding individual comportment, and indeed for the modern state's role in defining and maintaining social order. According to this argument, Calvinist church discipline proved to be an especially powerful form of social discipline; over time, it helped to create a collective religious identity among the Reformed in some regions that was "socially inclusive and territorially exclusive," and that was ultimately mobilized by political leaders to aid them in their own efforts to instill obedience, loyalty, and order.[35] How then does the practice of public apology or reconciliation in the context of sixteenth-century church discipline compare to modern examples of public apology?

33. De Boer, "Calvin and Borromeo," 91. See also de Boer, "Politics of the Soul," 116–33; de Boer, *The Conquest of the Soul*; and Luria, *Sacred Boundaries*.

34. De Boer, "Calvin and Borromeo," 92–93.

35. Gorski, "Calvinism and State Formation," 147–82, quotation on 148; Schilling, "Calvinism and the Making," 40–68.

Nowadays it seems that we are bombarded with apologies. Delivered by politicians, religious leaders, and celebrities, whether in newspapers, on television, or on the Internet, there is no shortage of instances in which public figures seek to acknowledge wrongdoing and request pardon for their offense. "At the end of the twentieth century," writes Susan Wise Bauer in her book *The Art of the Public Grovel: Sexual Sin and Public Confession in America*, "Americans increasingly expected their erring leaders to publicly admit their sin and ask for forgiveness."[36] While Bauer's study focuses on the specific examples of sexual sins confessed in twentieth-century America, sociologists and political scientists have also analyzed the phenomenon of public apologies, including those made by people in the present for offenses in the past, and by individuals or governments for collective crimes against various categories of victims. Examples include the Roman Catholic Church's apology in 1992 for placing Galileo Galilei under house arrest for life in 1633 and the state of Virginia's General Assembly's 2007 apology for slavery and mistreatment of Native Americans, which called for "reconciliation among all Virginians."[37] On the surface, this phenomenon would seem to indicate that the public apologies and reconciliations that were part of sixteenth-century church discipline, and which were sometimes avoided or resisted by the men and women who were ordered to perform them, are alive and well in our day.

Yet the ubiquity of modern public apologies suggests an important difference, one that perhaps derives from a very different conception of community. For the people of sixteenth-century Geneva (or Nîmes, or Emden, or Edinburgh), the power of public apology lay in the fact that one had to express repentance before a known community consisting of one's family, neighbors, and religious leaders in order to be reconciled with them and with God. The community or "public" to which one apologizes now is often so large, diffuse, and impersonal that the meaning of such expressions of regret or repentance may seem to be more

36. Bauer, *The Art of the Public Grovel*, 2.

37. See, for example Tavuchis, *Mea Culpa*; and Nobles, *The Politics of Official Apologies*. South Africa's Truth and Reconciliation Commissions represent another example of this phenomenon, which time and space do not permit me to explore here. It is worth noting that Geneva itself contains a "monument expiatoire" that commemorates (and seems to express an apology for) the execution of Michael Servetus in 1553, an event in which John Calvin played a leading role; see Choisy, *Calvin et Servet*. The monument was installed with great ceremony in 1903.

ritualized than real. Nevertheless, our continuing preoccupation with acknowledging offenses, expressing repentance, and seeking reconciliation suggests that the myth of sixteenth-century church discipline as a factor in creating modern societies, sensibilities, and identities may retain some reality, after all.

PART 2

Appeal of and Responses to Calvinism

5

The Elders' Gaze

Women and Consistorial Discipline in Late Sixteenth-Century France

GRAEME MURDOCK

In the story of Susanna and the elders, Susanna, the wife of Joakim, was a "very beautiful woman ... who feared the Lord." Two elders observed Susanna in her garden in Babylon and "began to lust for her." Turning "their eyes away from looking to heaven," the elders "day after day ... watched eagerly to see her." One "opportune day" the elders "were watching" Susanna when she was alone bathing. The elders demanded that Susanna consent to lie with them. When she refused, the elders falsely denounced Susanna for meeting secretly with a young man. When Susanna appeared before her accusers veiled, the elders ordered her to be unveiled "so that they might feast their eyes on her beauty." Susanna was condemned to death on the testimony of the elders. However, she called out for justice, and Daniel was inspired by God to intervene. Daniel questioned the elders separately, uncovering their lies by asking them under which tree in the garden they had seen Susanna meeting with her supposed lover. Daniel condemned the elders for their dishonesty, concluding that "beauty has beguiled you and lust has perverted your heart." The elders were put to death.[1]

This story of Susanna and the elders is a morality tale about truth and virtue prevailing over deceit and lust. There are a number of lessons intended to be drawn from the narrative about sight, sin, and sexuality, about the corrupt nature of the lustful male gaze, about how beautiful women are the objects of male desire, and about how women should protect their virtue by veiling themselves from the sight of men. Also implicit in the story are gendered notions of both sight and language; men look at women, and women are looked at by men; and men's words are more powerful and credible than those of women. Susanna's story attracted renewed attention during the Renaissance from a number of artists. However, portraits did not depict Susanna as a veiled woman of virtue but as a bathing beauty coming under the lecherous gaze of two elderly men.[2] Viewers of such pictures were thus offered the opportunity to scrutinize an idealized representation of the female form. It is not altogether obvious that such paintings were entirely in keeping with the authorial intent behind the story of Susanna.

Reformers followed some early church authorities in deciding to remove the chapter on Susanna from the book of Daniel. The story of Susanna and the elders was deemed to be apocryphal partly since, unlike the rest of Daniel, the text only survived in Greek.[3] Reformed church leaders were also quick to criticize visual representations of Susanna, as well as images depicting female saints, Mary, and other biblical characters. Calvin denounced Catholic pictures and statues of women as "exhibitions of the most shameless . . . obscenity." He suggested that "brothels exhibit their inmates more chastely and modestly dressed than churches do images intended to represent virgins." Those who allowed their eyes to commit "fornication" with such images and

---

1. For the story of Susanna and the elders see Daniel 13 or the Apocrypha.

2. Clanton, *The Good, the Bold, and the Beautiful*. Among many sixteenth-century portraits of Susanna see, for example, works by Jacopo Tintoretto from the 1550s.

3. Both Evangelical and Reformed churches set Susanna's story along with other apocryphal texts apart from the Old and New Testaments in printed Bibles. Susanna was also well known through a 1548 poem, "Susanne un jour," by Reformed writer Guillaume Guéroult, which became a popular song thanks to settings by a number of Catholic composers.

idols were, according to Calvin, covered "in the mire of Satan."[4] Calvin repeatedly warned of the problems associated not only with men looking at depictions of women but also with men catching sight of women's bodies in daily life. This, Calvin argued, was since eyes are "excessive in gazing about" "to the end we should become like brute beasts, full of wild and unruly lusts." Calvin highlighted the dangerous consequences of sight since a man need only "look upon a woman with an unchaste look . . . [to be] condemned for a whore-monger before God."[5] Calvin therefore urged women to take action to restrict visual access to their bodies, and instructed that men and women should not sit together in church, should not bathe together or dance together. Calvin even warned of the danger of catching sight of one's own naked body in private.[6]

This analysis of sight, sexuality, and the human body informed the advice which Calvin offered to women on how they should dress. Based on his interpretation of Paul's letters and other biblical texts, Calvin advised that "two things are to be regarded in clothing; usefulness and decency, and what decency requires is moderation and modesty."[7] In a sermon on "female modesty in clothing," which was published in France in 1561, Calvin stressed the importance of moderate expenditure on clothing. He suggested that the issue of how to dress represented a particular moral challenge to the wealthy since "there is scarcely anyone whose means allow him to live sumptuously, who does not . . . plume himself amazingly on his splendor." Clothing must also be modest, since Calvin suggested "not only all parts of the body" but also "clothes are adulterous."[8] Clothing that was too revealing, or that attracted attention to particular parts of the body unveiled

---

4. Battles, *Institutes*, 106-7 (I.xi.7); Calvin, *Of Shunning the Unlawful Rites of the Ungodly and Preserving the Purity of the Christian Religion* (1537), in *Selected Works*, 3:372, 402.

5. From the English translation by Arthur Golding of Calvin, *Sermons*, 522a and 528a-29a.

6. Calvin, *Commentaries on . . . Genesis*, 1:137, 151, 159, 163, 300-301, 303; Cottret, *Calvin*, 252.

7. Calvin, *Commentaries on the Catholic Epistles*, 96.

8. Calvin, *Sermon où il est montré*, with a preface probably by the former abbess Marie Dentière, wife of Antoine Froment; Calvin, *De Luxu* (1546/7) in Battles, "Against Luxury and License," 182-202; Battles, *Institutes*, 840-42 (III.xix.9); Beaty and Farley, *Calvin's Ecclesiastical Advice*, 84-85.

the wearer's vanity and shamelessness and fostered sin in the eyes and hearts of others. The need for greater modesty in clothing applied especially to women, who were identified by Calvin as far more culpable in this area. For women to appear in immodest clothing was not only ungodly but also unnatural, since such displays of provocative female sexuality aimed to usurp social power that properly belonged to men. Calvin therefore insisted that women ought not to "be decked for allurement." He argued that although "harlots for the purposes of enticement, are wont to dress themselves elegantly, to paint their faces, and to use other allurements," "the dress of a virtuous and godly woman must differ from that of a strumpet."[9] Calvin offered further advice on other aspects of female modesty, warning that the use of makeup made women appear like whores or like "painted idols in a church."[10] Calvin also stressed that women should normally appear in public with their hair covered. He found fault with the excessive attention that women gave to their "curled locks," and censured any costly decoration added to women's hair. If a woman had "her hair wantonly curled and decked," then "her vanity could not be excused."[11]

Calvin therefore identified close connections between female modesty and preventing sexual immorality in thought and action. He demanded that visual access to the female body must be restricted, and that women ought to adopt modest standards of appearance. Calvin argued that sexual immorality flourished as a direct consequence of the corrupting effects of Catholic teaching and visual culture. Other Reformed writers were equally anxious to distinguish their ideas from those of their Catholic opponents, arguing that the clothing adopted by priests, monks, and nuns only represented a false and hypocritical claim to a holy lifestyle.[12] However, Reformed concerns about female modesty and sexual morality were certainly neither novel nor exceptional in many ways. Among Catholic writers who were concerned with questions of female modesty was François de Sales, who, like Calvin, in-

---

9. Battles, *Institutes*, 407-8 (II.viii.44); Calvin, *Commentaries on the Prophet Jeremiah*, 1:247.

10. Calvin, *Sermon où il est montré*, 13, 31.

11. Calvin, *Commentary on . . . Isaiah*, 1:450; Calvin, *Commentaries on Paul's Epistles to . . . Timothy*, 66; Calvin, *Commentaries on the Catholic Epistles*, 96-97.

12. Battles, *Institutes*, 1264-65, 1472-73 (IV.xiii.10; IV.xix.25); Calvin, *Commentaries on . . . Ezekiel*, 107; *Chrestienne instruction*, 7.

terpreted the advice provided in the letters of St. Paul. However, de Sales also made comments about appropriate clothing for women, which had no parallel in Calvin's writings. For example, de Sales conceded that in matters of appearance "we may grant somewhat greater latitude to maidens, who may lawfully desire to attract many, although only with the view of ultimately winning one in holy matrimony."[13]

There were therefore some parallels between Reformed and Catholic ideas about female modesty. Reformed communities were also far from unique in adopting detailed regulations about clothing during this period. Many sixteenth-century states had sumptuary laws that attempted to uphold differences in social rank and to protect domestic economic interests. However, Reformed societies were distinctive in both the character of their regulations about clothing and in the determined efforts made to enforce changes to standards of appearance. In Geneva, the consistory's early efforts to proscribe certain forms of dress, hairstyles, and jewelry were clearly informed by concerns about sexuality and social justice. Geneva's ministers and consistory also urged the council to introduce civil regulations to restrict excesses in women's appearance. After discussions between ministers and the council a first set of regulations was eventually introduced in 1558.[14] In France, state laws already restricted the right of different social groups to wear certain materials and items of clothing. However, the Reformed church introduced its own guidance to church members about how to dress, and denounced immodest forms of appearance among women in particular. In the church's *Discipline Ecclésiastique*, ministers were required to warn congregations to refrain from all excesses in their clothing. Ministers and their wives were also instructed to set a good example to their communities on how to dress.[15]

Concern about women's clothing and appearance continued to be raised at Reformed synods during the 1570s and 1580s. In 1575 the Lower Languedoc provincial synod that met at Nîmes decided that some women's hairstyles had brought scandal to the church. Fashions of

13. De Sales, *Introduction*, 178–80.

14. Gallatin, "Les ordonnances somptuaires," 193–275; Murdock, "Calvin, Clothing and the Body," 481–94.

15. "La Discipline Ecclesiastique des Eglises Reformées de France," edited in Sunshine, "French Protestantism," 357, 375; Murdock, "Dressed to Repress?" 179–99; Romane-Musculus, "Histoire de la robe pastorale," 307–38.

twisting false hair into real hair, having long tresses and curls on display, using wire frame to raise the height of hair and to shape hair into horns, as well as decorating hair and headdresses by adding lace and gems all came under criticism. The Lower Languedoc synod decided that all necessary steps must be taken, particularly by the "brothers of Nîmes," to deal with excessive and immodest hairstyles. The next meeting of the Lower Languedoc synod in November 1575 expressed further concern about the dissolute ways in which some women were dressed, causing "great scandal to weak" members of the community. The synod confirmed that women, as well as their husbands and fathers, must be summoned to appear before their local consistory if they curled their hair or raised and shaped their hair using wire, or applied makeup to their faces or bosom. In 1581 the Lower Languedoc synod again deplored the consequences of women who adopted low necklines, while the same year another provincial synod complained about the indecency of women who revealed too much of their bosom to public view.[16] The issue of women's appearance was also discussed at the national synod in 1581, which reached the conclusion that those who wore clothes with "certain marked features of impudicity," including revealing their bosoms, would be denied the right to receive Communion.[17]

This urgent moral priority of dealing with excesses in the appearance of women and in particular of restricting visual access to the female body was taken up by Reformed communities. The issue was particularly significant in large urban centers that included many wealthy families who could afford new styles of clothing and costly forms of decoration. Attention here will focus on the town of Nîmes during the 1580s and 1590s to assess the consequences of Reformed church regulations about female appearance. Reformed religion had attracted significant support in Nîmes from the early 1560s. Among the first to convert were some of the town's wealthy judges and lawyers, including some consuls and councilors. A Reformed consistory began to meet in March 1561 under minister Guillaume Mauget. In 1561 the Reformed party seized control of the town, but this was reversed in 1563 when the governor of Languedoc installed Catholic consuls. In March 1565 a royal edict ordered the restoration of Catholic services but also conceded the right

16. Paris, La Bibliothèque de la Société de l'Histoire du Protestantisme Français (hereafter BSHPF), MS 566/ 1, 88v, 92.

17. Aymon, *Actes Ecclesiastiques*, 1:152–53.

for the Reformed community to build their own place of worship. The Reformed temple de la Calade opened in January 1566 with the central focus of the building on its pulpit. Prominent benches were assigned to the town's consuls, councilors, judges, and lawyers, and separate seating was provided for women and for men.

Competition for space and power in Nîmes descended into violence in 1567 with the Michelade massacre of leading Catholic citizens and clergy. This Reformed coup was directed by members of important local families, including the noble François de Pavée, the seigneur de Servas, and by the lawyer brothers Pierre and Charles Rozel. Catholic churches, including the cathedral, were attacked and badly damaged. After the peace of Longjumeau in March 1568, royal troops regained control over Nîmes. Over one hundred people believed by the royal authorities to have been involved in the Michelade massacre were condemned by the Toulouse *parlement*. Most of those named fled justice, but four (including Charles Rozel) were executed, and their heads were mounted on the town's gates. After the resumption of conflict across France, the Reformed party gained power once more in Nîmes with a further massacre of over a hundred local Catholics in November 1569. The August 1570 peace of St Germain offered Reformed communities the right to exercise their religion in towns that they controlled, including Nîmes. Nîmes then withstood a royal siege in 1573, and Reformed rights were confirmed by royal edict in 1576.[18]

Thus, by the early 1580s Nîmes was governed by Reformed consuls and councilors drawn from legal, professional, and merchant families. Around three-quarters of the town's population of over ten thousand people were Reformed. Nîmes stood at the center of a colloquy of between twenty and thirty Reformed churches in surrounding villages, and the town hosted both provincial and national synods as well as political assemblies of the Huguenot cause. A substantial Catholic population still lived inside the town, and some nearby villages also remained solidly Catholic. The town's civil authorities mostly worked in close cooperation with three resident ministers: Jacques Pineton de Chambrun, Claude de Falguerolles and Jean de Serres. Chambrun was the longest serving of the three, having worked in Nîmes since 1562, while his two colleagues had arrived in the town during the late 1570s. One of these

18. Ménard, *Histoire civile*; Tulchin, "The Michelade in Nîmes," 1–35; Guggenheim, "Calvinist Notables," 80–96.

ministers presided over Wednesday meetings of the town's consistory of four deacons and eight elders, a structure that mirrored the town's civil governance by four consuls and eight councilors. Members of the consistory were appointed each December by co-option, subject to the formal approval of the whole congregation. Some elders remained in post after one year's service to provide continuity and experience to the new consistory. Deacons were generally appointed from the ranks of judicial officeholders and lawyers, while elders were drawn more broadly from among merchants, professionals and artisans. For example, the list of elders for 1581 and 1582 includes merchants, a surgeon, a baker and a cloth maker.[19]

Membership in the consistory certainly carried a degree of social prestige in Reformed Nîmes, but it was also a time-consuming and demanding role. The consistory was responsible for all aspects of the organization and management of local church affairs, including donating charity to the poor and exercising moral discipline. The elders were particularly busy with disciplinary matters in the weeks leading up to four annual Communion services. Members of the congregation who had committed some offence then hurried to express repentance for their sins, to accept censure from the consistory, and to be reconciled with the church in time to receive a token from their elder, which permitted them to gain access to Communion. The consistory's powers were restricted to a range of spiritual sanctions, but these seem to have carried social authority. The elders first privately reprimanded offenders, then called repeat and serious offenders for formal interview and censure in front of the consistory. Persistent offenders could be required to offer public repentance for their faults before the whole congregation or be excluded from access to the sacraments or very rarely be excommunicated from the church.

The consistory kept private minutes about the business conducted at their formal meetings. These minutes sometimes refer to prior conversations held between an elder and a church member about his or her behavior. However, the records mostly summarize the interviews conducted with members of the congregation in front of the whole consistory. Some cases are reported in considerable detail while others are treated very briefly. Some entries involve a single offence by one named

---

19. Nîmes, Archives du Gard (hereafter RCN), "Registre du consistoire," 264.

individual, while others involve a number of different offences being dealt with at the same time, and others involve groups of people. The minutes set out the reaction of offenders to accusations made against them, and explain the decisions reached by the consistory. However, the minutes do not reveal any discussions or disagreements among members of the consistory on how to deal with offenders. It often remains unclear how elders had learned about the offending behavior of church members. While elders were active in monitoring daily life in their own districts of the town, they also seem to have received support from many ordinary people who passed on information about their neighbors. Nîmes certainly formed an excellent physical environment for both official surveillance and mutual observation. Town houses faced each other across narrow streets and winding alleys, which opened into small internal courts and into public spaces around the market and Roman amphitheater.

The surviving minutes of the consistory offer details about efforts to ensure that women were modestly dressed when they attended church services and went about the town. The consistory was concerned about clothing that revealed too much cleavage, although quite how much was too much is difficult to interpret. They were also worried about the vanity and pride of women who adopted extravagant hairstyles, used makeup or wore farthingales. The elders were concerned that women were trying to attract male attention by accentuating the prominence of certain parts of their bodies, or by altering and disguising the natural shape and color of their bodies. There are significant difficulties in analyzing the recorded information in the consistory's minutes about the campaign for female modesty in Nîmes. The minutes cannot be seen as comprehensive of the consistory's actions, and were only intended to provide some institutional memory for ministers, deacons, and elders. The minutes also reflect the perception of the consistory about the place of sin in Christian society, and present Reformed Nîmes as a sinful but penitent community. The elders did not expect to conquer sin, but sought to foster repentance in the hearts of individuals when they fell victim to temptation as well as establishing an environment in which people were helped to avoid sin.[20]

20. For approaches to Reformed disciplinary records in different contexts see Garrisson-Estèbe, *Protestants du Midi*; Vogler and Estèbe, "La genèse d'une société protestante," 362–88; Pollman, "Off the Record," 423–38; Todd, *Culture of*

Historians have subjected the records of the Nîmes consistory to detailed analysis.[21] This research has relied in part on counting the numbers of cases or incidents recorded in the consistory's minutes according to imposed categories of offences. Raymond Mentzer's analysis of the consistory's minutes between 1578 and 1583 suggested that around half of all formal cases were concerned with matters he described as interpersonal disputes and quarrels. Mentzer found that slightly less than a quarter of all cases during this period dealt with other "behavioral offences," including dancing, frequenting taverns, and excesses in clothing, and that less than one in ten cases involved sexual misconduct. The elders interviewed more men than women in all these categories of offences, except in the area of sexual misconduct and the intimately related problem (at least in the eyes of the elders) of immodest or inappropriate appearance.[22] Philippe Chareyre counted 12,442 cases in the consistory's minutes between 1578 and 1684. Of this total, only one hundred cases dealt with issues relating to clothing and appearance. Eighty-nine of these cases about personal appearance occurred between 1578 and 1594 out of a total of 4,173 cases counted by Chareyre during this period. Chareyre's statistical analysis reveals that there were only two formal cases relating to clothing, hairstyles and appearance considered between 1578 and 1581, while forty cases were heard during 1582 and 1583, and then twenty-five cases between 1584 and 1591. There were no recorded cases dealing with clothing and appearance after 1614.[23]

The early 1580s therefore marked a period of particular moral anxiety about female modesty in Nîmes and across French-speaking Reformed communities. The issue was a subject of discussion in print, was debated at provincial and national synods, and was dealt with in weekly meetings of urban consistories.[24] These strands of a concerted campaign to ensure that women adhered to acceptable forms of appearance were interrelated. For example, on 21 June 1581 the Nîmes

---

Protestantism; Mentzer, "Morals and Moral Regulation," 1–20.

21. Mentzer, "'Disciplina nervus ecclesiae,'" 89–115; Chareyre, "Le Consistoire de Nîmes;" Chareyre, "'The Great Difficulties,'" 63–96; Mentzer, "Organizational Endeavour," 1–29; Mentzer, "Ecclesiastical Discipline," 163–84.

22. Mentzer, "'Disciplina nervus ecclesia,'" 109, 111.

23. Chareyre, "Le Consistoire de Nîmes," 2:502–4.

24. Daneau, *Traite de l'estat honneste*; Daneau, *Deux Traitez de Florent Tertullian*.

consistory noted that the following Sunday one of the ministers would explain to the congregation the decisions made by the recent Montpellier meeting of the Lower Languedoc synod against low necklines and extravagant hairstyles. The elders believed that there were "several women" in the town who particularly needed to reform their appearance to avoid the impression of immodesty and of dishonorable attitudes and conduct.[25]

The consistory implicitly acknowledged at this meeting that many women in Nîmes were not guilty of adopting immodest standards of appearance. Many, indeed the great majority of women in the community, to judge by their absence from the consistory's records, came to cover their bodies and hair from the sight of men in ways that largely satisfied the ministers, deacons, and elders. Some women seem to have embraced the opportunity to visibly signal their commitment to Reformed religion in their clothing, also ensuring that their daughters were modestly attired, and perhaps informing their elder about other women whose appearance did not meet the required standards. Other women in Nîmes we can assume were less enthusiastic about abiding by the demands made on them but nevertheless decided to comply with the church on this issue because they accepted the authority of the consistory. The willingness of some to conform to Reformed ideas about clothing was in all likelihood bolstered by consideration of the social advantages of such apparent piety, or in reaction to the risk of the humiliation of being reprimanded by the elders. To be dressed in a modest way advertised an individual's honor, particularly important for the unmarried, and lowered the risk of public challenge to a woman's reputation and respectability. Such thinking may have also extended to influence women among the minority Catholic community in the town. Many women did not in any case have the financial resources to adopt novel or expensive styles of clothing and decoration that would have attracted the attention of the elders. They presumably continued to dress in ways that adhered to conventions for their social status and to the traditional norms of the local community, slightly adjusting their appearance if necessary in response to calls for greater modesty.

We know little from the consistory's minutes about what progress was made by the minister and elders in 1581 as they sought to enforce

25. RCN (42 J 27), 292.

norms of female modesty and talked with those whose appearance they deemed inappropriate. There is no further mention of the issue of women's appearance in the formal minutes of the consistory until February 1582. Each elder was then asked privately to warn women under "their watch" to avoid clothing that revealed too much cleavage and to abandon inappropriate hairstyles.[26] There were also a small number of formal interviews with women about their appearance, after other offences had first drawn them to the attention of the elders. These offenders were highborn and wealthy women, who had the means to adopt distinctive styles of clothing and to purchase decorative embellishments for their hair. Many belonged to leading Reformed clans in the town, connected by profession, marriage and patterns of sociability with some of the deacons and elders.

For example, on 14 February 1582 a group of people was named as having taken part in dances at the house of councilor Besserier. The dancers included members of some of the town's most significant Reformed families, including Rostan Rozel, Suzanne Rozel and the son of the seigneur de Servas.[27] The following week Suzanne, the daughter of lieutenant Charles Rozel, was the first of this group to appear before the consistory to confess to having danced. She was sternly admonished, and promised not to return to trouble the elders again.[28] However, on 7 March Suzanne Rozel was back in front of the elders to confess to having danced once again. On this occasion, the elders also told her to cover her bosom from sight and to stop raising and shaping her hair with wire.[29] At the same meeting, the elders instructed the daughters of Monsieur Boitier to cover their bosoms from sight and told them off for dancing.[30] Members of the Rozel clan were in trouble again when Louis Abraham confessed to having danced after taking supper at the house of Charles Rozel. On 21 March Captain Engarran also admitted to having danced at the Rozel house on several occasions. He was given

26. Ibid., 292.

27. Ibid., 288v, 292v, 294v, 295v, 296v and 298v. Rostan Rozel served for eight years on the consistory as a deacon after 1586. Chareyre, "Le Consistoire de Nîmes," 1: 614.

28. RCN (42 J 27), 290v.

29. Ibid., 297v, 300v, and 303.

30. Ibid., 299.

a severe censure by the elders and was warned to wear more modest clothes and to get his hair cut to a decent length.[31]

In February 1582 the consistory also investigated the behavior of Damoiselle Claude de Tuffan, who had gone to visit Avignon in the company of a Catholic noblewoman. The elders suspected that de Tuffan had attended Mass and danced while in Avignon.[32] When de Tuffan appeared before the consistory on 7 March 1582, she confessed to having attended three Catholic services, but only "out of curiosity," and denied the charge of dancing. She offered repentance for her offence and was reprimanded. However, the elders were evidently uncertain about the sincerity of de Tuffan's confession, and warned her that they would be checking on her behavior in future. De Tuffan was informed that her offences had caused a public scandal and greatly displeased God. She was instructed to attend sermons, to adopt a more modest hairstyle, and to cover her bosom from sight.[33]

On 20 June 1582 the elders considered the case of the daughters of Monsieur de Marguerites. Minister Jean de Serres was instructed by the consistory to exhort these girls to show greater restraint in their clothing, and in particular to cover their "open bosoms."[34] On 4 July the consistory noted that the ministers and elders were continuing to issue private warnings to women and girls in their districts to "close their breasts" from sight.[35] Many of these women were not called for formal interviews by the consistory, having apparently complied with their elders' demands, no doubt with varying degrees of conviction and enthusiasm. Perhaps such women had dressed wishing to gain the attention of another, or dressed with little calculation, but were alarmed to be identified as having appeared in immodest and sexually provocative ways. The elder's knock at the door of the family home and a stern private reprimand were all that was required to prompt such women,

---

31. Ibid., 296 and 304v. Other young men were also warned about their hair, 304v and 317. Captain Engarran was soon in trouble again for playing bowls, 314 and 319r. Another Rozel, "the young doctor," was among a group accused in October 1582 of attending Mass while at Toulouse, 353v, 356, and 366v.
32. Ibid., 287, 293v, and 294.
33. Ibid., 297–v, 310–v, and 313.
34. Ibid., 337v.
35. Ibid., 339v.

or their fathers and husbands, to ensure that they adopted more modest standards of attire in future.

Whatever progress was made by the elders in their campaign for greater female modesty in the spring and summer of 1582 was not enough to satisfy other Reformed communities in the region. On 7 November 1582 minister de Chambrun reported that the consistory had received a letter from the church at Orange. This letter raised concern about the dissolute clothing worn by some women in Nîmes. According to their colleagues in Orange, the women of Nîmes were causing a great scandal and providing a bad example to all the other churches of France. The Nîmes consistory discussed this letter and decided that the ministers should warn the congregation that those who disobeyed the church in this matter would be named in the pulpit, deprived of the sacrament, and then excommunicated in accordance with the regulations of the national church.[36] Evidently spurred on by this fraternal reproach, a week later the elders decided to take formal action against seven women from elite families. This group comprised some who were already well known to the consistory, including Suzanne Rozel and Catherine de Malmont.[37] Rozel had been warned about her appearance in the spring, while de Malmont had come to the attention of the elders in February for going to visit Avignon along with Claude de Tuffan. After she returned to Nîmes, the elders issued repeated calls until a reluctant Catherine de Malmont finally appeared to be admonished for her offences.[38]

In the following weeks the consistory interviewed other women whose clothing was deemed to be particularly offensive. On 29 December 1582 the daughters of doctor Pierre Lansard and of Monsieur de Recolin were reprimanded for disobeying the church's regulations against raising their hair with wire and shaping it into horns. The women promised to lower their hair and to go about the town in decent and honest clothing.[39] On 5 January Mademoiselle de Mirman also promised to lower her hair, and expressed her desire not to cause a scandal

---

36. RCN (42 J 27), 359.

37. RCN (42 J 27), 361.

38. RCN (42 J 27), 298, 303, 305v, 309v, 329v, and 331v. Catherine de Malmont and her father were in trouble again with the elders in August on suspicion of dancing; 348v.

39. RCN (42 J 27), 365v.

for the church. Other women proved rather less cooperative. Madame de Lacroix had been asked by her elder in late December to attend the consistory to discuss her appearance. The elder reported on 5 January 1583 that he had spoken with Madame de Lacroix, who had replied that she would certainly like to come to the consistory but could not because here husband did not want her to do so. This response was a common tactic of evasion used by women, which played on the elders' own ideas about women's place within marriage. The elder could only report that de Lacroix had agreed to "lower her hair as much as they wished." This statement has an air of sarcasm about it, and the consistory insisted that de Lacroix appear in person before them to be reprimanded.[40]

At the same meeting on 5 January there was a contrasting piece of business that may have only heightened the elders' annoyance at the excessive concern of some women in Nîmes about their clothing and appearance. The elders decided to write a letter to Madame de Châtillon thanking her for thirty écus that she had donated to clothe the poor of the town. The consistory frequently noted sums of money that had been spent to provide the poor with basic items of clothing, including coats and shoes. One poor woman was apparently so badly dressed that she was "almost naked," and such examples must only have exacerbated the sense of offence in the consistory at the immoderate spending on clothing and immodest display of some affluent members of the community. At any rate the elders determined on 5 January to call in a further "good number" of women about their shaped and raised styles of hair at a special meeting to be held two days later.[41]

When the consistory convened again on 7 January 1583 a group of women was interviewed about their hairstyles, their "open bosoms," and other forms of dress judged "indecent for the faithful." Women from a range of wealthy families in the town were reprimanded about their appearance, including mothers and daughters from the de Servas, de Nages, de Lagrange, de Maltrat, Dupin, Galepin and de Chabot families, as well as the wife of Captain Ducros and the wives of Jacques and Maurice Baudan. Mademoiselle de Seynes was specifically warned about her having fashioned her hair into horns and also for having "open bosoms." The daughter of Jacques Rozel, the daughter of Charles

40. Ibid., 366 and 368.
41. Ibid., 366r and 367.

Rozel, and the fiancée of doctor Lansard were all told to alter their style of appearance and to dress more modestly. The elders warned that if these women failed to change their appearance, then they would face the disgrace of being refused access to Communion. Each of these women was recorded in the minutes as expressing her desire to obey the consistory. Some mothers who appeared before the elders also promised that they would ensure that their daughters would adhere to the church's demands on this issue.[42] It is of course difficult to assess the sincerity of this apparent repentance and obedience. However, under threat of public humiliation, this group of women acknowledged that they had behaved improperly and offered expressions of repentance that the consistory accepted.

On 12 January 1583 the ministers and elders reviewed the progress made against scandalous clothing and hairstyles. They decided to continue to try to use publicity to shame offenders into repentance and obedience. Those who persisted in dressing immodestly were to be required to appear for formal interviews with the clergy and elders. The consistory also decided that elders should check for any recalcitrant offenders in their districts and pass on names where necessary for formal discipline at their next meeting.[43] These instructions were evidently carried out, and on 19 January the elders began to deal with those who had resisted demands for greater modesty. The Boitier family was in trouble with the elders again, and Monsieur Boitier's wife and one of his daughters were given a severe reprimand about their hairstyles and use of makeup. These women were warned about their future conduct and told that any further faults would lead to their being named in the pulpit and deprived of the sacrament. In addition, Monsieur Boitier was censured for allowing such insolence in his family.[44]

On 19 January the consistory considered what to do with other women who were defying their instructions about hairstyles, "open bosoms," and farthingales. Alongside private warnings and calls for women to appear for formal interviews, the consistory agreed on a new tactic of surveillance. The deacons and elders were to station themselves at the entrances of the temple on Sunday to check the hair, makeup,

42. Ibid., 367–68.
43. RCN (42 J 27), 368v.
44. Ibid., 369v.

and cleavage of women as they came into the service.[45] This seems to confirm the social significance of appearance during Sunday services and perhaps hints at notions of "Sunday best" in clothing. Women were very much on public display at church services, seated on benches near the pulpit under the gaze of the minister. Social rank was important in seating in Reformed churches, with particular prestige ascribed to the benches closer to the front, and disputes arose over the occupation of benches particularly when the church was full during Communion services.[46] If some women from elite families were arriving at church in their finery and in revealing clothing, then they were coming under pressure not to use services as an opportunity to advertise their wealth and beauty. They were also possibly coming under pressure from women seated behind them, who may have resented their claims to social precedence, and been angered by the display of costly forms of decoration beyond their means.

At the next meeting of the consistory on 26 January 1583, elders gave reports on the progress of their campaign for greater female modesty. All those women with raised and shaped hairstyles had been warned again, and had apparently either obeyed instructions to lower their hair or at least promised to do so. There was certainly some sense that the close observation of women as they went about the streets and attended church was having some effect. The elders decided "once again" to exhort women to lower their hair, and to call anyone who disobeyed to appear at their next meeting.[47] The following Wednesday no women were in fact interviewed by the consistory about their hairstyles or revealing clothing. The only case related to appearance tends to confirm the impression that the elders' campaign was having some impact. Monsieur Bernard was reprimanded for making "defamatory remarks against the word of God and the ministers" after his wife received a censure for her hairstyle.[48]

In the following months and years the consistory's formal minutes contain only a small number of cases brought against women on account of their appearance. We cannot be certain if the elders continued

---

45. Ibid., 369v. Farthingales were described in the minutes as "vertugadins" or "cache-bâtards."

46. Mentzer, "Les débats sur les bancs," 393–406.

47. RCN (42 J 27), 370–v.

48. Ibid., 370v.

to engage in private conversations with women in Nîmes about their clothing and hairstyles. However, it seems rather unlikely that the consistory had suddenly given up altogether on their campaign for female modesty or had changed their view about the sinful attitudes and actions associated with immodest appearance. Indeed the elders' perceptions about some of the families who had caused such difficulties on this issue must have been confirmed on 9 March 1583. The chambermaids who lived in the de Malmont and Lansard households were then called to appear before the consistory, both believed to be pregnant.[49]

During the late 1580s the issue of women's appearance was again highlighted both at the Nîmes colloquy and at the Lower Languedoc provincial synod. In 1587 the provincial synod required that the church's regulations on clothing be strictly enforced, and that anyone who continued to use makeup, wore farthingales, or dressed with "open breasts" should be suspended from Communion.[50] In 1590 the Nîmes colloquy complained about scandalous clothing and the use of makeup by some women in Nîmes. In 1593 the provincial synod repeated its demand that the church's rules on hairstyles and clothing be strictly applied. When the synod met at Nîmes in 1593, complaints were raised again about extravagant hairstyles and farthingales. The minister from Uzès complained that his efforts to apply the church's rules on modest appearance were being undermined because women under discipline in his town had gone to Nîmes to participate in Communion. The ministers from Nîmes responded that only those who had been given a token by their elder were allowed to receive Communion.[51]

Although this complaint from the church in Uzès suggested that a lax approach was being taken in Nîmes to dealing with the issue of female modesty, the authorities had in fact issued bans to local apothecaries against the sale of rouge and makeup in 1589 and 1592. However, in December 1592 the consistory acknowledged that their town compared badly with Montauban and Castres where there had apparently been a "great reformation" in appearance. The elders were prompted into a further bout of concerted action. In late 1592 and early 1593 around twenty women were interviewed about their clothing and appearance.

49. Ibid., 374v.
50. BSHPF, MS 566/ 1, 195v–96.
51. Ibid., 267–267v and 274v–75.

The consistory also discussed what to do about women who persisted in wearing items of "vain and dissolute clothing," and who had extravagant hairstyles that scandalized the faithful and dishonored God.[52] In December 1592 the ministers, deacons, and elders visited the homes of those who wore inappropriate clothing or who used makeup. Warnings were given to individual women about their immodest appearance, and any who defied the consistory were threatened with being denied access to Communion.[53] Among persistent offenders called in for formal interviews in early 1593 were members of the same circle of families who had caused the consistory problems during the 1580s, including Jeanne Rozel and Suzanne Lansard.[54] Only a small number of women were formally interviewed about their appearance by the consistory during the rest of the 1590s. In 1596 the Languedoc provincial synod repeated the need for churches to remain vigilant in dealing with women with "exposed breasts," with excessive hairstyles, and with women who wore farthingales. At Nîmes in 1598 there was criticism of the hairstyles adopted by the ministers' wives, and especially by the wife of Claude de Falguerolles. Meanwhile the community heard sermons preached about the problems associated with farthingales in 1595, and on the dangers arising from women who wore revealing clothing in 1600.[55]

What were the consequences of these efforts made by the authorities in Nîmes during the 1580s and 1590s to enforce Reformed norms of moderate and modest appearance? The evidence is inconclusive. It is certainly possible to argue that the consistory proved unable to alter standards of appearance in their community. The consistory only formally interviewed a relatively small number of women and did not strictly apply the church's own rules, which required that offenders ought to be excluded from participating in Communion. Instead the elders only reprimanded even those whose appearance was found to be particularly offensive. The ministers and elders in Nîmes also seem to have been prompted into taking action by external criticism, and by the decisions reached at national and provincial synods. Although some

---

52. RCN (42 J 30) (1593), 127v, 128, 134, 136, 137, 139v, 141, 145v–146, and 164v; Chareyre, 'Le Consistoire de Nîmes," 2:503–4.

53. RCN (42 J 30), 129v, 132, and 134v.

54. Ibid., 142.

55. Frossard, *Recueil de reglements*, 66; Chareyre, "Le Consistoire de Nîmes," 2:503–4.

efforts were made to alter the appearance of a group of wealthy women during the winter of 1582–83, this campaign might be seen to have faltered in the spring of 1583. Repeated complaints and calls for action during the 1590s might only seem to confirm the limited impact of the church's campaign, and highlight the persistent resistance of some women in Nîmes to the church on this issue.

However, such a conclusion takes an unduly limited view of the authority of the consistory and of the social appeal of Reformed religion in Nîmes. The freedoms of the Reformed community had after all only recently been secured and defended through violence, and remained threatened by ongoing conflict in the kingdom. It seems that momentum developed during 1582 among the members of a well-organized and widely respected consistory to engage directly with a visible moral problem in their town. Some women from elite families had adopted revealing styles of dress and dramatic hairstyles influenced by court and noble fashion. Such women certainly did not seem to have thought that they were acting inappropriately. However, the consistory responded with a determined and intense burst of activity to curb this scandalous conduct, even though it brought them into conflict with significant local families. The elders employed the more serious disciplinary sanctions at their disposal rather sparingly but with some skill. They spent a good deal of time in private conversation with women discussing their clothing and hairstyles, seeking to establish a broad consensus for the church's ideas about female modesty. This allowed the elders to isolate a small minority of the most flagrant offenders and to use formal disciplinary techniques to shame these women into changing their appearance. By the spring of 1583 the elders had clearly marked out boundaries of acceptable appearance for women in Nîmes, and limited to some degree visual access to women's bodies in the streets and at church. The elders remained vigilant on questions of female appearance in later years and took further concerted action when necessary during the early 1590s against excessive display of parts of the female body.

Insofar as the Reformed authorities in Nîmes were able to curb what they regarded as immodest forms of appearance, were they able to achieve the objective behind this campaign of taming sexual immorality and assisting men in not falling victim to lust? To what extent had Reformed writers and elders accurately diagnosed how the mind, body, and clothing related to one another, and whether the adulterous mind could be tamed by introducing restrictions on adulterous clothing?[56] The corruption of visual culture associated with the Catholic past had been largely excluded from sight in Nîmes. In this largely Reformed urban space there were no alluring paintings, indecent statues, or images of women visible in public that could lead men's eyes to commit fornication. In addition, it would seem that visual access to female bodies was somewhat restricted. However, to achieve this result an avalanche of language and conversation had been launched into the community from the pulpit and through elders' conversations about the tempting dangers of the female form. Was the male gaze in Nîmes thereby tamed or rather instructed about the sinful potential of sight? It seems conceivable, if not likely, that the consistory's focus on the dangers of the female body only succeeded in engaging the minds and directing the senses of some men in Nîmes towards women in their community, perhaps as never before. While there is no evidence of any misconduct by elders, such prurient interest may have been expressed by some of the self-appointed experts who discussed and closely scrutinized the female form as part of their official duties.

Urban Reformed communities contained a range of characters from the most spiritual and pious believers to those who were merely compliant with the church's demands to more difficult and contrary characters. For those on the less obviously pious end of the spectrum there was a profound risk from the church's perspective of reducing religion to a matter of being seen to abide by formal regulations. The church might have only succeeded in encouraging some to wear modest clothing as a useful way of signaling acceptance of its moral norms without any genuine spiritual convictions. The church also risked simply training people to learn a script of repentance when they were being interviewed about their offences. While forms of modest appearance may have established markers of sectarian difference between Reformed and Catholic communities, for some members of Reformed congregations clothing had quickly become only an empty and hypocritical gesture of piety. This mirrored the perceived problems in Catholic material culture of dress that Reformed leaders had been so quick to identify. While for some modest clothing merely represented a veil of respectability, others who listened to Reformed teaching on sight, sin, and

56. Arthur, *Religion, Dress and the Body*; Hollander, *Seeing through Clothes*; Roche, *The Culture of Clothing*.

sexuality seem to have welcomed the opportunity to express their piety and social respectability through their appearance. Such women and men responded to demands to turn their backs on ostentatious forms of appearance and to turn their eyes away from physical display and revelation in order to bridle the base lusts of the flesh. Some perhaps even adopted a life of acting as nervous jailors of their own bodies— a life marked by a strong sense of inhibition and a profound sense of shame about their own bodies. This diverse range of consequences of the campaign for female modesty in Nîmes thus highlights the complexity of following the gaze of elders to assess life under Reformed moral discipline.

6

Elements of Calvin's Theology and Practice in the Establishment of Reformed Churches in Java in the Seventeenth Century

YUDHA THIANTO

Introduction

Calvinism planted its roots on the island of Java soon after the arrival of the Netherlanders at Bantam (or Banten), on the northwestern coast of the island in 1596. Under the leadership of Cornelis de Houtman the expedition of four Dutch ships that left the Netherlands in the summer of 1595 arrived safely in Bantam, the great pepper port of Java, in the fall of 1596.[1] Before the arrival of the Dutch, other European nations had set foot on the East Indies archipelago now called Indonesia in their search for spices. The Portuguese and the Spaniards arrived at the East Indies around the middle of the sixteenth century, and with them came Roman Catholicism. But when the Dutch came to the island, they brought with them a different form of Christianity: Calvinism.

The Dutch wanted to monopolize the trade of spices between Asia and Europe. In order to accomplish their goal, they started the

---

1. Nagtegaal, *Riding the Dutch Tiger*, 16; Tuck, *The East India Company*, 143. See also van Loon, *The Golden Book*, 99.

Verenigde Oostindische Compagnie or the United East-India Company. The establishment of the company, the VOC for short, was fully explicated in the charter written in 1602.[2] The States-General of the United Netherlands gave the VOC full rights to act as sovereign government to accomplish the goal. The VOC was led by a group of seventeen gentlemen, collectively called the Heren XVII.[3] The preamble of the *Octrooi*, or the charter, stated that the VOC was formed in order to provide direction and to prescribe navigation of trading and commerce in the East Indies.[4] The charter specified that the VOC must necessarily perform three tasks: getting rid of the Portuguese from the region, preventing the Spaniards from invading the eastern part of the archipelago, and forcing local rulers on Java to trade only with the company.[5] At first the headquarters of the VOC was located in Ambon, in the eastern part of the Moluccas islands, but the headquarters was moved to Batavia (now Jakarta), on the western part of Java, in 1619, after the Dutch defeated and took over the region from the local regent. Batavia then became the most important port and was the only harbor for ships to and from Europe throughout the seventeenth century.

Since the VOC represented the Dutch government in the East Indies, and religion was an important part of the government, the VOC had to ensure that it maintained the practice of the true religion there.[6] For the Dutch government, the true religion was the Reformed, Calvinistic faith as expressed in the Belgic Confession. With regard to the relationship between church and state, the Belgic Confession article 36 stated that the civil government must "contribute to the advancement of a society that is pleasing to God," and that the government must remove "every obstacle to the preaching of the gospel and to every aspect of the divine worship."[7] The first step to fulfill this requirement

2. Verenigde Oostindische Compagnie (VOC), "Octrooi van de Verenigde Oostindische Compagnie (1602)," in Valentyn, *Oud en Nieuw Oost-Indiën*, 186–91.

3. VOC, "Octrooi 1602," article 2.

4. Ibid., preamble.

5. Ibid. articles 34, 35, 36, 37.

6. The VOC's responsibility to ensure the teaching of true Reformed religion was explicitly mentioned in the second charter of the VOC, published in 1622. The first charter (*Octrooi*) was good for twenty-one years, and thus in 1622 the new charter was published (VOC, "Octrooi 1602," article 7). See also VOC, "Octrooi, 1622."

7. It is worth noting that the literature on the history of the Reformed churches in the Dutch East Indies consistently used the term "the Dutch Confession," or *De*

was to drive the Portuguese and the Spaniards—who were Roman Catholics—out of the area. Here we see that the application of this article of the Belgic Confession in the East Indies also functioned as a political tool to drive away the enemies of the Netherlands. In Europe the Dutch were fighting battles against these two nations. So, in the East Indies the article of the Belgic Confession added a strong religious reason to fight and to drive away these enemies in the effort to gain monopoly and power over the whole region.

As soon as the Dutch established themselves in Java, they started church worship on the island. Understandably, the new churches were replicas of the Reformed church in their homeland. The theology and ecclesiastical practices of these new churches were shaped by the decisions of the Synod of Dordt of 1618–19. In 1624 the ministers who were sent to the island worked together to draft the *Batavische Kerkenordening*, or the Church Order of Batavia, to provide guidance and direction for the conduct of worship in the newly established churches.[8] This church order generally followed the Church Order of the Synod of Dordt, but with significant modification to make the church order applicable to the daughter church in Java. The publication of this church order in 1624 marked the beginning of the presence of the Calvinistic churches on the island. When the Church Order of Batavia was revised in 1643 to further address the issues that specifically arose in Java, it became more apparent that the theology and ecclesiastical practices of Calvin's Reformation occupied a strong place on the island and the rest of the archipelago.[9]

Some works on the history of missions in Java and other parts of the Dutch East Indies in the seventeenth to the nineteenth centuries had been done in the past few decades. The work of Hendrik Kraemer is still very fundamental for those who want to study the history of missions in the Netherlands East Indies.[10] Equally important is Johann Bavinck's

---

Nederlandsche Geloofsbelijdenis, instead of "the Belgic Confession." This custom continued well into the nineteenth century; Coolsma, *Zendingseeuw*, 49.

8. "Kerken Ordeninge Gestelt voor de Kercken in Oostindien Articulen," Batavia 1624, [hereafter: Batavia Kerkenordening 1624]. The archival document used in this study is a part of the collection of The Oud-Synodaal Archief of the Nederlandse Hervormde Kerk, catalogued by Janssen, *Catalogus van het Oud-Synodaal Archief*.

9. *Batavische Kerkenordening*, 1643.

10. Kraemer, *From Missionfield to Independent Church*.

John Calvin, Myth and Reality

detailed study of missions in the Dutch East Indies.[11] However, not much attention has been given to the study of the establishment of the Reformed churches in the archipelago, let alone particular attention to Calvin's influence in the theology and practices on these churches.[12] In Indonesia, church history and history of missions are academic fields that rarely receive attention. The few books on Indonesian church history do not focus much on the character of the Calvinism that became the root of many churches in Java.[13] At best, what we currently have are general histories of the Reformed churches in Java in the time of the VOC, published by Dutch authors at the end of the nineteenth century.[14]

In order to bridge this gap, this chapter attempts a close look at how elements of Calvin's theological and ecclesiastical practices were transplanted to Java at the beginning of the seventeenth century.

---

11. Bavinck, *Zending*. There are some other works on the history of missions in Java, such as Partonadi, *Sadrach's Community*; Hoekema, "Kyai Ibrahim Tunggul Wulung," 89–110; Ruff, "A Viewpoint from Migrant Churches," 265–67; van den End, "Transfer of Reformed Identity," 113–30.

12. The small number of scholarly works devoted to this particular topic include De Jong, "Early Reformed Missions," 33–74, and Soleiman, "The Propagation." A short study of the history of Reformed worship in Indonesia has been done by Widiasih, "A Survey of Reformed Worship," 175–94. Widiasih's study, however, covers a very broad area of all churches in Indonesia, and the article relies too heavily on secondary material, especially on Van den End's *Ragi Carita*.

13. The most recent study of Indonesian church history is Aritonang and Steenbrik, *History of Christianity in Indonesia*. This massive work covers over 400 years history of the Indonesian church. While this work helps readers with the big picture, it lacks details of how each theological tradition was brought to the archipelago. In addition, in the section that deals with the early history of the Indonesian churches, this work relies too much on secondary literature. The most widely used textbook on Indonesian church history is the two-volume work of Van den End, *Ragi Carita*. The first volume covers the period between 1500 and 1860, and the second volume covers the history of the Indonesian churches from 1860 to the end of the twentieth century. The only textbook that directly discusses aspects of Calvinism in Indonesian Reformed churches is De Jonge, *Apa Itu Calvinisme*. However, given the character of this book as a textbook that introduces Indonesian students to Calvinism, including historical background of Jean Calvin as a theologian, Calvin's theology in the context of sixteenth-century Reformation, and how Calvinism was brought to Indonesia, this book does not offer focused analysis on the theology and ecclesiastical practices of Calvin and how they were transplanted in the Reformed churches in Java.

14. Among other works, see, for instance, Van Troostenburg de Bruyn, *De Hervormde Kerk*; Reitsma, *Geschiedenis van de Hervorming*, and Van Hoëvell, *Tijdschrift voor Nederlandsch Indië*.

Elements of Calvin's Theology in Java

Particularly, it will focus on three areas that marked the presence of Calvinism in these churches: the use of the Heidelberg Catechism, the view of the sacraments, and the singing of the Psalms in the churches. I will attempt to achieve this objective primarily by way of studying and comparing the Church Order of the Synod of Dordt, the 1624 and 1643 Church Orders of Batavia, and the 1541 Ecclesiastical Ordinances of the Reformed Church in Geneva. By doing this comparison I hope to show clear threads of Calvin's influence on the Church Order of Batavia and thus to demonstrate that Calvin had a strong voice in the establishment of the Reformed churches on the island. But at the same time, while showing the similarities that these documents bear, I will also pay close attention to differences in order to accentuate the fact that adaptation was necessary as Calvinism started to find a place in the new land.

Transplantation of Calvinism in Java in the Early Seventeenth Century

The founding of the headquarters of the VOC in Batavia in 1619 coincided with the end of the Synod of Dordt in the Netherlands. With the revision of the 1585 church order of the national synod of The Hague, the Synod of Dordt increased the power of civil authorities over ecclesiastical matters.[15] At Dordt, discussions about certain articles of the church order happened between May 13 and 29, 1619, between the 145th and 180th sessions.[16] The decisions of the Synod of Dordt were affirmed by the Committee of the States on July 15, 1619, and were then sent to magistrates and officers of every town throughout the United Netherlands to be applied.[17] The ministers who drafted the church order in Batavia were very well versed in the Church Order of the Synod of Dordt. Three ministers deserve special attention in this matter, namely, Sebastian Danckaerts,[18] Justus Heurnius, and Georgius Candidius.[19] Together they received permission from the synods of

---

15. Brandt, *The History*, 314. See also Kromminga, *Christian Reformed Tradition*, 34.

16. Brandt, *The History*, vol. 3, book 42.

17. Ibid., book 44.

18. Sebastiaan Danckaerts (1593–1634) was a minister at Bantam, Java from 1616–1617, Ambon 1618–1622, and Batavia in 1624–1634. He died in Batavia in 1634.Van den End, *Ragi Carita*, 1: 252, see also van Boetzelaer, *Protestantsche Kerk*, 35.

19. Van Boetzelaer, *Protestantsche Kerk*, 30.

North and South Holland to proceed in the planning of the church order. The initial meeting to draw up the church-order draft was authorized by the VOC governor general Pieter de Carpantier on August 6, 1624. Sebastiaan Danckaerts was named the chair of the committee, and Michael Seroyen functioned as scribe.[20]

Like the Church Order of the Synod of Dordt, the Church Order of Batavia placed emphasis on the significance of the four offices in the church: ministers of the word, teachers (or doctors), elders, and deacons.[21] Both church orders emphasized that the office bearers should not be allowed to preach the word or administer sacraments without being lawfully called, examined, approved, and ordained by the classis.[22] The Church Order of Batavia specified that the minister of the Word who would work in the East Indies must have a letter of appointment from their particular classis in the Netherlands.[23] Being realistic about the possibility of the need for assistance from laypeople to work with the ministers in the new land, the church order provided some regulations to allow schoolteachers and visitors to the sick to have some ministerial capacity. However, the church order insisted that these people be allowed to lead in worship only after they had gone through close examination by the ministers, and after the individual had shown good understanding of Reformed doctrine and had demonstrated upright Christian character. The individual had to be observed for six months before the person could gain permission to lead worship.[24] The Church Order of the Synod of Dordt did not have an article about the visitors to the sick. This difference between Dordt and Batavia serves as a good example of how the Church Order of Batavia was adapted to the need of the East Indies churches.

All ministers of the Word, visitors to the sick, and the schoolteachers had to subscribe to the confession of faith of the Reformed churches of the Netherlands. In particular, the Church Order of Batavia specified the Heidelberg Catechism and the Canons of Dordt as the

---

20. Batavia Kerkenordening 1624.

21. Ibid., article 2.

22. The Church Order of the Synod of Dordt 1618–1619, article 4; Batavia Church Order 1643, article 5.

23. Batavia Kerkenordening 1643, article 7.

24. Batavia Kerkenordening 1624 article 5, Batavia Kerkenordening 1643, article 8.

two documents to which they must subscribe.[25] It is worth noting that even though article 40 of the Church Order of Batavia is very similar to articles 53 and 54 of the Church Order of the Synod of Dordt, Dordt's articles do not mention the Heidelberg Catechism by name.[26] This article in the Batavia church order marked the beginning of the significant role that the Heidelberg Catechism played in the Reformed churches in Java.

The two church orders in some ways mirrored the Ecclesiastical Ordinances of the church of Geneva at the time of Calvin. In Geneva the same four offices were affirmed.[27] While the church orders of Dordt and Batavia lacked the minute details that characterized the 1541 Ecclesiastical Ordinances of the church of Geneva, especially on matters regarding ministerial discipline, all three documents demonstrated similarity in their emphasis that no one should be allowed to preach and to administer sacraments without being lawfully called. Thus we see a strong influence of the practice of the Reformed church in Geneva at the time of Calvin on the ecclesiastical practices of the churches in the Netherlands—an influence then brought to Java.

Baptism was explained as the sign of God's covenant that is sealed to the children of believers in both Dordt's church order and the Batavia church order.[28] The two church orders insisted that baptism should be administered as soon as babies are born, in the public assembly when the Word of God was preached. The Church Order of Batavia clarified that these public assemblies were the ones celebrated on Sunday or Thursday mornings, when a sermon was preached, whereas Dordt's church order did not mention baptism as appropriate in midweek worship services.[29] In Batavia, baptism on Thursday morning was mostly intended for babies who were born weak and who might not survive until the following Sunday. Here we see that the flexibility to allow bap-

---

25. Batavia Kerkenordening 1624 article 21, Batavia Kerkenordening 1643, article 40.

26. The Church Order of the Synod of Dordt 1618–1619, articles 53 and 54.

27. "Ecclesiastical Ordinances 1541," in Hughes, *The Register*, 36.

28. The Church Order of the Synod of Dordt 1618–1619, article 56, Batavia Church Order 1643, article 45.

29. Batavia Kerkenordening 1624, article 22; Batavia Kerkenordening 1643, article 45.

tism during Thursday-morning worship was intended to ensure that there would still be sermon delivered when the baptism occurred.

In rural areas where there were not many church services, baptism could be administered privately on any day of the week. One main requirement still remained, namely, that a sermon must be said at baptism. In the Batavia church order the ministers were reminded that even in the case of emergency baptism, they should still preach a short sermon or a homily, in order to avoid the impression that conducting the sacrament was a practice of superstition.[30] This particular article in the church order was an indication of a fight against the Roman Catholicism brought by Portuguese and Spaniards before the arrival of the Dutch. Carrying the medieval practice into the seventeenth century, Roman Catholics allowed midwives to baptize newborns in cases of emergency. Calvin saw this practice of baptism as superstition. As a step to further prevent baptisms performed by laypeople, the Church Order of Batavia even prohibited visitors to the sick from baptizing. Only ministers were allowed to baptize. This requirement was similar to what happened in Calvin's church in Geneva. The 1541 Ecclesiastical Ordinances of Geneva explicitly mention that baptism should only be administered at church during regular service where preaching, obviously, was done. Baptism should be administered only by ministers or coadjutors.[31]

The ministers had to ensure the presence of the baby's father at baptism. The requirement for the father to be present at baptism was a practice that Calvin insisted on in the Reformed church of Geneva. This practice, as Karen Spierling has explained, was a new one at the time of Reformation and received a lot of resistance from some men, as the records of the consistory of Geneva at the time of Calvin indicate.[32] When we compare the Church Order of Batavia and how the Reformed church in Geneva required the presence of the father at baptism, we can see how the influence of Calvin's theology and practice flowed from Geneva to Java.

The Church Order of Batavia also added that if other witnesses (besides the father of the baptizand) were present at baptism, they should be

30. Batavia Kerkenordening 1624, article 22; Batavia Kerkenordening 1643, article 45.

31. Hughes, *The Register*, 44.

32. Spierling, *Infant Baptism*, 91–99.

Elements of Calvin's Theology in Java

people well instructed in the teaching of the Reformed Church. While the church order does not explicitly mention what it means by these witnesses, we could assume that they must be the godparents. Unlike the Church Order of Batavia, the Church Order of the Synod of Dordt explicitly mentions them as godparents.[33] While partly echoing Calvin's view of baptism, the Church Order of Batavia also showed departure from this view. In Batavia we see that the deliberate omission of the term *godparents* might have been triggered by the effort to separate the Reformed from the Roman Catholics. The Spaniards and Portuguese must have baptized babies in the presence of godparents. This omission became necessary in order to provide a clear distinction between the Roman Catholic and the Reformed beliefs.

Theologically, the Church Order of Batavia reflects Calvin's view that baptism is the new sign of the covenant that was established between God and Abraham and his descendants. Calvin closely connected the sign of circumcision, given in the old covenant, and baptism.[34] He believed that to Abraham God gave circumcision as sign and seal of the covenant, and to the church God gives baptism.[35] For Calvin, circumcision and baptism as signs of the covenant are similar in that they show God's fatherly favor of forgiveness of sins and eternal life. Just as circumcision brought the infant into the covenantal community of God's people Israel, so baptism consecrates us to God so that we can be reckoned as God's people.[36]

According to the Church Order of Batavia, the partaking of the Lord's Supper was contingent on baptism and proper instruction in the Reformed faith. The church order stated that native people must first be catechized in the Reformed faith, be properly examined to prove their pious life, make their profession of faith, and be baptized before they could participate in the Lord's Supper.[37] The church order further stated that native people, both children and adults, should be baptized using the form that had been prescribed for the sacrament before being allowed to partake of the Lord's Supper. The children of the native people

33. The Church Order of the Synod of Dordt, article 57, Batavia Kerkenordening 1643, article 46.
34. Battles, *Institutes*, 1325–27 (IV.xvi.3).
35. Calvin, *La Forme des Prières*, l2r.
36. Battles, *Institutes*, 1327 (IV.xvi.4).
37. Batavia Kerkenordening 1624, article 25; Batavia Kerkenordening 1643, article 50.

John Calvin, Myth and Reality

who were baptized in infancy should be instructed in the Reformed faith in their native language when they were older. Only after they had made their profession of faith could they participate in the Lord's Supper.[38] Again, this reminds us of Calvin's Geneva. The Ecclesiastical Ordinances of Geneva explicitly state that on the Sunday before the celebration of the Lord's Supper, the ministers were to announce that only children who had made their profession of faith based on proper instruction in the catechism could receive communion. The Genevan church also made sure that strangers to the city first presented themselves to the church and were properly instructed, if necessary, before they were allowed to celebrate the Lord's Supper.[39]

In Batavia, the Lord's Supper was celebrated on Easter, Pentecost, and Christmas, as well as once every three months: on the first Sundays of January, April, July and October.[40] This regulation was a slight modification of the Church Order of Dordt, since at Dordt it was decided that the Lord's Supper should be held once every two months, and when circumstances allowed, it should be celebrated on Easter, Pentecost, and Christmas.[41] Thus in Batavia the total number of celebrations of the Lord Supper could be as many as seven in a year, except when Easter fell on the first Sunday of April, in which case the Lord's Supper would be celebrated six times that year. In Geneva the sacrament was celebrated four times a year, namely, on Christmas, Easter, Pentecost, and the first Sunday in September.[42] This practice reflected Calvin's willingness to compromise with the Geneva city council. Personally, Calvin believed that the sacrament should be celebrated as often as possible.[43] In Java, while the Lord's Supper was not celebrated as often as had been Calvin's wish, the church order moved closer to what Calvin wanted, in celebrating the sacrament more than just four times a year.

The Church Order of Batavia added several articles as an appendix, which was not found in the Dordt church order. One significant issue addressed in the appendix was the role of the visitors to the sick.

38. Batavia Kerkenordening 1643, article 47.
39. Hughes, *The Register*, 44–45.
40. Batavia Kerkenordening 1643, article 55.
41. Church Order of the Synod of Dordt, article 63.
42. Hughes, *The Register*, 44.
43. Battles, *Institutes*, 1420–22 (IV.xvii.43).

Initially, these visitors to the sick were needed to help when the people were on the ship sailing from the Netherlands to the East Indies, as well as when the Dutch settled in the new land. But then, after the people settled in the land, their responsibilities of the visitors to the sick grew into more pastoral and ministerial duties. They were to deliver God's word to the sick, to comfort and strengthen their faith, to lead them in singing, and to read to them parts of the catechism or sermons from the *Decades* of Heinrich Bullinger, or from any of the Reformed books available to them, with prayer before and after the reading.[44] They were also to lead prayers in the morning and in the evening and to remind their hearers to repent of their sins, especially from swearing and cursing God or from using the name of the Lord in vain when they were sick. At church the visitors to the sick had the duty to lead prayers at the appointed time in the evening and to lead in the singing of certain verses of the Psalms. Outside the church, at a fort or a hospital, when people needed to hear the word of God, they were to be the ones to read the Scripture and led the people in singing the Psalms. They were also to visit the sick in their homes at least once a week.[45] They were to come to the hospital in the morning and evening to read one chapter from the Scripture, and to lead people in singing.[46] In all these tasks, the visitors to the sick were to remember that they were not ordained preachers or ministers.

The elaboration of the tasks of the visitors to the sick in the Church Order of Batavia was an expansion of that of the practices in the church of Geneva. Ordinances of Calvin's church in Geneva stated that ministers must help the sick by continuously admonishing and teaching them the Word of God so that they would not die without the admonition. Therefore, the ministers in Geneva had to see to it that a sick person who had been confined in bed for three days be visited. The task of visiting the sick was not to distract the ministers from their ministerial duties but had also to be done diligently. The ministers were not to wait until the sick person was about to die to visit, since their consolation to the sick would not mean so much for one nearing death.[47] Both the

---

44. Batavia Kerkenordening 1643, appendix, article 72.
45. Batavia Kerkenordening 1643, appendix, article 76.
46. Ibid., appendix, article 77.
47. Hughes, *The Register*, 46.

Dutch Reformed churches in Java and the Reformed church in Geneva wanted to make sure that the sick were comforted as well as taught and admonished so that they could repent.

In reality, in many rural churches outside Batavia it was the visitors to the sick who had to do most churchly duties. While ministers did come from the Netherlands to Java, church work could not be done by these ministers alone.[48] The visitors to the sick or the schoolteachers often led worship. Although they were not allowed to deliver their own sermons, they were allowed to read sermons written by ordained ministers. The place of these visitors to the sick in the churches was very strategic. They could lead worship in Malay, the language of most people in the East Indies.[49] In remote areas the visitors to the sick even baptized babies, although, as I already noted earlier, this practice was prohibited by the church order.[50]

Often tensions arose within the churches in the Netherlands about the duties and responsibilities of the visitors to the sick. The mother church in the Netherlands understood the significance of their work, not only in helping the sick Dutch people in the East Indies, but also in spreading the gospel among the natives; but church leaders in the Netherlands also realized that these visitors to the sick were not allowed to do the duties of ordained ministers. In addition, the churches in the Netherlands criticized the lack of training and education among visitors to the sick.[51] In the end, however, seeing the need of the churches in Java, some classes in the Netherlands agreed to give visitors to the sick special permission to baptize.

Schoolteachers held another position very much emphasized by the Church Order of Batavia. These teachers had the duty to teach the young the fundamental teachings of the church as explicated in the catechism, to instruct them how to pray and also to lead in the singing of

---

48. It was reported that in Batavia in 1622 there were 31 church members; in 1630, Justus Heurnius, the minister in Batavia, reported there were about 500. In 1639 there were 150 children to be baptized. In 1652 there were 5 ministers, and the number grew to 6 in 1669, and to 7 in 1675. In the following year there were 13 ministers—7 permanent and 6 from other areas. In 1683 there were 10 ministers, in 1729 there were 15 and the next year the number grew into 17. By 1706 there were 4110 members of the churches in Java. See van Troostenburg de Bruyn, *Hervormde Kerk*, 13-14.

49. Van den End, *Ragi Carita*, 1:67–68.

50. Van Boetzelaer, *Protestantsche Kerk*, 9.

51. Brouwer, "Het Onstaan der Protestantsche Zending," 35.

the Psalms. In addition, the schoolteachers had also to teach the youngsters to obey their parents, the government, and their ministers; to read and write; and to live morally.[52] Schoolteachers in the orphanages were to lead the morning and evening prayers before meals, and also to lead in the singing of the Psalms. Every week all schoolteachers had to read the questions from the catechism, and expected the children to give correct answers to the questions.[53] The particular question and answer from the catechism for a given week were based on the previous Sunday afternoon's sermon on the catechism.[54]

The tasks of schoolteachers explicated in the Church Order of Batavia demonstrated the application of Calvin's insistence on educating the young. In Geneva, Calvin taught that parents must bring their children to catechism on Sunday afternoons. For Calvin, the children had to be able to show that they understood the meaning of the questions and answers of the catechism before they were allowed to make their profession of faith.[55] As I mentioned above, in Batavia, catechization and the profession of faith went hand in hand as requirements for children to participate in the Lord's Supper. In an effort to include native children in the church, the Church Order of Batavia declared that unbaptized children of the local people who received blessing from the church through the laying on of hands were bound to the church and therefore should be included as children who belonged to the church.[56]

The Church Order of Batavia emphasized that preaching, singing of the Psalms, and instruction and catechization of schoolchildren should be done in the vernacular.[57] This led to the need to translate the Bible, the Psalms, and the catechism into Malay. In Batavia, church services in Malay started the day after Christmas in 1621 with Jacob Dubbeldrijk preaching. From that time onward, every Sunday the church had a service in Malay.[58] Translations of the Ten Commandments and the Apostles' Creed had been made even before the Church Order

52. Batavia Kerkenordening 1643, article 78.
53. Ibid., article 79.
54. Ibid., appendix, article 82.
55. Hughes, *The Register*, 47.
56. Batavia Kerkenordening 1624, "Middelen om de bekeeringe," article 2, see also Van Boetzelaer, *Protestantsche Kerk*, 34.
57. Batavia Kerkenordening 1643, Appendix, article 3.
58. De Bruyn, *Hervormde Kerk*, 15.

of Batavia was published.[59] Then in 1623 Sebastiaan Danckaerts translated the Heidelberg Catechism into Malay.[60] Danckaert's translation was widely used in the East Indies throughout the seventeenth century, and it became the foundation of the teaching of Reformed Christianity in Java. Because the need was so great, in 1665 the classis of Amsterdam sent one thousand printed copies of this edition of the catechism to Batavia.[61]

Besides Danckaerts, Justus Heurnius (1595–1651) was another very influential figure in the transplantation of Calvinism in Java during this time period.[62] As a missionary and a well-educated minister, he saw the need for the people in the East Indies to have the most important texts of Christianity translated into the language of the people.[63] In 1637 Heurnius published the Malay translation of the four Gospels, which he made directly from Greek and conformed to the Low Dutch translation of the Gospels, and in 1651 he added the book of Acts to the four Gospels. This work was later republished in England by the British East India Company in 1677.[64] Heurnius also published a Dutch-Malay dictionary to help other ministers learn the language in order to be more effective in preaching. Heurnius acknowledged that he used the works of others who had attempted to translate the Bible and other Christian texts from Dutch into Malay as the sources of his dictionary. He credited the works of Sebastiaan Danckaerts, his predecessor; Caspar Wiltens; Jan van Hasel; and Albert Ruyl as sources for his dictionary entries.[65] These ministers had preached in Malay, and Heurnius used words from their written sermons to construct his dictionary entries. He insisted that all ministers in the East Indies should be able to speak and preach in Malay in order to reach out to the people.[66] In the

59. Van Boetzelaer, *Protestantsche Kerk*, 33.
60. Danckaerts, *Cattechismus*.
61. De Bruyn, *Hervormde Kerk*, 91.
62. Justus Heurnius was born in the Netherlands in 1595. Between 1624 and 1632 he became minister of the Dutch Reformed church in Batavia, and then minister in Saparua, Ambon from 1634 to 1638. Van den End, *Ragi Carita*, 1:253.
63. For the most comprehensive work on Heurnius see Callenbach's published doctoral dissertation from the Rijks Universiteit, Utrecht, *Justus Heurnius*.
64. Heurnius, *Jang Ampat Evangelia*.
65. Heurnius, *Vocabularium*, A2v.
66. Ibid., A3r.

dictionary he also included a brief introduction to Malayan grammar and a guide to pronouncing the words to assist anyone who wished to learn the language. This effort showed how much he cared about the spreading of the gospel to the native people.

Following the practice of the Reformed Church in the Netherlands, the Reformed Church in Java only sang the Psalms in their services. The Dutch taught these psalms to the people by way of the "English method."[67] The church used a leader, who would sing the first line of the psalm, with the congregation repeating the same line, and then the leader moved to the second line and so on. This was called the English method because this way of singing was commonly practiced in the Church of England in the seventeenth century. This method was useful in introducing the new tunes. It was also helpful for teaching illiterate people to sing the Psalms. As singing the Psalms was an important part of Reformed worship in the Netherlands, it became important too in the Reformed churches in Java and in the rest of the East Indies. The Dutch Psalter was soon translated into Malay so that the native people could sing them. Caspar Wiltens was the first minister to translate some of the psalms into Malay.[68] With the introduction of psalm singing, the Reformed churches in Java started to become familiar with a tradition that was an integral part of the Reformation era, most notably for Calvin in Geneva in the middle of the sixteenth century. Calvin's insistence that the church sang only the Psalms and a small number of biblical songs was also brought to Java.[69] In the new place the tradition continued, but a noticeable adaptation also took place. Through this method of singing, new Christians in Java were led step by step to embrace the ecclesiastical practice of the Genevan Reformer.

Conclusion

This brief study of the early establishment of the Reformed churches in Java at the beginning of the seventeenth century shows that the influence of Calvin's theology and ecclesiastical practices was far reaching. It also shows the reality of the influence of Calvin outside Europe. As

67. Batavia Kerkenordening 1643, appendix, article 3.
68. Heurnius also used Wiltens's works as the source of his dictionary; Heurnius, *Vocabularium*, A3r.
69. Calvin, *La Forme des Prières*.

Calvinism was brought by Netherlanders to the East Indies, certain elements did not change. Seriousness regarding office bearers of the church, theological positions on the sacraments, and the manner of worship, including the singing of the Psalms, came to Java by way of the Netherlands. Close comparison of the Church Order of Batavia and the Synod of Dordt reveals how these elements remained strong when Calvinism was introduced to the people of Java. Equally strong was the use of the Heidelberg Catechism, which stood as the standard of belief. However, these theological and ecclesiastical practices also needed to be adapted to the new situation. It is evident that Calvin's influence on these churches was more directly connected to worship and the life of the church rather than to doctrinal issues, such as election and predestination. The ministers and other church workers who worked hard to establish new churches in Java were much more concerned with issues related to ecclesiology and ecclesiastical practices than with debating doctrine. This does not mean that these doctrines were completely absent from these ministers' thought. But in their situation, practical matters such as making sure worship and sacraments were done properly took primacy.

This chapter has demonstrated that adaptation was necessary in order for the theology and practice to become useful for the people. One reason for adaptation was the cultural and linguistic differences that stood between Java and the western European land from which this theology had come. The native Javanese had to be able to know the content of the theology that was offered to them, and so translation was necessary. That is why we see that many dedicated ministers worked very hard to translate the Bible, the catechism, and the Psalms into Malay. Another reason for adaptation derived from necessity. As we have seen, in the Church Order of Batavia, the removal of the presence of godparents in baptism, the frequency of the celebration of the Lord's Supper, and most notably the effort to allow visitors to the sick to perform baptism were adaptations that became necessary if Calvinism was to be made applicable by the new churches on the island of Java.

7

A Devil's Siren or an Angel's Throat?
The Pipe Organ Controversy among the Calvinists

RANDALL D. ENGLE

In 1687 in the Dutch city of Wemeldinge, an elderly widow with no children prepared her last will and testament. Like many other Calvinists in the Dutch province of Zeeland, Anna Maria Koopman had contempt for organ music; she considered the sounds that belched from organ pipes to be a vainglorious, distasteful remnant of Catholic worship that were best suited for accompanying the kinds of songs sung in alehouses. At the same time, she was a faithful member of her local Reformed congregation. Consequently, when she bequeathed her entire estate to her church, her gift came with a strict codicil: the church could never install a pipe organ. If it did, the value of her estate, which was quite substantial, would be withdrawn from the church and deposited instead into an endowment to support the town's poor.[1]

The condition of Mevrouw Koopman's will put Wemeldinge's church council and city fathers in a bind. Both groups hoped to benefit from the generous bequest, but neither group wanted to submit to her conditions because they did not agree with her distaste for organ music. Their solution honored only the letter of the widow's will; they ordered

1. Van Winkelen, *Wemeldinge in oude ansichten*, 1–43.

that a mural of a pipe organ be painted in the church in the exact spot where a pipe organ would have been placed had they not inherited the conditions of Mevr. Koopman's will.[2] As a result, the Reformed congregation in Wemeldinge worshipped without the sound of an organ for over two hundred years, though they viewed an image of one at each worship service. Only in 1927 did a Dutch court nullify the conditions of the will, after which the church purchased a reed organ in advance of finally installing a pipe organ in 1952.[3]

Stories of such organ strife abound during the period of the Protestant Reformation in the Netherlands. The break with Rome brought about obvious changes in Christian liturgy, but Reformed churches dramatically altered the role of music in public worship, especially the use of the pipe organ. This dramatic difference from Roman Catholic practice can be traced in part to the writings of reformers such as Jean Calvin. Calvin wrote that the organ was a popish instrument, and that the organ was an invention of the prince of darkness. Admittedly, instrumental music ranked low on the list of Calvin's and other reformers' concerns—their preferred targets were Catholic indulgences, church administration, and clerical depravity in general—, but the subject of organ music was addressed, and then most often unfavorably not only by Calvin but by many other reformers. In fact, most all Protestant churches across Europe initially silenced the pipe organ during worship. But, curiously, roughly one hundred years after Calvin's death, with a ban on organ use officially adopted, nearly all Protestant churches heard again the sound of windblown pipes in their sanctuaries, even the more strict Reformed churches of the Netherlands, despite the continued protestations of anti-orgelists such as widow Koopman.

What is more, my research shows clearly that most Calvinist churches never did stop using the pipe organ. While the ideals of Geneva were seemingly sacrosanct, Calvin's proscriptions of instrumental music did not—could not—stand. This tension between the liturgical ideal and the local practice of instrumental music in worship in the face of these ideals fueled a little-known yet virulent controversy.

We begin by understanding the reasons the reformers were opposed to the use of the pipe organ in worship. First, and probably

2. Kist, "Het kerkelijke orgel-gebruik," 299; Philipse de Groene, *Wemeldinge zoals het was*, 153.

3. Van Winkelen, *Wemeldinge in oude ansichten*, 43.

the least surprising and most obvious, the organ was considered too Catholic. Though scholars disagree on exactly how much organ music was used by the Roman Catholic Church of Calvin's day, organ music was often used in Roman Catholic liturgy, even though the a cappella music of Palestrina was also used at this time.[4] Calvin lamented that Catholic priests in his day did not understand the words of the Latin liturgical chants, and he found the Catholic Church's misuse of pipe organs especially worthy of complaint—for instance in his commentary on 1 Samuel 1 and in the *Institutes*: "Thus in the papacy has been a too ridiculous and inept imitation, when they started to embellish the churches and to make God's worship more ornate, if they had added organs and many other theatrical devices of that kind."[5] "The songs and melodies which are composed to please the ear only, as are all the quaverings and trills of Papistry and all that they call broken-music and composition and four-part songs, in no wise accords with the majesty of the Church, and cannot be other than gravely displeasing to God."[6]

Reformers pleaded for an uncomplicated style of worship free from ceremony and ostentatiousness that, to the Reformed mind, characterized the Catholic Church, and they distanced themselves from it. Over a century later, an uncouth comment from Gisbertus Voetius testifies to the depth of this disaste for "Catholic" organ music: "the organ, like all new novelties, is dangerous and suspicious, especially as the churches would appear to return to that which they had just discarded like a sick dog to its vomit."[7]

This assertion that the organ use was "too Catholic" is an interesting one, because there is equal evidence that the Roman Catholics were struggling with musical abuse as well and had established a strict guideline for organ use that predates the Reformation. Local gatherings of

---

4. Arnold Schering argued that even then many vocal masses were really rendered as solo pieces played by the organ, *Die niederländische Orgelmesse*, as quoted by Smith and Dineen, "Recent Work on Music," 55.

5. CO 30:259.

6. Ibid., 4:420. It should be noted here that the clause "fringots et fredons de la papisterie" is only in the 1559 edition of the *Institutes*. This leads many scholars, chiefly Doumergue, to believe that this portion is corrupted, not of Calvin, and added later as an assertion by an editor.

7. "Quia omnis novitas periculosa, & meritò suspecta; imprimis si aliquâ ex parte per eam Ecclesiae nostrae viderentur redire ad vomitum aut palinodiam canere" (Voetius, *Politicae Ecclesiasticae*, 1:585, no doubt recalling 2 Pet 2:22).

Catholic clergy, such as the regional Synod of Kamerijk, and the larger-scale Council of Trent, bellwether of the Counter-Reformation, devoted three sessions to the role of music and decided that instrumental music should be used only in proper ways and in a manner that enhanced singing.[8] Both these gatherings were careful to point out that the papal chapel did not (incidentally, still does not) own or use an organ. When the Council of Trent met on 17 September 1562, in the twenty-second session, it formulated a "Decree Concerning the Things to be Observed and to be Avoided in the Celebration of Mass." Particular consideration was given to the expectation of proper and dignified behavior during the worship service. The Council decreed that all bishops must "banish from churches all those kinds of music in which, whether by organ or in the singing, there is mixed up anything lascivious or impure, as also all secular actions; vain and therefore profane conversations, all walking about, noise, and clamor, that so the house of God may be seen to be, and may be called, truly a house of prayer."[9]

What is important for this study is the Catholic Church's statement on the role and use of the pipe organ: so long as it remained pure and added to the solemnity of worship, the pipe organ was permitted to retain its position.

Nonetheless, primary sources abound with assertions that the pipe organ was a dangerous vestige of Catholicism. Thus, said the Protestants, organ music must go the way of all other semiotic reminders of the corruption of the papacy such as bells, salt, candles, oil, holy water, feast days, funerals, vestments, veneration of the altar, festal processions, and the like.

Beyond the organ's being a caricature of Rome, the second objection to the pipe organ was that it was an idol. Like a statue, windows of stained color, or a painting, the organ was a tactile object. Oftentimes pipe organs from this period had large doors affixed to their cases. This was because when a church building was nearer a sea climate, the humidity and changing temperature made it almost impossible to use wooden pipes. Instead, metal pipes were used. But metal pipes, though not susceptible to humidity, would subtly change in size depending on the air temperature. When a metal organ pipe changes size, it can

8. Particularly the sessions of 17 September 1562, 15 July 1563, and 11 November 1563.

9. Waterworth, *The Canon and Decrees*, 161.

go out of pitch. To alleviate this problem, these large doors were constructed and the organ kept closed except when in use. Now herein was the problem: When these magnificent doors of these instruments were thrown open, artisans saw a huge canvas waiting to be painted and decorated. Thus, like the space above Catholic altars reserved for triptych paintings, these case doors were painted and gilded with images of saints or biblical scenes. The result was that the organ became a double idol, if you will—an object of Rome now painted with graven images. It was therefore doubly destructive.

If Protestants still were not convinced of the evils of either the pipe organ, or its presence in the worship space, the coup de grâce was that this idol was a working, breathing, *sounding* idol. This idol produced sound. Pipe organs breathed and exhaled. They had lungs. They wheezed and ciphered in their lofts. They were sibiliant. In a very real sense, pipe organs lived. They were sound machines, engineered by human hands and played by wild organists assisted by bellow pumpers. How could such a contraption ever be holy or even used in a holy, dignified manner? Jan Jansz. Calckman, a beer-tax collector from Den Haag who was so opposed to organ use that he wrote an entire tome against organ use, wrote: "What are the organ pipes other than idols when they are used for a worship service? Have they not been manufactured from all sorts of materials: lead, iron, copper, tin, silver and gold, yes, don't they even make all sorts of images from them such as priests' heads, human faces, and gargoyles of devils, through which the pipes are shown and give their sound? Is that done in any way differently from the blind heathen and the followers of the Roman Church which also does this for its religion?"[10]

Furthermore, what if a sinful organist (which they all were, were they not?) were not honest in the style of music he played? Did an organist not have the power at hand to lead an entire congregation astray by the music he piped? Jan Jansz. Calckman posited a worst-case scenario: what if unknowing and unsuspecting congregants were to go to

10. "Wat zijn de Orghel-pijpen anders als Afgoden / alsse gebruyckt worden tot eenen godsdienst / sijnse niet gemaeckt van alderhande specien / loot yser / koper / tin / silver en gout / ja maectmen daer aen niet alderhande fatsoen van Paters hoofden / menschen aengsichten / en grijnsen van Duyvelen / door welcke de Pijpen steccken / en geven door de selve haer geluyt? Ist anders gedaen als de blinde Heydenen / ende navolgers der Roomsche kercke / de welcke het oock houden voor haeren godtsdienst" (Calckman, *Antidotum*, 137–38).

John Calvin, Myth and Reality

church and hear not a sacred melody but, because of the sinful nature of the organist, a song about a woman sitting by a river?[11] The dangers were too great. Organ music was too great a force to distract the mind and heart and thoughts of pious worshippers. Rather than risk its misue, the organ, along with all other superfluous sound such as choir and instruments, best be silent.

With the pipe organ wheezing and hissing in the organ loft, only to produce unwanted and needless sound, it was just one small step to finally label the organ demonic. Said Voetius, "If the organ were to be used, the workload of the minister would be substantially increased because they would have to then be vigilant to ward off other possible abuses and tricks of Satan."[12]

Thus *anti-orgelists* were convinced that the organ was the devil's voice (*duyvelschen fluytenkast*) in disguise. Calckman posed the question this bluntly:

"What is the difference between the organ and the idols through which the devils spoke? . . . Are not the organ pipes hollow as well, do they have a might or knowledge from which to speak or to make sound by their own power? . . . Have not the pipes themselves been fashioned from many different materials like the idols of the heathens?"[13] If organ music is the sound of the devil, then clearly its use must cease.

Finally, the Reformed labeled all accoutrements for worship, such as the pipe organ, an unnecessary and luxurious expense. Such human-

---

11. "Wat doetmen vorder om tot zijn werckinge te brengen / men huyrt een Man om gelt / dat hy alle de Pijpen vant Orgel vol blaest: vol wint zijnde / so comt de Meester vant Musijck / die gaet daer op speelen / dickmael een byant van Godts Woort / die liever na zijn Natuyr soude speelen / een Meysjen op een Riviertge sat / dan eenen geestelijckē Psalm." [What else do they do in order to make it work, they hire a man for money so that he fills all the pipes of the organ with air, being full of wind the Master of the music comes, he will play on it, often an enemy of God's word who would rather play according to his nature about a girl by the riverside than a spiritual psalm] (Calckman, *Antidotum*, 171).

12. "Ratio; quia crescet labor noster, & cogemur semper ad vigilare, ne abusus irrepant; ne Satan & mundus obrepat, ne falsi fratres insidientur; haut aliter ac illi qui picturas, aut imagines, aut altaria retinent in Templis" (Voetius, *[Liber de] Politicae Ecclesiasticae*, 585–86).

13. "Waer in bestaet nu het verschil? tusschen het Orgel / en haere Afgoden daer de Duyvelen door spraken . . . Sijn de Orgel-pijpen niet mede hol / isser eenighe macht of wetenschap in om te spreecken / of geluyt te maken uyt haer selven?. . . sijn de Pijpen selve niet van veelderhande materien gemaeckt / gelijck de Afgoden der Heydenen?" (Calckman, *Antidotum*, 157).

made, vainglorious items were simply not becoming of the simplicity of true, focused worship of the heart. Nor did these noisy idols keep with the modest and simple ideals of the early church to which the Reformed aspired. Thus many organs were not just recklessly destroyed, but carefully and intentionally recycled for another use that benefited the poor. In Winterthur metal organ pipes were melted down and recast as a roof for the prison tower there. In Geneva the metal pipes were refashioned into dinnerware for use in the city's hospital.[14]

Take these five predispositions against the organ together (that it was too Catholic, that it was an idol, that it was a sounding idol, that it was demonic, and it was vainglorious), and it is hardly surprising to read of the anti-organ rhetoric during the first wave of the Reformation.

Theologians, preachers, and laymen alike minced no vulgar or uncouth words to describe their distaste for the instrument. For example, the organ was variously called "the devil's bagpipe" (*eüffels Sackpfeiffe*), "the pope's bagpipe" (*Papsts Sackpfeiffen*), the "Idol's Pipes" (*Götzen Pfeiffen*), the "devil's trumpet" (*Teufels Trompete*), and a "seducer to Roman, antichristian worship" (*Lockvögel zum Römischen Antichristischen Gottsdienst*). Even the organist was styled a "Bagpiper," and his wife, children, and assistants represented as costly to maintain and "wanton" in their "playing and piping." Like the Catholic "idols" and "images" (*Götzen* and *Bilder*) with which they were classified, the organs were condemned to burn in Vulcan's Oven (*Offen Vulcani*) for the sake of the Reformation.[15]

A final example needs an apology, and I must ask you to "excuse my French." I offer this uncouth, verbatim quote so that you will get the idea of the disgust with which people spoke of the instrument. When our friend Jan Calkman tried to explain why some churches were slow to stop organ use during their services of divine worship, his only rationalization was (and I quote): "Because sometimes even after a cow shits herself, she continues to wag her tail."[16]

---

14. Jakob, *Orgelbau im Kanton Zürich*, 1:88–91.

15. Erinnerung der Kirchendieneren zu Schaffhausen: 1597 (26 July) (Zurich: Zentralbibliothek, Ms. A 134, 424r-v), reprinted in Ex. 2 of Davies, "Destroying the Devil's Bagpipe."

16. "Als de Koe bescheten is / soo üaetse garen met de staert om" (Calckman, *Antidotum*, 165–66).

Thus it was clear that the organ was to be done away with. Where organs were not dismanted, destroyed, or recycled for other purposes they were simply not used. Further, almost all Calvinist cultures rode the anti-organ wave to enact official ecclesiastical and civic legislation against their use.

In fact, in the Netherlands, the first national synod of 1574 held in Dordrecht decreed that organ use would be done away with, using 1 Corinthians 14 as a proof text to do so.[17] Four years later, in 1578,[18] that judgment was upheld at the second national synod held in Dordrecht; these do not take into account numerous provincial-synod bans on the use of the instrument during worship.

But the Reformers were not merely reactive against instrumental music; they were also proactive and articulated their own ideal of proper church music. Thus, simultaneous with these anti-organ judgments, a new church-music model was being instituted. Instead of a human-made instrument of praise (i.e., the pipe organ) being used in worship, now the God-made instrument (i.e., the human voice) was to be used in worship by all people—men, women, and children alike. These voices were to be used alone, with no musical accompaniment that would distract or cover up the sound of this supreme instrument. Still further, this sound was not to be corrupted by "sweet harmony," lest the harmony distract from the text, or lest one should become more enamored with the medium used to convey the message than with the message itself.

---

17. "Aengaende het spelen der Orgelen in de Gemeenten, houd men dat het gantsch behoort afgeset te vvesen, volgens de Leere Pauli I Cor. 14. vers. 19." [Regarding the playing of the organs in the church we are of the opinion that it should be completely discontinued, according to the teachings of Paul in 1 Cor 14:19.] Schoock, *Exercitationes variae*, 538 (Exercitatio XXX: "De Musica organica in Templis").

18. "77. Het ghebruyck der orghelen in den kercken houden wij niet voor goet insonderheyt voor de predicatie. Daerom achten wij dat de Dienaren behooren te aerbeyden, ghelyckse voor eenen tyt gheduldet worden, dat se alsoo metten eersten ende op het aldervoeghelijckste wegh genomen worden." [We do not consider the use of the organs in the churches to be appropriate, especially not before the service. And that is why we recommend that the ministers should strive as they were tolerated for a while, to have them removed at the earliest and most suitable time]; Rutgers, *Acta van de Nederlandsche synoden*, 253. The Dutch word *predicatie*, usually translated into English as "sermon," can also refer to the entire worship service, and is so here and elsewhere translated. See Tel, "Gebruyck of Ongebruyck," 315 n. 6.

As to the message, the content, of human song, the Reformed turned not to human-composed texts, but to God-composed verse found in the Bible's hymnal itself, the book of Psalms. Since no extant Jewish melody or notation survives, Jean Calvin asked that the biblical Psalter be rhymed in the vernacular and set to simple tunes of weight and majesty. This result, as you all know, is the famous Genevan Psalter. The original music of this Psalter is impressively simple: the range of the melody rarely exceeds a fifth, and the tunes, which to today's ears seem to have difficult syncopation, as Dr. Emily Brink unforgettably pointed out to me once when I was her student, are simply a combination of long and short notes. These melodies were to be composed with requisite gravity so that they would guarantee a "weighty and majestic" sound when sung. Ironically, in the end, a musical idiom that sounded not all that different from Catholic chant.

But Calvin's "sound theology" did not stop with music. In addition to the visual iconoclasm, which is well understood and studied (where icons, statues, colored glass, and crucifixes were removed from Reformed worship), there was also what I like to call an "aural iconoclasm." Calvin was consistent: he wrote that elaborate sound could confuse the ear and distract a worshipper no less than visual objects; thus, he objected to all foreign verbiage, florid music, and unintelligible speech in worship.

The purpose of these sweeping changes was to focus worshippers more clearly on the meaning of the gospel rather than on the medium used to transmit it. In other words, Calvin simplified worship from its existing Catholic and Lutheran forms, made worship didactic, and emphasized the spoken word of the minister. Thus, where the Catholic priest had turned his back on the congregation while consecrating the eucharistic host, now the Reformed minister stood in a central pulpit and faced the congregation at all times; "sound boards" were now placed above pulpits to ensure the minister's words would project distinctly to the farthest corners of the church. The priest's homily became a preacher's sermon, and the sermon replaced the Mass as the central act of worship. A choir of monks either chanting plainsong or singing complex polyphonic motets behind a gated transept was replaced by an entire congregation singing a psalm in one unaccompanied, unison voice. Liturgical Latin was replaced with vernacular dialects, and from the pulpits preachers read no missal but only the Bible. Whereas

Catholic priests chanted prayers, the Gospel, and other parts of the Mass, Reformed pastors simply spoke their prayers, the Scripture lesson, and their sermon in clear, phonated speech, lest any musical decoration distract the congregation from Almighty God, the author of the Bible and the recipient of human prayers.

It was all so clear, thought out, beautiful, and—dare I say it?—predestined. But the fact remains that in less than one hundred years' time after Calvin's death, organ use was employed in nearly all Reformed churches, save those in Scotland. And further research shows that most churches defied immediately the official organ bans. Other congregations ignored the bans from the start and never did stop using the organ, hymns, and in some cases, even choirs. How can we explain such a disregard for such a clear Genevan ideal?

Ironically, it is Calvinism itself that may have ensured, not discontinued, organ use. First, as ingenious as the Genevan Psalter was in theory, in reality it did not sing well. In reality, most congregants could not afford to purchase their own Psalter, and it appears that access to the Psalter was initially limited. And even if you owned a Psalter and brought it with you to worship, chances were that you were not able to read it: most congregants were illiterate. Further, the French paraphrases of the Psalms did not always translate well into other languages such as Dutch; these translations from the French were strained linguistically, requiring contractions of syllables and grammatical contortions in order to suit the meter of the music. In short, all accounts confirm that initially Reformed congregations singing the Genevan Psalms yielded a sound that was anything but majestic and weighty. More likely, it was cacaphonous.

The immediate solution was to place a precentor in front of the congregation. This person was literate, usually the schoolteacher of the village. He would lead the psalmody by "lining out." In this type of musical direction the precentor would sing each line of a psalm first, and then the congregation would repeat that line immediately and a cappella. But many worshipers could not see or hear the precentor. So he was then given synodical approval to hold a baton and stand in front of the pulpit.[19]

---

19. Dirk Balfoort documents one entertaining experience in the Church of St. Eusebius in Arnhem. See Balfoort, *Het muziekleven in Nederland*, 26ff.

A Devil's Siren or an Angel's Throat?

But there was still another problem. However useful "lining out" might have been for illiterate worshippers and for those who could not afford their own Psalters, the ultimate success of lining relied on the skill of the precentor. That is, with no instrumental support, some precentors were better able than others to stay in tune, keep a steady tempo, or even sing the tune as printed. Others were not.

In Scotland, according to William Maxwell, many Scottish precentors were more remarkable for their idiosyncrasies than for their musical skill.[20] It appears that some precentors embellished the tunes with grace notes or melismas (whether intentionally or out of poor skill is not known) such that the congregation's attempts to copy the precentor's example were disastrous if not certainly comical. Such a situation prompted a late-arriving worshipper in Berwickshire to ask the question, "What tune are they at?" He received the reply, "I no ken, I'm at the Auld Hundert."[21] Later some churches attempted to resolve the confusion by displaying the name of the tune on a chalkboard or printed card set in clear view of the congregation upon the precentor's desk.[22]

These problems with the precenter, however, point to a larger, more fundamental problem at this time with congregational song. Though it seems obvious, it was not just that the Genevan Psalms were new; it was that *congregational singing* was a new experience. Before the Reformation, liturgical music was provided for the worshippers by trained musicians and well-rehearsed clergy. Congregants were not asked to sing as a group. Most worshippers might have sung privately in their homes, but not until the Reformation would they ever have done so corporately in a church. As our friendly and colorful beer-tax collector Jan Jansz Calckman said, of congregational singing "we know as much as a cow in Flanders."[23]

Churches began frantically to instruct their congregations how to sing beautifully and as an ensemble. Interestingly, their focus began in the schools, and they insisted that the children learn how to sing, and they could model beautiful psalm singing for older worshipers on Sunday.

---

20. Maxwell, *A History of Worship*.

21. Millar, *Four Centuries of Scottish Psalmody*, 136–37.

22. Maxwell, *A History of Worship*, 165.

23. "daer het meestendeel vande gemeynte so veel verstants van heeft / als de Koe van Vlaenderlant" (Calckman, *Antidotum*, 194).

As for the adults, in the province of Zeeland in the Netherlands, the congregation was instructed how to sing with this advice: "1. Stretch the notes; 2. Turn them in the mouth; 3. Chew; 4. Through numerous raisings and elevations between the teeth and in the palate move the tongue back and forth like a snake; 5. Make the notes whirl."[24] Incidentally, the advice apparently worked, and the author of this account made the picturesque comment that his advice led to a kind of singing that he compared to the sound of waves and of the murmuring of the sea.

Nevertheless, by almost all contemporary accounts, congregational singing was disastrous, and the culprit was, ironically, the Genevan Psalter, whose use was supposed to have yielded simple, congregational song of weight and majesty put in the hands of people who had never sung as an ensemble before. Thus after a very short time even the most dogmatic Reformed leaders gradually began to question the ban on the pipe organ. And they looked, literally behind them or in front of them, at the silenced pipe organs. These silent instruments stood before them offering a key to successful congregational singing.

The fact is that while some organs were removed or destroyed during the Reformations, most stayed. In the case of the Netherlands, this was because the actual church buildings in which the Reformed worshiped were not owned by the congregations but by the cities. As a result, Calvinists curiously found themselves with large, ornate, and conspicuous pipe organs in their worship spaces. Seventeenth-century paintings by Pieter Saenredam and Emanuel de Witt show whitewashed Reformed church interiors and empty niches that had held statuary and altarpieces, yet these canvases clearly show Reformed churches with incongruous accoutrements: stained-glass windows, heraldry banners, and memorial plaques in honor of dearly departed congregants, and worship spaces that had intact pipe organs.

Like church buildings elsewhere in Europe, Dutch church buildings served many important public functions for Dutch daily life. For example, church towers served as manned lookout posts against fire, flood, and other dangers. Clocks were often placed in the church tower, and they were used to announce the time of day to the citizens. Under the wings of the church town markets were held. Churches were the

---

24. "1. De noten uitrekken; 2. in den mond draaien; 3. kauwen; 4. door ettelijke verhogingen en de verheffingen tussen de tanden en 't gehemelte slangswijze henen slingeren; 5. ze doen dwarrelen." (Van Iperen, *Kerkelijke historie*, 2:442–43).

places where soldiers were recruited and quartered. Fishermen hung their nets to dry in the cavernous, roofed spaces.[25]

And there pipe organs were built, expensive instruments funded by citizens though city subsidies. In a real sense, the citizens, not the church, owned their pipe organs because of their residency in the town and their status as taxpayers, not because of their membership in the church. Moreover, in many cities the organ in the church was used to provide secular musical entertainment during the week, special recitals were offered, and the organ played during the market as a sort of entertainment.

Thus in most Calvinist locales, even when pipe-organ music was banned during worship, that did not stop the organ from being played before and after worship (so we have the origin of our prelude and postlude) and throughout the week. The times before and after worship were, technically, not worship, and so the organ entertained the flock who were shopping, gossiping, or selecting their seats for worship. But the moment the preacher's foot touched the step of the pulpit, however—that was when the music was to conclude: that was the signal that worship had officially begun.

Not only did organ music continue because organs were owned by cities, but it is also undeniable that many supposedly Reformed ministers did not mind organ music before, after, or even during the hour of divine worship. After the Reformation, a significant number of Catholic priests converted to Protestantism, leading their followers into the new faith with them. Although some professed Reformed theology and practiced Reformed worship, these priests were used to chanting the liturgy themselves, supported by a skilled organist, and their parishioners were used to enjoying the organ music and trained choirs. Many examples exist of such congregations, who, because of the leadership of their minister, never did question organ use, or even stop it. This explains records like the one unearthed in De Lier. In 1566 church records document that their new pastor was an adherent of the Protestant teachings. Nevertheless, the record contines to record that "on five or six Sundays, both before and after the sermon, [he allowed]

---

25. Van Swigchem, *Een huis voor het Woord*; see also Spicer, "'So Many Painted Jezebels,'" 249–76; Spicer, *Calvinist Churches*; and Frijhoff, "Votive Boats or Secular Models?" 215–34.

Dutch psalms to be sung in the church together with some boys, *while the organ was playing.*"[26]

Within a generation's time, most all villages were to follow suit. By 1638, a provincial synod declared that organ playing was a matter of medium importance, and each congregation was free to judge for itself whether or not to use the organ.[27]

Nearly simultaneous with this decree, the pipe organ evolved into a new kind of instrument. This is because it was now no longer functioning solely as a concert instrument or as an instrument to support small monastic choirs. Now it was to accompany entire congregations in song. Thus, its sound, volume, design and construction had to change drastically.

The idea of organ builders was that if the instrument was going to be used to support the human voice, then the organ's design should be humanly guided wherever possible. Diameters of organ pipes were scaled to the classic proportions of the human body—its width being one-sixth of its height—because, it was thought, by more closely matching a pipe's dimensions to the classic proportions of the human body, the organ would be better suited to support the human voice. The organ's pipes and machinations were given decidedly anthropomorphic terms: for example, the parts of the organ pipe are to this day referred to as the foot, the mouth, the labia, the ears, the beard, and the waist; and organ pipes "sit" on a "chest."

The organ was made visually and audibly more conspicuous as well. A principal chorus, complete with pitches from sixteen feet through the upper work mixtures, and solo stops such as the trumpet and the cornet were often placed in a new organ division called the *Rugpositief* (literally: "organ at the back") since this division of the organ hung on the balcony rail, against the organist's back, so that the solo pipes were lower than the others and closer to the singing congregation.

---

26. "Vyf of zes zondagen zoo voor zoo na die preeke, Duytsche psalmen in die kercke met eenige jongens gezongen, terwijl het orgel eronder speelde" (Vente and Vlam, *Documentaet archivalia,* 196, supplement 147, italics added).

27. ". . . is geoordeelt, dat hetselve is een middelmaetijghe zaecke; en wert daeromme gelaeten in de vrijheyt van yedere kercke, omme to doen tot stichtinge." [It is determined that the playing of the organ is a matter of medium importance and is therefore left to the freedom of each church for the purpose of edifying [the congregation] Den Haag, Koninklijke Bibliotheek, Hs KA XLVIII, fol. 629.

A Devil's Siren or an Angel's Throat?

These new solo stops could trumpet the melody (literally) into the ears of the singers.

Organ builders invented the *vogelgesang*[28] organ stop, which mimicked the sound of singing birds, and they brought back the sound of bells into the sanctuary by adding the *zymbelstern*[29] to some organs. The *vox humana* organ stop (literally: the "voice of the human") was invented;[30] contests were held by organ builders to see whose *vox humana* stop sounded most like a singing child.

Even more surprising than changes to organ construction were changes in the perception of the organ. Some Reformed began to see their pipe organs now as allegories of the church itself. Far from the devil's minions of a previous generation, the rows of pipes standing in regimented ranks now praised God just as the rows of church pews filled with worshipers also did. The renowned poet Jacobius Revius penned:

> The organ is properly used for psalms and prayer
> Oh bliss whose throat opens the glory of the Lord![31]

Dutch worshippers also began to view the organ as a work of art to be appreciated; that is, that the organ builders' art reflected the very creativity and artistry of God.

Nothing could be less "Calvinistic," to be sure, but the designs and installations of organs from this time period are irrefutable proof of the change in Reformed thinking about the organ. Figurines of angels were displayed on the outsides of some organ cases, while statues of important biblical characters decorated the exteriors of other pipe organs.

---

28. This voice was made by three or four pipes that were inverted in a pan of water. When the pressure forced air up through the pipes, it simultaneously made the water gurgle, and the result simulated a warbling bird whistle.

29. The "cymbal stars" are actually complex sculptures that make sound. A paddlewheel is set in motion by air jets when the organist pulls a stop on the console. The paddles move a metal beater, which is surrounded by a set of bells hanging from an outer frame. When the paddles move the beater, the arms of the beater strike the bells, making a charming sound. The whole machinery is covered by a glittering, decorative star; when the air jets blow the paddles, this air current also spins the star around in circles on an axle.

30. A thinly scaled reed used with tremulant to mimic the human voice.

31. "Tot psalmen en gebee'n wort 't orgel recht gebruycket / O Salich welcker keel des Heeren roem ontluycket" (Revius and Smit, *Over-ysselsche sangen,* 66)!

John Calvin, Myth and Reality

Less lofty but perhaps more visually impressive were mechanical statues whose arms moved to beat a drum or to lift a trumpet to wooden lips. Over time weathervanes, clocks, heraldic imagery, civic mottos, and even sculpted animals and figurines were placed on the organ cases. My favorite instrument of this era is probably the organ at Edam, whose three façade towers are each topped with obelisks sculpted as mounds of cheese, the town's signature export. Some organ builders added an extraordinarily pedestrian invention for the convenience of the organist: a hidden "drink drawer" where a bottle of spirits could be secretly stashed for discreet use as needed.

As you may well imagine, not all were pleased with such sacrilege encroaching upon the Reformed worship space. Thus, with no recourse from secular officials (remember, they most often owned the organ), the *anti-orgelists* had to rely on church authorities. However, here too the Reformed church order worked against them. The Reformed distinguished the essence of worship from the circumstances of worship. Items that in the confessional statements of the Reformed received no explicit mention were variously labeled "indifferent matters," "middle things" or adiaphora—things neither forbidden nor approved but nevertheless introduced into the church in the interest of good order. That organ music fell into this category was generally assumed, indeed affirmed by a provincial synod in 1638 when it attempted to put the organ controversy to rest for the churches in its classis. This Provincial Synod of South Holland, which met in Delft between 2 and 14 August 1638, decided that playing the organ to support the congregational singing of psalms was "a matter of medium importance [best left] to the decision of the churches." Further, they declared that "those that use this organ playing can best judge whether it happens in an edifying way in their churches or not."[32] These decisions implied that there was no longer any official objection to the sound of organ pipes in Calvinist worship within this classis.

As it was now clear that organ use was accepted because it enabled a more beautiful psalmody, most Protestant cultures grappled with contigent issues of organ use. For example, there was the sticky issue of the organ postlude. As it is in many churches today, the postlude was

---

32. "dat de classis dese zaecke als middelmatich zijnde dern kercken bevolen laet, welcke did orgelspelen gebruijcke, als best connende oordelen off het met stichtinghe in haere kercken gebryckt wert ofte niet" (Knuttel, *Acta der particuliere synoden*, 175).

A Devil's Siren or an Angel's Throat?

seen merely as a moment for the organist to shine. Bravura voluntaries pointed solely at the skill of the player and the capabilities of the instrument to produce thunderous tones. Because this music was being played technically beyond the temporal boundaries of the worship service proper, believers should have been able to enjoy the organ postlude guilt free. However, synodical delegates feared that the postlude would distract the congregation's attention from divine matters and cause people to forget everything they had heard in the sermon, which was (and is) of paramount importance in Reformed liturgy.[33] Besides, one Polish Reformed minister remarked that the thunderous tones of the organ postlude had a "negative effect on nervous women."[34]

The solution was that where organ postludes were used, closing organ voluntaries could continue to be played. However, they must be "serious and grave" pieces. Further, the melodies played should be psalm tunes so that people could have another chance to hear these melodies as they were leaving. No secular songs would be allowed, nor would any "frivolous pieces."[35]

I'd like to now play an exerpt of such a "serious and grave" postlude. The piece I'd like to demonstrate is from the pen of Henderick Joostensz Speuij. Briefly, Speuij was organist in Dordrecht at both the Great Church and the Augustine Church. He was also the town's harpsichordist. It is documented that Speuij was the organist who played a prelude before the National Synod of Dordrecht in 1618.[36] But seven

---

33. "Ende al hoe vvel men het alsnoch in sommige deser Kercken, alleen in 't eynde der praedicatiën gebruyckt op 't scheyden van den volcke, soo dienet nochtans meest om te vergeten vvatmen te voren gehoort heeft: ende is te besorgen, dat het hiernaer tot superstitie sal gebruyckt vvorden, gelijck het nu tot lichtvaerdigheydt dient; d' vvelck soo 't afgeschaft vvare, men soude de Aelmoessen bequamelijcker aen de deuren in 't uytgaen des volckx, versamelen, dan datmen sulckx in 't midden der Predicatie, tot groote hindernisse des Dienstes, doen moet." [And although it {the organ} is still used in some of these churches at the end of the sermon when the people are leaving, it mostly serves to make the people forget what they have just heard, and we need to worry that afterwards it will be used for superstition, just like it now serves for frivolity; and if this were to be discontinued, it would be easier to gather in the offerings at the door when the people are leaving rather than to do so in the middle of the service, at which time it greatly disrupts the worship of God.] (Schoock, *Exercitationes*, 538).

34. Sapalski, *Przewodnik dla organistow*, 131.

35. Vente and Vlam, *Documentaet*, 2:93

36. Van den Borren, *Les origines de la musique de clavier*, 55; Eitner and Springer, *Biographisch-bibliographisches quellen-lexikon*; Goovaerts, *Histoire et bibliographie*,

John Calvin, Myth and Reality

years before that international synod, Speuij published *De Psalmen Davids, gestelt op het Tabulatuer van het Orghel*, a folio of twenty-four bicinia based on Genevan psalm tunes for organ that met the criteria of "serious pieces."[37] This collection is the first of its kind for the Reformed church: this is the first published manuscript we have of organ music from a Reformed church, for a Reformed church, written by a Reformed organist. Though it was not recorded which of his psalm settings he played before the Dordrecht synod, I'd like to think that it could have been his setting of the famous Geneva 100.[38]

Our conference theme is "John Calvin: Myth and Reality." One myth (kept alive especially among non-European scholars) is the commonly accepted fallacy that the newly birthed Reformed church wielded a unified, central structure with an authority that controlled the activities of its affiliate congregations and clergymen. A corollary to this fallacy is the assumption that the Reformed churches of any particular country used a single, common liturgy based upon Calvin's teachings. However, if these assumptions were true, then the early Reformed synodical declarations that the pipe organ was unfit for worship would have been observed by all Reformed churches without delay or objection. However, the very fact that this did not happen proves these assumptions are not correct. The reality is that the Reformed left indifferent, nonsalvific issues (such as organ music) to local discretion along with other liturgical decisions such as funereal practices, weekday services, and the use of hymns.

As Reformed theology met entrenched local customs, congregations, consistories, laymen, and theologians jostled for power. They in turn wrestled in some way with secular powers who demanded equal control over the religious lives of their citizenry. Still further, these secular leaders would not necessarily have known what the right "Reformed" decision would be, nor would they necessarily even vote in that direction.

307; *Nieuw Nederlandsch Biografisch Woordenboek*, 2:1349, and 5:786; Zwart, "Hendrik Joosten Speuy," 97–98, 129–32.

37. Extant copies exist only at British Museum and at the University Library of Glasgow. However, Frits Noske has edited and published them under the title *Psalm Preludes*. See also Curtis, "Henderick Speuy," 143–62.

38. Here Engle performed Speuij's organ voluntary on Geneva 100.

A Devil's Siren or an Angel's Throat?

Dutch *orgelists* were willing to set aside clear directives for church music in their country in order to ensure musical beauty. Because the sober liturgy of the Dutch Reformed called for the unison, unaccompanied singing of new, complicated French psalm tunes, congregational singing became nearly impossible and, by all contemporary reports, no longer worshipful or practical. This process was only checked by the gradual, local reacceptance of the pipe organ, and by Reformed congregations' ignoring the ban of instrumental music.

Ironically, Calvinism itself may help explain the apparent divide between Reformed theory and actual, varying practice. While Calvin did set forth clearly his liturgical ideals, he worked equally hard to underscore the necessity of democratic church governance that could accommodate cultural and local variations of practice. Further, because Reformed church buildings and their pipe organs were not owned by the church but by the city, the Dutch Calvinists had little control over all components of their worship, especially sound. Within such a political setting, civic and church powers conflicted, sometimes harshly, and local congregations varied in how fast or faithfully they carried out Calvin's aural iconoclasm. By the late seventeenth century, the Dutch Reformed had largely reached compromise about liturgical sound, and they viewed worship's aural elements to be at least as important as its visual ingredients. The consequence of these ecclesiastical, theological, artistic, and practical compromises among the Dutch Calvinists remains significant for a clear understanding of this period in Reformed worship.

This is not to suggest that all Reformed folk everywhere immediately and fully accepted the organ; indeed, some remained convinced for centuries that the devil himself and his minions blew their vices through organ pipes directly into the hearts and minds of worshipers. At the same time, others heard organ music as angel voices that called worshipers to join their voices in song with those celestial choirs. While the theological arguments at the root of this controversy were never truly settled by the Reformed, in the end the pipe organ did indeed help them sing their beloved psalms more reverently, which was something—perhaps the only thing—to which they could all finally sing a resounding amen.

8

"Cruel, Cold and False"
Calvin and the Calvinists through the Eyes of Their Dutch Opponents (1566–1619)

MIRJAM G. K. VAN VEEN

During the Reformation the Dutch Republic developed a unique religious landscape. Primarily because the magistrates were unwilling to persecute deviant religious groups seriously, dissident churches like the Anabaptists and the Catholics could maintain a significant place beside the Reformed Church within this landscape. Both Catholics and Anabaptists were tolerated.[1] To be sure, this tolerated status was far from desirable. Catholics in particular always ran the risk of being suspected of supporting a foreign enemy, and a vast number of Catholic priests working in the Republic had a shorter or longer "prison experience."[2] But despite these difficulties, Catholics and Anabaptists were able to remain a strong and vital presence within the Republic. Around 1600 the Reformed Church was split between the orthodox Calvinists and the Arminians. After a short period of persecutions, the Arminians

---

1. Parker, *Faith on the Margins*, 46–58; Zijlstra, *Om de ware gemeente en de oude gronden*, 340–44.

2. Ackermans, *Herders en Huurlingen*, 51.

"Cruel, Cold and False"

obtained a status similar to the Anabaptists'.[3] In addition to these organized churches, a large part of the Dutch population remained aloof from the visible churches. Some of these "Neutralists" defended this position in public writings and urged their readers to leave the visible churches as they had done.

The sixteenth- and seventeenth-century religious landscape of the Dutch Republic became a sort of a religious market with four competing groups: Catholics, Anabaptists, Reformed, and Neutralists. These groups used various means to win the competition for souls. In this competition the orthodox Calvinists were granted a head start. They were the public church and could always hope for the magistrates' support. In marked contrast to this dominant position, Reformed ministers felt they were a minority. They were forced to defend themselves against, in their eyes, an overwhelming majority of Catholics, Neutralists, Anabaptists, and Arminians, who put the Reformation at risk. The ministers saw their inheritance seriously threatened.[4]

In this competition the churches did their utmost to draw clear boundaries between themselves and the others. Members were discouraged, to say the least, from visiting other churches or from marrying outside their own church. Members were encouraged to set a clear example of a true Christian life. Catholics, Anabaptists, and Reformed believers were urged to sanctify their lives in order to attract others to their churches. Religious leaders especially had to be sober, strict, and moderate. Reformed ministers, for example, were urged to avoid luxurious clothes, since many believers were attracted to Anabaptist sobriety.[5] Churches used various means to teach their members their true doctrine. Catholics and Reformed published catechisms to explain their own right and the opposite's wrong. Priests and ministers preached against each other and used their sermons to prove their own truth. Ministers and priests were trained to maintain themselves within this polarized religious landscape. They were taught about the differences between the churches: priests were well trained in Scripture so that they were able to counter the Reformed attacks, and both ministers and priests were trained in disputations.

3. Van Deursen, *Bavianen en slijkgeuzen*, 227–371.
4. Augustijn, "Reformierte Kirche," 112–13.
5. Synod of Friesland, 3 Mai 1585, art 10; Reitsma and van Veen, *Acta der Provinciale en Particuliere Synoden*, 6:16.

Within this religious landscape, religious polemic flourished. The competing groups wrote against each other to encourage their own members to be steadfast and to discourage the others. In addition to these writings, competing groups used pictures to blacken the others and to show one's own excellence. In this chapter I will analyze the polemic against the Reformed as a part of the competition between these different religious groups within the religious landscape of the Dutch Republic. I will confine myself to polemical writings against the Reformed published between 1566 and 1619. Various scholars have written about these polemical works, but they have focused on the polemic between two confessions. Books have been written on Catholic polemic against the Reformed and on the polemic between Anabaptists and Reformed, but no attempt has been made to grasp the whole picture.[6] There is reason enough, however, to study this polemic as a whole. Anabaptist, Catholic, Arminian, and Neutralist polemic was interrelated: they each used the same stereotypes against the Reformed, and sometimes they supported each other against the Reformed. In my description of this polemic against the Reformed, I will focus on the image the opponents created of the public church and of its members. So far scholars have primarily paid attention to the theological arguments authors used, but there are strong indications that image was at least as important as theology. Theological arguments on, for example, predestination and justification were difficult to grasp; accusations of hypocrisy and avarice against Reformed ministers were easily understood by everyone.

In 1566 the Reformed stepped into the open with an outburst of iconoclasm, which provoked a fierce Catholic reaction. In fact, Catholic polemic against the Reformed only started in the mid-1560s. Earlier, the defenders of the Catholic faith had confined themselves to polemic against Lutherans and Anabaptists. The same is true of Neutralist polemic against the Reformed. With his defense of Nicodemism, the Neutralist Dirck Volckertsz Coornhert wrote against the Reformed at a comparatively early date (1560), but he did not continue his polemic against the Reformed until 1572.[7] Anabaptist polemic against

---

6. Andriessen, *Die Jezuïeten*; Buitendijk, *calvinisme*; Vermaseren, *katholieke Nederlandse geschiedschrijving*; Wessel, *De leerstellige strijd.*

7. Van Veen, "*Verschooninghe van de roomsche afgoderye,*" 165–72. On Coornhert's polemic against the Reformed and especially on his disputations with the Reformed

the Reformed started earlier, but this polemic changed after the 1560s because the Reformed movement changed. Up to the sixties the Anabaptists and the Reformed had shared a similar fate: they were both clandestine movements. But whereas the Anabaptists remained a minority movement, the Reformed succeeded in obtaining a majority position. The Reformed Church became closely linked with the Dutch Revolt and obtained the status of the public church. Although the Reformed never became a State Church (church membership remained voluntary), the young Republic presented itself as a Reformed state. In the 1570s this Reformed majority position and Reformed cooperation with secular authorities became a major issue in Anabaptist polemic, along with the ongoing doctrinal issues and sanctification. Something similar can be said of Catholic polemic. In the 1560s Catholics pictured the Reformed as revolutionaries and as thieves of church property. After the Reformed had become the public church, their changed position from a minority movement to a majority church became an important target of Catholic polemic as well.[8]

During this same period, the Reformed Church defined its own identity. Within a short time the Reformed succeeded in developing into a well-defined group with clear boundaries. The Dutch Confession and the Heidelberg Catechism became the two pillars of Reformed identity: these two documents marked the difference between Reformed and non-Reformed and became symbols of Reformed unity. The process of finding and establishing an organization and an identity ended in 1619 with the Synod of Dordt.[9] This Reformed identity was a second target in the polemic against the Reformed.

Opponents of the Reformed used a variety of literary means to criticize the public church. Arminians and Catholics wrote history books to picture orthodox Calvinism as a brand-new invention; priests and Catholic laity wrote songs in which they pictured the Reformed in the darkest tones; Catholic theologians wrote treatises to explain Reformed errors in doctrine; and Abraham Verhoeven, an Antwerp printer, invented the *Tijdingen* (a forerunner of the newspaper) to describe all the evils that occurred in Reformed countries. These various types of

---

see also Roobol, *Landszaken*.
8. Van Veen, *Een nieuwe tijd*, 62–117.
9. Ibid., 133–79.

anti-Calvinist polemic were intertwined. Authors from different confessional backgrounds used each other's arguments, and Catholics were especially happy to support the publication of other polemics against the public church.[10] The Arminians were granted the possibility of using Antwerp's printing presses, and on some occasions Catholic authors published Arminian treatises with a Catholic preface.[11]

This polemic was embedded in an international context, but it also had its own specifically Dutch marks. The Catholic reproach, for example, that the Reformers were a sixteenth-century invention, was, of course, not typically Dutch but was instead the stereotypical reproach of breaking with apostolic tradition. Catholics and Neutralists took over Jerome Bolsec's famous depiction of Calvin. Using Bolsec as a reliable source, they portrayed Calvin and his sympathizers as "loose fishes," who not only chased every possible woman, but who also committed the sin of sodomy.[12] According to the Catholic writer Franciscus Coster, who followed Bolsec in this respect, Calvin's reworking of his *Institutes* was the very proof of the Reformer's inconstancy.[13] In addition to Bolsec's work, the old stereotypes of medieval heresy were an important source of inspiration for Reformed opponents. The Reformed were the inheritors of early-church heresies such as Arianism and Manicheism, they were driven by haughtiness and curiosity, they always disguised themselves and concealed their true beliefs, and they lacked morality.[14]

The specifically Dutch marks of polemic against the Reformed were largely due to the concrete historical context in which the Reformed church in the Low Countries was born. The birth of this church, taking place between 1566 and 1619, was closely linked with the Dutch Revolt. The Reformed had wholeheartedly supported this revolt, and they regarded their liberation from the Spanish king as the sixteenth-century reiteration of the exodus from Egypt. The Republic was the new Israel, and the Reformed Church was called to play a vital role within this

10. *Vant swingelsche calff*, fol. b3r; *Christelijcke waerschouwinghen*, 51–52.

11. Sabbe, *Brabant in't verweer*, 36. Catholic authors published the Arminian treatise, *Ioannes Calvinus*. The Antwerp canon Aubertus Miraeus supported the Arminian point of view publicly, Vermaseren, *Katholieke Nederlandse Geschiedschrijving*, 180.

12. [Richard Verstegen], *Oorspronck ende teghenwoordighen staet*; Coster, *Antwoorde*, 330–31; Petronius, *Kettersche spinnecoppe*, 67.

13. Coster, *Antwoorde*, 210.

14. Grundmann, "Der Typus des Ketzers," 313–27.

new Israel. Neutralists, Anabaptists, and Arminians agreed with this positive picture of the revolt. They too described the revolt in terms of freedom and liberation, but they had a different opinion of what this freedom and liberty meant. According to them, their ancestors fought and suffered during the revolt in order to obtain the liberty to worship not in a Reformed way but in accordance with one's own conscience.[15] Consequently they did not regard the public church as the inheritor or the safeguard of the revolt. According to these dissenters, the Reformed put this inheritance at risk. By urging secular authorities to check the influence of other religious groups, Reformed ministers turned against religious freedom and thus betrayed the revolt.[16]

The Catholic picture of the revolt was completely different: the revolt had brought nothing but misery. Catholics reminded their contemporaries that due to the revolt, the unity between the northern and southern part of the Low Countries had been broken. The wealth of churches and monasteries had been violated by Calvinists who were, Catholic authors knew for sure, driven by greed. The attempts to introduce a religious peace and a form of coexistence between the different churches had failed because the Calvinists were not ready to keep their word. The Calvinists had undermined the Pacification of Ghent as well as the Satisfactions in different cities.[17] The Calvinists had broken the old peaceful order of society, for they had revolted against the legitimate king. Instead of the old normal order, a monarchy, they had introduced a Swiss type of democracy. This Swiss type of democracy implied that normal, unlearned people and even women were allowed to read and explain Scripture; democracy allowed these normal people to contradict their masters and fostered contempt of the old nobility. The logical consequence of the introduction of democracy was the disruption of the old peaceful order, and immeasurable bloodshed.[18] A dialogue written in 1580 makes this Catholic picture of Calvinism and revolt abundantly clear. In it, the king of hell complains about the

---

15. On these different opinions on the exact meaning of 'liberty,' see van Gelderen, "De Nederlandse Opstand," 27–52.

16. *Antwoordt*, 42; *Retortie ofte weder-steeck*, a2v; *Voor-looper*, 12, 13, 15.

17. *Vant swingelsche calff*, c1v, e4r; *Balladen*, 315, 317.

18. *Vant swingelsche calff*, b4r; Coster, *Antwoorde*, 76–77, 115; *Balladen*, 61.

Calvinists entering his kingdom and wants to refuse them entrance to the underworld because they disrupt the order of hell.[19]

In spite of their very different evaluations of the revolt and of the Reformed role in it, the Calvinists' opponents largely agreed on the main characteristics of the Calvinists. One striking trait was their hypocrisy, which was clearly shown by the changed attitude of the Calvinists toward religious tolerance. According to the Arminians, Anabaptists, Neutralists and Catholics, the Calvinists had pleaded for religious tolerance during the revolt. But now that they had gained a dominant position, the Calvinists denied others what they had gained for themselves.[20] According to Catholic authors this plea for tolerance had been only a trick to gain dominance. Tolerance had been a mere word to seduce people to choose the Calvinist side.[21]

Both Catholics and Protestant dissenters regarded this hypocrisy as a hallmark of international Calvinism. Dutch Calvinists had not been the only ones to seduce people with the promise of religious tolerance. Calvin himself had done the same. He had claimed the freedom to worship in accordance with his own conscience, but once he had gained a dominant position in Geneva, he was ready to persecute his opponents. To prove Calvin's hypocrisy, Protestant dissenters and Catholics used the Servetus case.[22] In the Republic the Calvinists' calls on the magistrates to check the influence of other churches showed their hypocrisy. According to Anabaptists, Neutralists, and Arminians, the Reformed ministers behaved like new popes. Arminans and Neutralists especially warned their contemporaries that the Calvinists were introducing a Genevan inquisition in the Low Countries.[23]

On this topic (the supposed Calvinist hypocrisy about religious tolerance) the reproaches made by Protestant dissenters were most far reaching. According to these dissenters, the Calvinists had not only changed their minds because it suited them better, but they had also

19. "Eenen poeetsche dialogus genaempt Calvinus," in van Boelaere, *Twee XVIe eeuwsche dialogen*.

20. *Vant swingelsche calff*, c4v; *Protocol Leeuwarden*, 50.

21. Petronius, *Kettersche spinnecoppe*, 68.

22. *Vant swingelsche calff*, 3r; Coster, *Antwoorde*, 259–260; Coornhert, "Proces van't ketter-dooden, ende dwangh der conscientien, deel 2," in Coornhert, *Wercken*, 134ab.

23. *Ioannes Calvinus*, 2; *Ratelwachts Roep*.

"Cruel, Cold and False"

betrayed the liberty and freedom that were the inheritance of the revolt. The Anabaptist spokesman, Peter van Ceulen, reminded his Calvinist opponents of their common history of suffering religious persecution. He accused Calvinists of being ready to become persecutors themselves, thus betraying their own history.[24]

Calvinist hypocrisy came to light not only through Calvinists' changing opinion on religious tolerance. The Calvinists' view and use of the Scriptures was another example of their hypocrisy. The Reformed, their opponents were sure, did not stick to Scripture alone. *Sola scriptura* was a mere phrase in the mouth of a Calvinist. Calvinists ignored specific parts of the Bible and were even ready to distort Scripture.[25]

The Heidelberg Catechism, the Dutch Confession, and the authority ascribed to synods were further evidence that the Calvinists had abandoned their adage of *sola scriptura*. With the introduction of human inventions, the Calvinists erred in several respects, if we are to believe the Protestant dissenters. There was, first of all, a return to human traditions. Moreover, a synod received the authority to impose rules on believers. This, Arminians, and Neutralists were sure, was a reintroduction of the papal hierarchy, the return of a "Jus Canonicum."[26] The confession and the catechism were new burdens on the shoulders of believers. With these human writings Calvinist ministers prescribed what Christians had to believe. Catechism and confession thus set limits to the freedom of belief.[27] The introduction of a catechism and a confession was in the eyes of other Protestant believers a betrayal of *sola scriptura* and a threat to the freedom of individual believers.

Most far reaching were the Anabaptist reproaches. According to the Anabaptists, the Calvinists did not live with Scripture alone. They had (Reformed) doctrine alongside and above the Bible, and they wanted to know things about God and Christ that could not be found in

---

24. *Protocol. Embden*, 308v–309r; See also *Antwoordt op de malitieuse calumnie*, 31–32.

25. Coster, *Antwoorde*, 4; Coornhert, *Synodus vander conscientien vryheyt*, 42, 43–45; Jansenius van Hulst, *Een corte confutatie of wederlegghinghe*, d6r.

26. *Antwoordt op de malitieuse calumnie*, 34, 40. Coornhert, *Remonstrance of Vertooch by die van Leyden*, in Coornhert, *Wercken*, 187a.

27. *Antwoordt op de malitieuse calumnie*, 39–41; Coornhert, *Dolingen des catechismi*, in Coornhert, *Wercken*, 2:235a; Coornhert, *Theriakel teghen het venijnighe wroeghschrift*, in ibid., 2:254cd.

the Bible.[28] With sophisticated speech and with their university-trained ministers, the Calvinists once again took the Bible away from normal believers.[29] If one believes Peter van Ceulen, the Reformed were even more attached to human traditions than the Catholics: "I don't doubt that, at that time when the Reformed church will be a hundred years old, it will have far more human rules than the Catholic Church, which has existed for some centuries. Just look how many rules the Reformed have laid down during their first synods!"[30]

In short, according to Catholics, Neutralists, Anabaptists, and Arminians, the Calvinists were hypocrites. Their changing attitude towards religious tolerance and their introduction of human inventions like synod, catechism, and confession were clear examples that the Calvinists were faithful neither to the inheritance of the Dutch Revolt nor to the principles of the Reformation.

A second striking fault besides hypocrisy, according to their opponents, was the Calvinists' immorality. According to Catholic authors, Calvinists did not check the desires of the flesh and so lived in a libertine way. Protestant dissenters largely agreed. Neutralists were sure that the Reformation was unable to improve the lives of believers. Religious persecutions and the wars raging throughout Europe made it clear that the Reformation had failed to foster the most important mark of Christianity: love of one's neighbor.[31] Anabaptists largely agreed that the Calvinists failed to sanctify their daily lives. According to Anabaptist leaders, this was largely due to a lack of discipline. According to all anti-Calvinists, the doctrine of predestination undermined morality. Arminians and the Neutralists were sure that the whole idea of predestination killed every possible striving for moral improvement. According to an Arminian treatise published in 1620, everyday life made it clear that people used the doctrine of predestination as a cloak to live as libertines.[32] Coornhert severely criticized the Reformed doctrine of predestination for killing every good endeavor and for teaching

28. *Protocol Emden*, 120r.
29. Ibid., 241r.
30. *Protocol Leeuwarden*, 54.
31. "Het beginsel en voortganck der geschillen, scheuringen en verdeeltheden onder de gene die doops-gesinden genoemt worden," in: *Bibliotheca Reformatoria Neerlandica* 7:514.
32. *Antwoordt op de malitieuse calumnie*, 42–44.

that people were unable to overcome sin. The Anabaptist leader Hans de Ries agreed with Coornhert. His fellow Anabaptist Peter van Ceulen saw predestination as an easy escape; if the doctrine of predestination were true, people were no longer responsible for murder or theft but could easily defend themselves by saying that they had been predestined to commit these acts.[33] Catholics and Arminians fostered the notion of the predestined thief. The Arminian Slatius was the first to evoke this figure, and it became quite a success.[34] Other Arminians and Catholics also used the predestined thief in order to show that Reformed predestination put morality at risk.[35]

According to Catholics, predestination was not the only part of Reformed doctrine that undermined morality. The whole idea of justification by faith alone was a broad road to hell. According to Catholic authors, the Reformation had made faith far too easy. Lutherans and Calvinists had abolished good works and penance. In Catholic eyes, Calvinists taught that faith alone was enough, and that it was not necessary to refrain from sin.[36] In 1579 a Catholic writer accused the Calvinists of not taking the Ten Commandments seriously. Believing in Christ was enough for a Calvinist believer.[37] According to Cornelis Vrancx, the Reformed abolition of purgatory put the souls of believers at risk, since the fear of purgatory had caused them to refrain from sin. But Reformed ministers had done away with this fear, thus enabling a libertine life.[38]

According to Catholic writers, erroneous doctrine was not the only explanation for the Calvinist lack of morality. In the eyes of Catholic authors, this lack of morality was simply inevitable. The whole Reformation had started with Martin Luther's decision to listen to the desires of the flesh and to marry the nun Katherine von Bora.[39] The case with Jean Calvin was even worse, because he had even committed the sin of Sodom. Monks and priests who chose to side with the Reformation

33. *Protocol Emden*, 48v.
34. Sabbe, *Brabant in 't verweer*, 36.
35. Ibid., 49. [Richard Verstegen], *Scherp-sinnighe characteren*, 126.
36. Duncanus, *Catholijcke catechismus*, d4r.
37. *Balladen*, 140.
38. Ibid., 17.
39. Coster, *Antwoorde*, 135.

had generally been driven by their wish for sexual license.⁴⁰ Besides this sexual immorality, the whole Reformation was motivated by vain curiosity, by a longing for renewal, and by haughtiness. To Catholic authors, Calvin's idea that he was permitted to reject or correct the teachings of the church fathers, as well as his break with the old ecclesiastical tradition, was the height of human arrogance. Who was Jean Calvin to correct and criticize a tradition that was more than a thousand years old?⁴¹ Who were the Calvinists, that they knew better than the old tradition?⁴²

Again, according to the Catholics, the Calvinists had abolished all valuable measures the early church had introduced to check the desires of the flesh. Calvinists did not fast, and their ministers were allowed to marry. As Franciscus Coster put it, the Calvinists had exchanged churches and monasteries for inns and public houses.⁴³ Moreover in comparison with Catholics, Calvinist religious zeal was meager. Calvinists only attended church services once or twice a week, and they only prayed a couple of times a day.⁴⁴

Neutralist, Catholic, Anabaptist, and Arminian polemic against Calvin and Calvinism was of course not one and the same thing. Each group had different theological reasons for opposing the public church, and each had a different view of history. But these different polemics also had much in common: the negative pictures created by Neutralists, Catholics, Arminians, and Anabaptists strongly resembled one another. The Reformed were flip-floppers, who did not stay firm in their own principles. They used the whole idea of *sola scriptura* and of religious toleration only to seduce people. Moreover the Reformed lacked religious zeal. They did not sanctify their lives but lived like Epicureans and Libertines.

There are some indications that this dark picture of the Reformed had an influence in the Dutch Republic. New church members in Delft

---

40. Val, *Den spieghel der calvinisten*, 8r-8v; Petronius, *Kettersche spinnecoppe*, 112-13.

41. [Verstegen], *Oorspronck*; Coster, *Antwoorde*, 111.

42. Coster, *Antwoorde*, 29, 115-16, 346; Coornhert, *Synodus*, eerste deel, 135; Coornhert, *Een corte confutatie of wederlegghinge*, d4v; [Verstegen], *Nederlantsche antiquiteiten*, 87.

43. Coster, *Antwoorde*, 89, 131; cf. De Val, *Den spieghel der calvinisten*, 5r; Petronius, *Kettersche spinnecoppe*, 209; *Balladen*, 139.

44. *Vant swingelsche calff*, h1r.

"Cruel, Cold and False"

did not want to be mentioned by name because they felt ashamed to be members of the Reformed Church. And ministers complained about rumors that they were aiming for a Genevan inquisition. The Leeuwarden consistory, for example, complained that people tended to believe the Anabaptist picture of the Reformed as persecutors and murderers. If we are to believe the consistory, this picture seriously hindered the Reformed Church: while the public church was still in a poor condition, the number of Anabaptists was growing.[45]

The influence of this dark image of the Reformed is, I think, explicable. The common features of the Reformed images created by Neutralists, Catholics, Arminians, and Anabaptists gave this image credibility and strength. Reproaches and criticisms against the public church were always shared by a larger group outside the public church. Someone like Dirck Volckertsz Coornhert was never just one individual opposed to the Reformed Church: he was always the spokesman for a large part of the population. Accusations against the Reformed Church reinforced one another. According to these anti-Calvinist authors, the fact that so many writers from different backgrounds shared this image of the Calvinists proved its reliability. As a Catholic author who referred to Coornhert put it, even people outside the Catholic Church shared a negative picture of the Reformed Church.[46] A reader of a Catholic catechism was sure that the Heidelberg Catechism was not based on Scripture, since so many authors from so many churches questioned its biblical basis.[47]

As stated above, the Reformed ministers felt threatened. Although they had a majority position, they felt like a minority. And indeed the Reformed had some serious problems. They were able to counter the theological objections against them. Especially on the theological battlefield, the Anabaptists were simply not an equal match for the Reformed ministers. But it is questionable how important this theological victory

---

45. Augustijn, "Die Reformierte Kirche," 112; Consistory of the Reformed Church in Leeuwarden to the ministers and elders of the Dutch Reformed Church in London, Leeuwarden, 21 [31 NS] December 1596, in Hessels, *Ecclesiae Londino-Batavae Archivvm*, 3:994–995, ep. 1367; Consistory of the Reformed Church in Leeuwarden to the ministers and elders of the Dutch Reformed Church in London, Leeuwarden, 4 [14 NS] April 1597, in Hessels, *Ecclesiae Londino-Batavae Archivvm* 3: 1002, ep. 1378.

46. *Christelycke waerschouwingen*), 51–52; *Vant swingelsche calff*, b3r, c4r.

47. *Catholijcke catechismus*, ov.

was. The Delft church members who did not want to be mentioned by name, and the Leeuwarden complaints about the Anabaptists' picture of the Reformed, are strong indications that the Reformed had a serious image problem. Moreover these testimonies suggest that image was at least as influential as learned theological arguments.

9

Calvinism at the Borders of the Empire
Johannes Wigand and the Lutheran Reaction to Calvinism

IRENE DINGEL

In the second half of the sixteenth century the prospect of Calvinism at the borders of the Holy Roman Empire—and especially the prospect of its potential expansion within the borders of the Empire—was for the imperial princes a thoroughly disconcerting idea. That was due not only to the political and legal constellations within the so-called Holy Roman Empire of the German Nation, though they certainly played a significant role. Since the Religious Peace of Augsburg of 1555 within the Empire, only those who had accepted the Augsburg Confession and were officially designated as the adherents of the Augsburg Confession were supposed to enjoy political toleration, along with the adherents of the traditional Roman faith. A principality or a free imperial city that could be suspected of Calvinism, or even of giving it preferential treatment, ran the risk of being excluded from the official Religious Peace and might well be subject to imperial penalties. Initially viewed as temporary, the Religious Peace can be seen as an epoch-making event in so far as it was the first time that politicians and legal experts had succeeded in setting aside the question of truth in determining the legal order of society and guaranteeing a politically and legally based coexistence¹ of two competing religious groups.²

This did not mean, however, that intentional support for tolerance had been developed. Even those who demanded that they themselves have a hearing and that their own particular system of belief be accepted did not develop a concept of tolerance.³ Before and after the Religious Peace, a social system that viewed the political community and the *Corpus Christianum* as congruent with each other could in fact have only *one* religious option claiming to have the truth. Competition among systems of belief, especially when it threatened to promote public disorder and to call God-established authorities into question, endangered both common life in society and political stability. This is the reason why neither the struggle between Roman Catholicism and Protestantism nor the struggle between the confessional groupings that were establishing themselves within Protestantism came to an end. On the contrary, the passion for converting people from the other side on the part of Roman Catholicism, and especially of the Jesuits, sometimes supported by political leaders, led in certain regions to regular waves of transferring allegiance. There were also fairly frequent conversions from Lutheranism to Calvinism. This shows that no one was indifferent to questions of religious belief and that the understanding of decisive ecclesiastical dogmas could penetrate the levels of society that had no academic training and could become a part of people's thinking at those levels.⁴ The entire sixteenth century and the early seventeenth century were marked by the power of unshakable religious convictions, which in no way were limited in their impact to a theological elite. They were rather conveyed to the level of the common people by extensive use of preaching and by propaganda, which brought the controversies into the vernacular in the form of pamphlets. Many people were prepared to do battle in rigorous defense of their own convictions, to present them publicly in confessional documents, and to defend them without

---

1. Cf. Schreiner, "Toleranz," 528-31.

2. On European peace agreements regarding religion, see Kohnle, "Konfliktbereinigung und Gewaltprävention," 1-19.

3. Cf. Schreiner, " Toleranz," 530.

4. See the study of Robert Christman on the "Substantialists" and the "Accidentalists," in the controversy over the proper definition of original sin: "Heretics in Luther's Homeland," and Christman's "'I Can Indeed Respond,'" 1003-19.

compromise. All of this set the stage for the debates that the confessional groups conducted as these groups consolidated. This explains the bitterness that marked such controversies.

This essay focuses on Lutheranism's polemic against Calvinism and attempts to place the mechanisms that were developing for the defense of confessional positions in their historical and theological context. This will above all bring the Lutheran perspective on Calvinism to light. It is obvious that one essay cannot cover the waterfront. Therefore, this investigation attempts to develop a model for analysis through a micro-study, which can serve as an example for the assessment of the confrontation between Lutheranism and Calvinism. Drawing on one of the most prominent producers of Lutheran polemic in the latter half of sixteenth century suggests itself as an appropriate approach. The writings of Johannes Wigand offer the necessary points for analysis in their construction, in their theological content, and in their argumentation. This chapter will first explicate Wigand's position in *history* before going on to address the Calvinistic challenge to the creation of the Lutheran confession of the faith. It concludes by looking at Wigand's developing the structure of his argument, which, depending on the situation, could be directed toward political authorities and was designed to legitimize the course of action he desired.

Johannes Wigand as a Spokesman against Calvinism

At first glance it may not necessarily be clear why the Lutheran theologian and later bishop of Pomesania and Samland in Prussia, Johannes Wigand, and his writings can be cited as an example for the long-lasting friction between Lutheranism and Calvinism. But for several reasons he can be taken as a typical representative of the second generation of reformers.[5] Born in 1523, Wigand had studied under Luther, Melanchthon, and Caspar Cruciger in Wittenberg and had experienced the Smalkaldic War and the Augsburg Interim of 1548, the imperial law of religion that aimed at recatholicizing the imperial principalities that had adopted the Reformation. Wigand did not evade the situation in which these controversies were ignited but rather developed into a controversial theologian who resolutely defended the teaching and per-

---

5. Cf. the overview on his life and work, Irene Dingel, " Johannes Wigand," in *TRE* 36:33–38.

son of Martin Luther, not only against the adherents of the old faith,[6] but also against those within the Protestant camp who oriented their further development toward Melanchthon, and against the Reformed alternatives to Luther.[7] The necessity of securing the Lutheran theological legacy and the public teaching associated with it against every deviation led him to formulate clear dogmatic boundaries for Lutheran teaching. To maintain them he was prepared to go into exile on at least two occasions.[8]

Wigand's many years of work on the *Magdeburg Centuries*, in close cooperation with Matthaeus Judex and the organizer of the project, Matthias Flacius Illyricus, sharpened his historical consciousness, particularly of the history of dogma. This made its mark especially in a series of works produced late in his career, in which he traced the historical development of those who stood outside the theological mainstream or supported noticeable deviations in doctrine. He denounced them as false. These works include writings that in part also made sources on their subjects available: *De Servetianismo* (1575), *De Anabaptismo* (1582), *De Schwenckfeldismo* (1586), *De Manichaeismo renovato* (1587), and also the volume aimed at Calvinism, a volume in 598 quarto leaves, *De Sacramentariismo* (1585).[9] It presented Andreas Bodenstein von Karlstadt, Ulrich Zwingli, Johannes Oecolampadius, and John Calvin as "patriarchs of the sacramentarians." With this repertoire of writings Wigand tried to provide historical and dogmatic documentation on all the contemporary heterodox movements that had arisen from the Protestant camp.

At this time Wigand was among the most influential theologians in the Empire. He had served as professor in Jena before he received the theological doctorate from the University in Rostock and—after a seven-year exile—returned to the University of Jena in 1568. At this time

---

6. Among his first polemical writings was his treatise of 1550 against the Roman Catholic Michael Helding. He criticized Helding's Mainz Large Catechism, *Ex Sidonii Catechismo maiore* (1550) cf. also his *Verlegung aus Gottes wordt* (1556); *Synopsis. Oder Spiegel des römischen Antichrists* (1560); and *Warnung vor dem Catechismo D. Canisii* (1570).

7. The publications that belong to the period after the Interim are legion. On them, see the Datenbank des Projekts "Controversia et confessio."

8. Examples include his exile from Jena in 1561 and the refusal of the city council of Magdeburg to give him a position the following year.

9. *De Sacramentarijsmo, dogmata et argvmenta*.

he voiced his criticism especially of the budding Crypto-Calvinism (so-called) within electoral Saxony. From 1573 on, Wigand held the position of Chief Professor of Theology at the University of Königsberg; his colleague Tilemann Heshusius had worked hard to obtain this position for his longtime associate. As Heshusius's colleague, Wigand became bishop of Pomesania in 1575, and in 1577 he also assumed Heshusius's former position as bishop of Samland, after the two of them had fallen into a theological dispute over the doctrine of Christ's two natures.[10]

Even if his conduct earned criticism from his contemporaries, Wigand achieved success both in ecclesiastical office and in the context of the university as a recognized theologian in the midst of controversy and as a leading spokesman for Lutheranism. As such he dedicated himself in a host of writings to opposing all tendencies that appeared to place the Lutheran theological legacy in question or seemed to threaten it. Among these were, of course, in a most prominent way every development that, in the usage of the time, could be designated "sacramentarian," whether within the Empire or outside its borders.

The Calvinistic Challenge to the Formation of the Lutheran Confession of Faith

Upon closer inspection of the later anti-Calvinistic writings of Wigand that fall into this phase of confessional consolidation, three different geographical focal points emerge, which are of interest in this study: electoral Saxony, France together with the Netherlands, and Danzig, Königsberg's neighboring city in Royal Prussia.

First of all, the so-called philippistic tendencies in *electoral Saxony* inclined it toward the Reformed faith. This caused Wigand to take pen in hand and to develop a heightened sensitivity to the threat he believed that Calvinism posed to the Wittenberg theological legacy. Against the background of this experience, he viewed the developments in Western Europe as a challenge that he must meet. Finally, he turned his gaze to

---

10. Heshusius had maintained that it was permissible to say that the divine attributes of omnipotence and omniscience not only "in concreto," that is, to ascribe them to the concrete person of Christ, but also "in abstracto," that is, to ascribe them to human nature of Christ. This caused animosity between Wigand and Heshusius and led to Wigand's demanding a retraction from Heshusius. Heshusius' refusal to issue a retraction led to his removal from office by the duke of Prussia (Dingel, "Wigand," 36).

the east, where in the neighboring city of Danzig, subject to the Polish crown, Reformed ways of thinking threatened to undermine the established confession of the church.

Of fundamental significance for Wigand's opposition—and for that of Lutheranism in general—to Calvinism was the realization that a way of thinking inspired by Melanchthon's theology but perceived as a form of Calvinism had secretly spread in the homeland of the Wittenberg Reformation. This development fostered in Wigand a deep mistrust, sharpened his sensitivity to all deviations from Martin Luther's teaching, and caused him to publish on the subject of the Lord's Supper. After a series of developments between 1546 and 1548 (Luther's death in 1546, the military defeat of the Evangelical Smalkaldic League in 1547, and the promulgation of the imperial policy aimed at eradicating the Reformation, dubbed the Augsburg Interim), a group of Philip Melanchthon's followers established their control at the University of Wittenberg.[11] Their publications in the 1570s revealed that they no longer understood the reformational doctrine of the Lord's Supper exclusively from the standpoint of Luther's theology but rather were striving to connect it with Melanchthon's teaching and bring these two doctrinal authorities into agreement to the greatest extent possible.

At the beginning of 1571 the publication of a new catechism, put together by Christoph Pezel,[12] which was advertised as a work of all the Wittenberg theologians, added to the tensions over these issues. This Wittenberg catechism was supposed to build upon the foundational education given in Luther's catechism and to replace the catechism of the Lutheran theologian David Chytraeus, who regarded himself as a

---

11. They included Georg Major (1504–1574), up to his death "Decanus perpetuus" of the faculty, Paul Eber (1511–1569) along with his successor after 1570 Friedrich Widebram (1532–1585), and Paul Crell (1531–1579, who was transferred to the leadership of the consistory in Meißen in 1569 and returned to a professorship in Wittenberg from 1574 on). Christoph Pezel (1539–1604) replaced Crell in 1569. In addition, the faculty included Johannes Bugenhagen the younger (1524–1592), who first served in the philosophical faculty, and Caspar Cruciger the Younger (1525–1597) and Heinrich Moller (1530–1589). Cruciger entered the theological faculty in 1569; Bugenhagen and Moller in 1570, as they earned their doctorates in theology. On this, see details in Dingel, "Historische Einleitung," 3–15.

12. *Catechesis continens explicationem;* the text is found in Dingel, *Controversia et Confessio* 8:79–289.

faithful disciple of Melanchthon but taught the Lord's Supper in a significantly different way from Pezel.[13]

Other publications during these years, among them the "Consensus Dresdensis" (1571), the *Grundfest* (*The True Church's Firm Foundation: on the Person and Incarnation of Our Lord Jesus Christ* [1571] and the anonymous *Exegesis perspicua* (1574)[14] also aroused suspicion among the strict Lutherans that the theologians of electoral Saxony had been infected by the Genevan Calvinists and particularly by the Christology of Theodore Beza. The theological collegium of the University of Jena, to which Wigand had belonged in the years 1560/1561 and 1569–1573, argued against the electoral Saxon position. Even after moving to Königsberg Wigand joined the battle to expose the theology propagated in electoral Saxony as dangerous Calvinism and to decisively warn against it.[15] He labeled these Wittenberg colleagues "the new ravers about the sacrament," who with the introduction of the Wittenberg Catechism were setting the stage to intentionally educate young people in Calvinistic teaching.[16] This makes it clear into which confessional camp he placed his electoral Saxon colleagues.

Philippism, that is, the theological tendency identified by Wigand as Crypto-Calvinism, lost its political dominance in electoral Saxony in 1574. The Saxon elector August changed the direction of his religious policy as he initiated the project to establish concord among the Lutherans, led by Jacob Andreae, with its conclusion in the Formula of Concord and the Book of Concord.[17] The acute danger of Calvinism appeared to have been headed off, even if those sympathetic to the movement remained in various territories and cities.

13. The *Catechism* of David Chytraeus, the first edition of which appeared in Wittenberg in 1554, was the most widely distributed textbook in Latin in the second half of the sixteenth century; up to 1614 it appeared in at least 114 Latin editions and translations; see Kaufmann, *Universität und lutherische Konfessionalisierung*, 622. On its being taken out of circulation, see Dingel, "Historische Einleitung," 10 n. 22.

14. An edition of the most prominent documents of each phase is found in Dingel, *Controversia et Confessio* 8.

15. Cf. e.g., *Christliche Erinnerung* and *Analysis Exegeseos Sacramentariae*.

16. A citation from B2b ("*fursetzlich junge Sacramentschwermerlein*") in [Johannes Wigand, Tilemann Heshusius, Timotheus Kirchner], *Von den Fallstricken Etlicher newer Sacramentschwermer zu Wittenberg*. The title alone of this publication says much; Wigand was the chief author of the treatise.

17. See Ludwig, *Philippismus und orthodoxes Luthertum*.

Nonetheless, Wigand encountered new points of entry through which Calvinist teaching could make its way into the Empire. This brought him to alter his view of where and how Calvinism was threatening. He began to focus on the borders of the Empire. For as it became known that the Formula of Concord contained repudiations of doctrines that directly concerned the Reformed churches, particularly in article 7, "On the Lord's Supper," and article 8, "On the Person of Christ," Western European Protestants lodged objections. Indeed, an initiative by Johann Casimir, duke and later elector of the Palatinate, attempted to bring European Calvinist churches together in a conference in Frankfurt am Main in 1577[18] and to unite them in a *Harmonia Confessionum*,[19] but that effort was not able to significantly counteract the Lutheran efforts to establish concord that had just been completed. Many Western European Calvinists suspected that the consolidation of Lutheranism around the confession of faith found in the Formula of Concord would have an impact on the Religious Peace in the Empire. This posed a problem because the Formula reverted to the Unaltered Augsburg Confession, with its article on the Lord's Supper, which presented Luther's theology of the sacrament. Thus, this clearly reduced those who could claim legal status as adherents of the Augsburg Confession to those who held to its "unaltered" version of 1530.

Calvinists also feared that the Formula of Concord could have an impact outside the borders of the Empire in renewed persecution of Protestants. If within the Empire the Calvinists could be defined as not adhering to the Augsburg Confession and thus outside the law, such status would only strengthen the argument of Roman Catholic political authorities elsewhere for the persecution of Calvinists. A letter from Dutch pastors to the authors of the Formula of Concord illustrates this fear. The Dutch viewed their situation as one in which they shared the fate of their fellow believers in France, the Huguenots.[20] The letter's author was the court preacher of William of Orange, Pierre Loyseleur de Villiers.[21] During the course of 1577 he published a penetrating call for

18. On Johann Casimir's efforts, see Dingel, *Concordia controversa*, 115-29.
19. *Harmonia Confessionvm Fidei*, esp. 123-27, 136-41.
20. *Sendbrieff Der Kirchen Diener*.
21. Loyseleur (ca. 1530-1590) served as court preacher of William of Orange. He had fled France and studied theology there. He became William's court preacher in the mid-1570s.

the unity of the various Protestant parties. His treatise, *Ratio ineundae Concordiae*, highlighted the political danger that was feared, and which was a real threat, as a result of the perception of Calvinism that the Lutheran confessional position had created.[22] Wigand reacted immediately to Loyseleur's appeal.

The situation in the city of Danzig, next door to ducal Prussia and under the Polish crown, also gave Wigand concern.[23] In 1562 the city had attempted to settle ongoing disputes over the understanding of the Lord's Supper by issuing a decree, a *Notula* or "Formula of Concord," which appealed to Holy Scripture and the Augsburg Confession as the norms for public teaching. Thirteen years later, one year after the collapse of the Philippist—labeled by many "Crypto-Calvinist"—movement in electoral Saxony, the city introduced the *Corpus Doctrinae Philippicum*,[24] which had set the doctrinal standard for Melanchthon's followers in electoral Saxony and beyond its borders. It was the standard to which the so-called Crypto-Calvinists had appealed. At the same time the duchy of Prussia, with the city of Königsberg, was finding its orientation in the *Corpus Doctrinae Prutenicum*,[25] a document authored by Wigand's fellow Lutherans Joachim Mörlin and Martin Chemnitz,

---

22. Loyseleur, *Ratio ineundae Concordiae*.

23. In 1454 Prussia and Danzig revolted against the Teutonic Order and submitted to the king of Poland. Danzig belonged to royal Prussia, not to ducal Prussia, where Wigand served. See Neumeyer, " Danzig," in *TRE* 8:354.

24. This publication was originally a private undertaking edited by the Leipzig printer Ernst Vögelin and contained only writings of Philipp Melanchthon, with the exception of the three ancient creeds (Apostles, Nicean, and Athanasian). In its German edition it contained the version of the *Confessio Augustana* published in 1533 (prima variata); the first Latin edition contained the edition of 1542 (tertia variata). Later editions in Latin printed the *Confessio Augustana invariata* (1531) and the *Confessio Augustana variata* (1542). Then followed the *Apology* of the Augsburg Confession (German 1540, Latin 1542), the *Confessio Saxonica* (1551), the *Loci Theologici* of 1556, the *Examen Ordinandorum* (1554), the *Responsio ad articulos Bavaricae inquisitionis* (1559), and the *Refutatio erroris Serveti et Anabaptistarum*, which Melanchthon had originally conceived as an appendix to the *Responsio*. In the Latin editions of this *Corpus Doctrinae* was also published the *Responsio controversii Stancari* (1553). What appears in the Melanchthon *Studienausgabe*, volume 6, under the title *Corpus doctrinae christianae* is therefore not the authentic *Corpus doctrinae Philippicum* (see *Melanchthons Werke in Auswahl*, 6:3–377; see also Dingel, *Concordia Controversa*, 15–16, n. 4.

25. Joachim Mörlin was at that time bishop of Pomesanien and Samland, Martin Chemnitz served as superintendent of the churches in the city of Braunschweig. On this document, see Kolb, "The Braunschweig Resolution," 67–89.

and therefore a document representing a strict Lutheran position. This meant that in contrast to its neighboring territory, Danzig had decided for a theology oriented toward the teachings of Melanchthon.

Wigand, the bishop of Pomesania, regarded Danzig's teaching as crypto-Calvinistic and as a bridge to Calvinism. Danzig did not accept the Book of Concord; Wigand favored its acceptance.[26] Rather, in Danzig Calvinistic tendencies gradually took hold (even if, it turned out, only temporarily[27]) with the calling of two theologians: Peter Praetorius,[28] as pastor of the large parish church, Saint Mary's; and Jacob Fabricius,[29] rector of the municipal secondary school, in the middle of the 1570s and the beginning of the 1580s. With their presence in Danzig, Reformed innovations were introduced.[30] The immigration of Dutch exiles to the region strengthened these tendencies.[31] Nonetheless, the city tried to remain pledged to the Augsburg Confession, which achieved the full recognition of the Polish king, Stephan Bathory, in December 1577.[32]

Viewed from the standpoint of confessional allegiance, the situation in Danzig was fundamentally confused, and such lack of clarity was reason enough for concern in Wigand's eyes and for those who shared his viewpoint. They viewed the situation as a Calvinistic threat to the true teaching of the Book of Concord, which had found acceptance in many Evangelical principalities in the Empire. They sought to clarify the matter with polemical writings and to denounce those who opposed their clarification.

---

26. See Mager, "Aufnahme und Ablehnung des Konkordienbuches," 295–96.

27. In the first half of the seventeenth century they were decisively suppressed; Müller, "Unionsstaat und Region," 135–37.

28. Praetorius came to the main parish church in 1575. On Praetorius and his interesting career, see Manfred Knedlik, "Praetorius, Peter," 1183–84, and the brief reference to Praetorius as a Philippist exile, in Müller, Zweite Reformation, 82 n. 207.

29. Fabricius had studied with Pezel in Wittenberg and later in Heidelberg, received his doctorate in Basel, and returned to Danzig in 1578. On Fabricius, see Klueting, "Reformierte Konfessionalisierung," 46–47.

30. Since 1569 the abolition of the exorcism in baptism became an issue of dispute again and again. Praetorius tried to introduce the Heidelberg Catechism and the Lobwasser Psalter through devious methods. See Hartknoch, Preussische Kirchen-Historia..., 710 and 721.

31. See Mannhardt, Danziger Mennonitengemeinde.

32. See Neumeyer, "Danzig," 355.

The labels that keep appearing in these denunciations and similar contexts ("sacramental raver," "profaner of the sacrament," "sacramentarian," "those who adulterate Christ's testament"[33]) are not only the frequently used insults of the time, but they also identify the point of dispute that determined the interconfessional controversies and the dividing lines between the two groups (Calvinists and Lutherans) at the time: the understanding of the Lord's Supper as the central sacrament of Protestantism. Designations such as "Zwinglian" or "Calvinist" were used more seldom, probably because they did not present the content of the dispute at issue in the controversies clearly enough.[34] The precise differentiation between these two groups was not a concern at this time, since those associated with Calvin and Beza had been identified as Zwinglians in the general polemic after the agreement between Calvin and Bullinger in the Consensus Tigurinus of 1549. Wigand and all his Lutheran contemporaries spoke most often—following Luther—of the "*sacramentarii*," and Wigand explained the term in one of his publications from 1579 as those "who are called in the vernacular Calvinists."[35] Calvin, Beza, and Bullinger won his designation as "the true, public sacrament-wolves." He warned the Christian church against them.[36] This designation that drew the line between the confessions indicates how dangerous the other confessional position was thought to be. The label was supported by arguments regarding the content of the doctrine, which could focus on different concerns depending on the context of the specific dispute.

Wigand's Argumentation against Calvinism

The structures of the argument that Wigand developed against Calvinism are clearly determined by the historical and geographical targets set by his own circumstances. There is, on the one hand, a certain thematic spectrum, in which not every one of his arguments is

---

33. See Wigand's treatise addressed to the mayor of Danzig, *Vrsachen*, passim *Sacramentschender, Sacramentschwermer; Sacramentirer*, 4, 19, etc.; "*Testamentsverfelscher*," 6. Wigand's *Christliche Erinnerung* does, in contrast, speak of "Zwinglischen vnd Caluinischen Jrthum," 1a.
34. See Wigand, *Christliche Erinnerung*, 8a–b: "Zwinglianer."
35. Wigand, *Commonefactio*, 1.
36. See Wigand, *Christliche Erinnerung*, 1a.

necessarily applicable to the broader gamut of questions. On the other hand, as a general comparison of his work with writings of his contemporary like-minded theologians demonstrates, his views can be seen as quite typical. The influence of his judgments is at any rate— to some extent up to our own time—immense.[37]

Before Wigand's treatments of the Calvinism of western Europe and of the events in the east, at ducal Prussia's borders in Danzig, come into our purview, his perspective on developments in Wittenberg and electoral Saxony deserve attention because only from this perspective can his later refusal to compromise be explained. That precisely in the place where the Lutheran Reformation began Calvinists had secretly been able to gain a foothold—from the point of view of his Lutheran contemporaries—was taken as a special provocation. From Königsberg in 1574 Wigand looked back to the development of so-called Crypto-Calvinism, which had in recent months been purged in electoral Saxony. He presented readers with a penetrating reminder of the ways in which a real infiltration of Calvinism had become possible there. His treatise *A Christian Reminder of the Confession of Theologians in Meissen on the Lord's Supper*, which was approved and subscribed by his colleagues in Prussia, particularly in Königsberg, presented nothing other than a warning in the face of possible points of entry through which Calvinism might advance[38] on the borders of the Empire.

The anonymously published *Exegesis perspicua*,[39] which offered a spriritualistic interpretation of the words of institution of the Lord's Supper (in fact the work was written by a physician, Joachim Curaeus) elicited Wigand's response. This volume had aroused the reaction of elector August of Saxony against Calvinizing tendencies in his lands, and Wigand commented:

> The insidious *Exegesis*, with its ravings about the sacrament, made its horrible attempt to take everything captive to its

---

37. That is true above all of the estimation of Melanchthon as sympathetic to Calvinism.

38. Subscribers to this document included Tilemann Heshusius, bishop of Samland, Benedictus Morgenstern, pastor of the "Domkirche" in Königsberg; Philippus Caesar, pastor in the "Altstadt" of Königsberg; Hieronymus Mörlin, pastor of the church of the "Löbenicht" in Königsberg; Johannes Weidmann, court preacher in Königsberg. See *Christliche Erinnerung*, 19a.

39. Edited in Dingel, *Die Debatte um die Wittenberger Abendmahlslehre*, 1015-89.

Zwinglian and Calvinistic error, to take hold of everyone's mind. But our wonderful God and Lord turned the tables in a wonderful fashion, so that several of these deceivers, those snakes, were revealed and exposed. Others, on the other hand, were moved to make a clearer confession of the truth regarding the holy, blessed Testament of Jesus Christ than they previously had, and to warn the Christian church about the real, public sacrament-wolves, Calvin, Beza, Bullinger, and others, to name names.[40]

Wigand saw Christ himself at work making it possible to eliminate the "Calvinistic and Bezian raving," and he thanked the government that had followed its duty so conscientiously that it was able to obligate its theologians to a renewed confession of the unadulterated doctrine of the Lord's Supper of 1530.[41] Wigand alluded to the "Torgau Articles" of 1574, a document that attempted in fact to demonstrate that the positions of Luther and Melanchthon on the Lord's Supper were in harmony with each other, and to avoid playing off the authority of one of the reformers against the other.[42] The electoral Saxon government had had this document composed with the purpose of laying it before its theologians for their subscription after the discovery of the spiritualizing efforts of the so-called Crypto-Calvinists.

Nonetheless, for the bishop of Pomesanien it was more than clear that someone had seduced Philip through "sacramentarian raving." Wigand regarded it as wrong to place Melanchthon's theological formulations alongside the biblical testimony and Luther's writings on the Lord's Supper, particularly if they were to be judged on the basis of

---

40. Wigand, *Christliche Erinnerung*, 1a. In 1574 Wigand had also published a refutation specifically dedicated to the *Exegesis perspicua*, his *Analysis exegeseos Sacramentariae*.

41. See Wigand, *Christliche Erinnerung*, 1a-b: Dafu[e]r dancken wir dem frommen getrewen Herrn Christo von grund vnsers hertzen / das er in dieser betru[e]bten letzten zeit der Welt / noch ein solch Liecht seinem heiligen Testament / in Deudschlanden auffstecket / vnd die Caluinische vnd Bezische Schwermereyen / etlicher massen außsteupert / vnd zu ru[e]cke treibet. Wir dancken auch der Oberkeit / das sie dem Herrn Christo (wie sie denn auch schuldig ist) darin dienet / vnd die Theologen darzu ermanet / vnd angehalten / die reine Lere vom Abendmal des Herrn / wie sie auff dem Reichßtage zu Augspurg Anno Domini, 1530. bekant / vnd von Luthero gantz herrlich vnd gewaltig / aus vnd nach Gottes Wort erstritten / zu widerholen vnd zu bekennen.

42. See Dingel, "Die Torgauer Artikel," 119-34. The text of the *Torgauer Artikel* is edited in Dingel, *Die Debatte um die Wittenberger Abendmahlslehre*, 1103-51.

Luther's fundamental understanding of the sacrament. The basis for his judgment and the arguments he introduced in his claim have shaped the negative estimation of Melanchthon as one who paved the way for Calvinism, a proto-Calvinist, and therefore made it difficult to take him seriously as an independent thinker in his own right, who had formulated his own understanding of the Lord's Supper. Not only, according to Wigand, had Melanchthon altered the Augsburg Confession without consulting Luther. He had also approved of the teaching of sacramentarians such as Albert Hardenberg of Bremen, and he had also failed to reject and repudiate the sacramentarian position in his Saxon Confession of 1551 and in his Examination of Candidates for Ordination of 1552.[43] (Wigand had accepted the former document as a worthy confession when it was first issued two decades earlier.) Melanchthon's disciples and colleagues in Wittenberg, such as Caspar Peucer, Christoph Pezel, Caspar Cruciger the Younger, and Heinrich Moller, had "become acquainted with the ravings of the Zwinglians through him."[44] Especially Melanchthon's son-in-law Caspar Peucer, according to Wigand, had gotten his ideas from Melanchthon's own mouth and therefore knew precisely "that he had held the position of Bullinger, Calvin, and Beza, and had apostasized from Luther's teaching."[45] The final definition of the Lord's Supper that Melanchthon offered was so "slippery, that is, as smooth as a marble," that both sides, Lutherans and Calvinists, had been able to appeal to it.[46] Wigand regarded this as one of the most disastrous developments of his time, for public teaching and confession had to be clear and unambiguous. Here there was no room for play in trying to reach consensus or for formulations that could be interpreted in more than one way. This touched both the usefulness and the clarity

---

43. See Wigand, *Christliche Erinnerung*, 3a–18b. Wigand extended his argument at this point (3a): Das der herr Philippus wol im anfang wider Oecolampadium / vnd in der Augspurgischen Bekentniß / vnd andern schrifften / etwas wider die Sacramentirer gethan. Aber darnach fast zeitlich hat er sich sehr geneigt zu den Sacramentirern / vnd ist endlich gar zu jnen getretten / vnd jre schwermerische meinung gebilliget / vnd solche ding vom Abendmal geschrieben / welche stracks wider die Lere vnd wort Lutheri sind / vnd ko[e]nnen nimermehr fu[e]r Gottes Augen vnd der Christenheit / mit einander gleich gestimmet oder vereiniget werden / vnd solches ist klar zu beweisen.

44. Wigand, *Christliche Erinnerung*, 8a-b.

45. Ibid., 9a.

46. Ibid., where the citation is found.

of the confession of the faith, and that was Wigand's chief concern in the disagreement with Western European Calvinism.

Pierre Loyseleur de Villiers served as the spokesman of all those at the western borders of the Empire who strove for interconfessional understanding and viewed the very existence of Protestantism as continually under threat. They also felt themselves theologically and politically isolated when efforts to consolidate the development of the Lutheran confession of the faith attained the acceptance of the Formula of Concord in 1577.[47] Loyseleur called for a general synod in which everyone would abandon the use of party labels and personal insults. This synod was to differentiate necessary from unnecessary articles of faith and to create a confession to bridge the rival positions.[48]

That this proposal lay outside the possibilities of Wigand's grasp of the situation is clear from his reaction to the developments in electoral Saxony. In 1579 the Prussian clergy subscribed to the Formula of Concord and unanimously adopted the Book of Concord as its new *Corpus doctrinae*, its standard for public teaching. Among them only the professors at the University of Königsberg hesitated and withheld their subscription.[49] Against this background, Loyseleur's proposal had to sound like a serious step backward, an effort to stop the process of the Lutheran consolidation of public teaching and to call it into question. Wigand insisted on the purity of the confession of faith and public teaching, and he focused quickly on the doctrine of the Lord's Supper. Public teaching was to be guaranteed not through ambiguous formulations but rather with carefully targeted repudiations of false teachings, which by their very nature cultivated not true fellowship in the faith but rather blasphemous dogmas.

"Our theologians do not condemn entire churches, which exist in great kingdoms and well-populated cities, but they condemn dogmas taught in an impure and blasphemous fashion, at odds with the words of the Lord's testament, and those who teach these dogmas provocatively and with an ill-will. They do not ignore the fact that in these kingdoms

---

47. Fears of an alliance of the pope with the French and Spanish crowns against European Protestantism ran high; see Dingel, *Concordia controversa*, 161-67.

48. On the exchange of polemics between Loyseleur and Wigand, see Dingel, *Concordia Controversa*, 176-83.

49. See Hartknoch, *Preussische Kirchen-Historia*, 487-89.

there are not a few who disapprove of these false dogmas as they groan under the cross."⁵⁰

Wigand reproached the Calvinists represented by the Dutch court preacher for their veiled tactics: seeking to avoid the kind of process for clarifying issues that had successfully brought concord to a majority of Lutherans, attempting to claim that they were adherents of the Augsburg Confession, or asserting that at the end of his life Luther had abandoned his insistence that the body and blood of Christ are truly present in the Lord's Supper.⁵¹ Wigand also sharply rejected the idea of a general synod, referring to examples from Holy Scripture, particularly the examples of Christ and the apostles, which demonstrated the necessity for decisive confession of the truth rather than discussions aimed at compromise. In Wigand's eyes it was clear that the guarantee of faithful teaching and an appropriate exclusion of error could not be produced through attempts to find consensus at a synod: "Certainly the patriarchs, prophets, Christ, and the apostles did not wait for the authority and decisions of general or provincial synods before they propagated divine teaching and condemned all false dogmas and worship. Indeed before the synod in Acts (the council of Jerusalem, Acts 15) Paul would never have withheld his anathema of the dogmas of the false apostles."⁵² It was totally unthinkable for Wigand, and for Lutherans in general, that it might be possible to produce a new confession through the deliberations of a synod in which participants could feel compelled to make concessions to the Calvinists on the doctrine of the Lord's Supper.

In the confrontation of these positions, which cannot be rehearsed here in detail, two things become clear. First, Lutheran confessional

---

50. Wigand, *Commonefactio*, 14: Neque etiam integras Ecclesias, quae sunt in regnis amplissimis & vrbibus populissimis nostri Theologi damnant, sed tantum impure & blasphema dogmata, cum verbis Testamenti Dominici discrepantia, & eorum doctores vehementes & maledicos: Neque ignorant in illis regnis non paucos, esse, illa falsa dogmata serio improbantes, licet sub cruce gemant.

51. Wigand probably was thinking of the attempt of the elector of the Palatinate, Friedrich III, to prove that his teaching agreed with that of the Augsburg Confession. He did so at the imperial diet in Augsburg in 1566, on the basis of Heinrich Bullinger's *Confessio Helvetica posterior*. In his *Wider die Landlügen*, Joachim Mörlin sharply criticized the rumor that Luther had revised his teaching on the Lord's Supper shortly before his death. See Dingel, *Die Debatte um die Wittenberger Abendmahlslehre*, 608 n. 17.

52. Wigand, *Commonefactio*, 14.

consciousness placed the Augsburg Confession at the center of public confession of the faith because these Lutherans prized this confession as an expression of correct teaching. Its position was ranged against the urgent attempt by the Calvinists, in view of the political threat of the time, to reach an all-embracing minimal consensus with a summary of the heart of the faith. Against the background of the electoral Saxon experience Wigand emphasized the priority of the purity of public confession over the attainment of integration in theology and political stance.[53]

Second, there was a clear difference in the evaluation of the authority attributed to public doctrinal formulations. While Wigand appealed uncompromisingly to Holy Scripture, to examples he gained from it, and to Luther as its interpreter during the increasingly sharp dispute, his opponents appealed again and again to the vehicle of the synod, which among Calvinists had been used a number of times. This difference certainly did not mean that consultation in a synod was foreign to Lutheranism, or that Calvinists avoided arguing on the basis of Scripture. Calvinists were indeed biblical theologians, while in the process of consolidating public teaching Lutherans utilized a number of such meetings and consultations in synods. But it is interesting that Wigand played off "divine teaching,"[54] which he viewed as vouchsafed in Holy Scripture, and which he believed could be clearly grasped thanks to the "clarity" of Scripture, against human exchange of ideas.

By the time Wigand published a sharply anti-Calvinist work a few years later, aimed to defend the legitimacy of governmental action against "sacramentarians," a number of further controversies had contributed to the hardening of the fronts between the two sides. All these exchanges in print were part of the experience that formed Wigand. The situation in Danzig described above brought him to dedicate to the mayor of the city at that time, Georg Rosenberg, his *Reasons Why Christian Governments May Not Tolerate Sacramentarian Teaching or Teachers*.[55]

---

53. See Wigand's preface to *Analysis exegeseos sacramentariae*,)(2a –)()(4b.

54. Wigand, *Commonefactio*, 17.

55. Wigand, *Vrsachen*. The argumentation referring to the doctrine of the Lord's Supper and the understanding of the words of institution in this treatise is not new. In a similar fashion Wigand had already commented on the matter, e.g. in his *Causae*.

John Calvin, Myth and Reality

In the dedicatory preface Wigand's entire mistrust of his confessional opponents, whom he viewed as dangerous not only for proper public teaching of the faith but also for the social order, found expression:

> Your Excellency knows what kind of unrest, nastiness, and other evil fruits the spirit of the sacramentarians brings to those places in which they make their nests. This spirit creates factions, divisions, and turmoil at all levels of society, hate and envy among both teachers and hearers, and fosters disturbances. It speaks with a forked tongue, and it deals with the words of Christ in his testament in a deceptive and misleading fashion. It steals and robs the poor little lambs of Christ of their most precious and salutary treasure from the testament, and it dares to claim that the body of Christ is as far from his testament as the heaven is from the earth, and that the words of Christ are not true as they stand and sound. This spirit is hard to pin down in what it confesses, and it fools the people in a mischievous manner.[56]

This alone demonstrated for Wigand the necessity of refuting this spirit. For, he believed, his confessional opponents' interpretation of the words of institution called into question the pastoral consolation of the sacrament of the Lord's Supper, which the Lutherans prized so highly. Wigand and his fellow Lutherans insisted on the true presence of the divine and human natures, that is, of the divinity and humanity of Christ in, under, and with the elements of the Lord's Supper. They also maintained the necessity of receiving the elements in a way that brought about an experience of consolation, especially in situations of spiritual struggle. His confessional opponents had countered this position with a statement of Beza at the religious colloquy in Poissy in 1561: that since the ascension of Christ to the right hand of God, the exalted humanity of Christ was as far from the bread and wine as the highest heaven was from the earth.[57] The doctrine of the two natures of Christ had been debated already in the first controversy over the Lord's Supper between Luther und Zwingli (1524-1529) and also in the second between Joachim Westphal and John Calvin (1552-1558). It was used by many, but not all, on the Lutheran side, which interpreted Christ's

---

56. Wigand, *Vrsachen*, A2a-b.

57. On Beza's role at the colloquy of Poissy, see Nugent, *Ecumenism in the Age of the Reformation*, 125-60; Dufour, "Das Religionsgespräch von Poissy," 117-26.

exaltation to the right hand of God as an exaltation to the full use of the omnipotence of God. This position served Lutherans as a subsidiary argument to support the real presence of Christ's body and blood in the sacramental elements,[58] so it was disparaged by the Cavinist opponents as "the doctrine of ubiquity," which became the subject of countless disputes. But Wigand largely set this issue aside, returning to Luther's original concern. Wigand did not belong to the group that had been eager to use such arguments. That in the recent past related questions had plunged him into disagreements with his longtime friend in the more radical Lutheran camp, Tilemann Heshusius, may have only strengthened his reluctance to use this argumentation.[59]

Most important was the clarity of the literal sense of the words of institution as a hermeneutical basis for defending the real presence and as the foundation for a clear—precisely not a "slippery"—confession of the truth. Temporal authorities had to bear responsibility for maintaining that confession since, as Wigand declared, "Anabaptists and defilers of the Sacrament" were leading Christianity away from proper teaching, and especially those who "rave about the Sacrament" were growing in numbers in villages, towns, and at noble courts.[60] On the basis of this interpretation of the clarity of the literal sense of the words of institution, Wigand labeled all other hermeneutical approaches as seductive attempts that would finally result in making Christ himself a liar and in denying his "witness to the truth and his omnipotence."[61] "The sacramentarians call the words of Jesus Christ our Savior lies. He makes an affirmative statement and says clearly, 'this is my body.' The sacramentarians make a negative statement and deny that [presence], against Christ's words, just as in Paradise in Genesis 3 the accursed devil, God's enemy, denied God's Word and presented the opposite against it."[62] Wigand found that his Calvinist opponents were continually invalidating the words of Christ, robbing Christ's body and blood from his testament, through which he bequeathed salvation.

58. Dingel, "Joachim Westphal," in *TRE* 35:712–15.

59. Ibid., 714. Wigand addressed this doctrine at another place and referred to the deprecatory nature of the term "ubiquity," see *De vbiqvitate*, esp. 1a.

60. Wigand, *Vrsachen*, 2.

61. Ibid., 9.

62. Ibid., 4.

Against such views governmental authorities had to proceed with definitive action, because in Wigand's opinion, it was "a dubious and inconsistent doctrine,"[63] which in terms of Christ's omnipresence went so far as to set human reason against God's order revealed in the New Testament.[64] Indeed, Wigand accused his opponents of intentional perversion of the clear word of God, which made the matter a governmental responsibility as a crime of "lese-majesty"[65] and would thus have to invite governmental suppression. Wigand expanded with a number of further arguments to justify governmental intervention against the so-called sacramentarians. He charged them with evading the article of faith expressed in the Creed through their interpretation of the right hand of God as a geographically determinable place,[66] and he did not neglect mentioning the danger of Arianism, which, he feared, might possibly result from the christological argumentation of the Calvinists. Misinterpreting patristic arguments regarding the Lord's Supper; setting aside Luther's catechism; changing the numbering of the Ten Commandments; rejecting private absolution and the accompanying instruction of the penitent, which were practiced as important elements

---

63. "Derwegen sollen solch Sacrilegium / Kirchenraub vnd Diebstal des Leibs vnd Bluts Christi / aus dem heiligen Testament Christi / da die wort klar vnd lauter fu[e]r augen stehen / keine Christliche Oberkeit noch Gemeine in keinem wege leiden," *Vrsachen*, 6. A bit later Wigand continued: "Alle vngewisse / zweiffelhafftige / vnd mit sich selbst streitige Lehre in der Kirchen Gottes / sol Christliche Oberkeit vnd Gemeine / abschaffen vnd nicht dulden" (Wigand, *Vrsachen*, 7). The idea that the government had the duty to intervene against unjustified ambiguity in interpreting Holy Scripture, against confusing doctrine, and against the accusation that God deceived in the words of institution is a constantly recurring theme in this treatise.

64. See Wigand, *Vrsachen*, 10: "Jtem / sie sagen / es sey dem HERRN Christo vnmu[e]glich mit aller seiner allmacht / das er ko[e]nne seinen wesentlichen / waren Leib / gegenwertig geben zu essen vnd sein Blut zu trincken / an allen den orten / da sein Abendmal laut seiner ordnung / gehalten vnd gebraucht wird. Denn es sey wider die natu[e]rliche eigenschafft eines Co[e]rpers / oder eines menschlichen Leibs / zugleich vnd auff einmal mehr als an einem ort wesentlich sein / welches denn alles aus der blinden menschliche[n] vernunfft herfleust / die aus jren sinnen daher Schwermet vn[d] treumet / vnd sihet nicht / das solches im Abendmal / da wir sollen den leib Christi nicht allein im glauben / sondern auch mit dem munde essen / vnd sein Blut trincken / eine ordnung Gottes ist / der ein Herr ist vber alle Creatur / vnd alles wz er will macht vnd wircket / vnd kein ding / was er nur ordnet / bey jm vnmu[e]glich / wie Gottes wort zeuget / Psalm 115. 135. Luce 1."

65. Wigand, *Vrsachen*, 9.

66. Ibid., 14–15.

in Lutheran pastoral care; misinterpreting the Augsburg Confession; reviling the Lutherans as "cannibals, who eat human flesh and drink blood and consume human beings";[67] the "zerzausen, zermartern, und zerpeitschen" ("tousling, torturing and whipping") of Martin Luther;[68] publishing religious works anonymously and pseudonymously; maintaining divisions within communities; the mobs' practicing iconoclasm; These and many others were the charges Wigand lodged against Calvinism.[69] Any government that took seriously its responsibility toward God simply could not tolerate them. For "God the Lord, whom we rightly are to fear and honor to the highest degree, cannot dwell with his grace and blessing where false teaching and teachers, blasphemers and enemies of his testament are tolerated, but there one will experience his disfavor and wrath . . . For Christian governments and communities cannot and should not tolerate sacramentarian teaching and teachers if they do not wish to bring the stern curse and great punishment of the Lord Christ upon themselves and their children."[70]

This book addressed to a temporal government by Wigand shows—without doubt reflecting the background of his own experiences and his development as a theologian—a clear intensification of his arguments against these opponents. Indeed, it was no longer only the theologian Wigand who expressed his position, but the watchman standing at the city wall, the one charged with prophetic admonition, who viewed it as his duty to make it clear to political authorities the direction they should pursue and the maxims they should follow in their actions.

Conclusion

Our consideration of the reactions of Lutheranism to Calvinism through the example of one theologian, whose writings, despite the uniqueness of this or any author, can be considered a suitable example of the larger interconfessional scene, has shown that interaction with confessional opponents at the borders of the German Empire were shaped by experi-

---

67. Ibid., 22.
68. Ibid., 23.
69. Ibid., 18–25.
70. Ibid., 26.

ences that Lutheranism had had with similar developments on its own territory. Without question, the rise of Philippism, which was identified quickly as leaning in the direction of Calvinism—and that in the land of the origin of the Reformation—had intensified sensitivities and heightened the inclination to regard confessional opponents beyond the borders of the Empire as stealthy deceivers motivated for political or other self-serving reasons simply to strive to disguise their teaching as that of the Augsburg Confession.

At every turn the publications of Johannes Wigand reveal his mistrust that began with the so-called Crypto-Calvinist developments in electoral Saxony. The strident polemic born there fed itself even on the ways each group labeled the others. Calvinism was perceived as an insidious threat, which placed Martin Luther's theological legacy in question at one of its most decisive and distinctive points: the doctrine of the Lord's Supper. The clarity of the literal sense of the words of institution, upon which Luther himself had laid great emphasis, was an essential element of the body of public teaching for Lutherans. This had led to an emphasis on the clear, unambiguous confession of that doctrine as it was to be found in the Unaltered Augsburg Confession. Confessional consciousness, and connected to it, the active confession of proper teaching, appeared in open conflict with the Calvinist appeal for doctrinal consensus, often—with good reason—fed by political necessities.

Lutheranism was not in a situation in which understanding of those necessities could be developed, given its completely different political and juridical situation according to the law of the Empire, especially according to the Religious Peace of Augsburg of 1555. Holy Scripture and the Augsburg Confession, grounded upon the Scripture, were accentuated as authorities over against what was seen as a misguided biblical hermeneutic and flawed ways of dealing with the church fathers. In this process the Augsburg Confession, which Melanchthon had composed, that is, in its unaltered form, became ever more the guarantee of Martin Luther's theology. At the same time, the simplistic assignment of Melanchthon to the camp of Luther's opponents in the controversies over the sacrament intensified the focus on Luther as the person who identified confessional Lutheranism.

Calvinism, on the other hand, as it could be observed across the imperial borders, aimed for a pluralism in so far as it was represented by a variety of territorial or national confessions of faith. It was strongly compatible with Genevan theology, but Genevan theology never gained the position as a secondary authority for doctrinal interpretation. In spite of the Calvinists' heightened awareness of the importance of their confessional documents for their identity, they were ready, in view of the prevailing distress, to negotiate new political alliances on the basis of new expressions of their confession. Nevertheless the controversies between the two consolidating confessions did not represent a simple search for political protection or the maintenance of the authority of different leaders of the Reformation but rather arose from deep theological perceptions and convictions as they took form in specific historical circumstances.

PART 3

The Impact of Calvin's Ideas

10

Respect for the Word
What Calvin and Wittgenstein Had against Images

CONSTANTIN FASOLT

> If you offer a sacrifice and are pleased with yourself about it, both you and your sacrifice will be cursed. The *edifice of your pride* has to be dismantled. And that is terribly hard work.
>
> All that philosophy can do is to destroy idols.
>
> —Ludwig Wittgenstein

John Calvin, the sixteenth-century theologian, and Ludwig Wittgenstein, the twentieth-century philosopher, are not exactly known for having much in common.[1] Their juxtaposition may therefore strike the reader

---

1. The epigraphs are taken from Wittgenstein, *Culture and Value*, 26e, and Wittgenstein, "Philosophy," 171. I would like to thank Amy Nelson Burnett for inviting me to the Calvin Studies Society Colloquium; the audience for lively discussion; Conor Smith Gaffney for help with the research; and Lawrence McEnerney, Linda Zerilli, David Terman; and the members of the Continuing Colloquium—Sean Dunwoody, Torsten Edstam, Christopher Fletcher, Elisa Jones, Uri Shachar, Jeremy Thompson, and Colin Wilder—for reading drafts with critical engagement.

as far-fetched.² The purpose of this chapter is to show that, on the contrary, reading them side by side opens an approach to the core of their thinking that would be difficult to find by reading either one in isolation from the other.

The core I have in mind is sketched in the title of this chapter: Calvin and Wittgenstein both had respect for the word, and they both had something against images. But this sketch is very rough indeed. It would be tempting to try and make it more detailed by delving straight into the writings of our authors. Tempting, but unlikely to succeed. What Calvin shares with Wittgenstein departs so widely from our most deeply rooted ways of thinking that it is bound to remain invisible without sufficient preparation. I should therefore like to start with the deeply rooted ways of thinking from which they both departed. Let me refer to those ways as conventional wisdom.

Conventional wisdom holds that I know nothing better than myself. My body is *my* body, and my mind is *my* mind. I know what I feel; I know what I think; and I know it better than anything else. Whatever I happen to think about the external world may be subject to doubt. But the knowledge I derive from introspection is different. I think, therefore I am. That much, conventional wisdom says, is absolutely certain.

From this certainty conventional wisdom infers a number of corollaries. Let me spell out some of the most important. First, con-

---

2. A review of the scholarship would corroborate that supposition. I have found no publications examining Calvin and Wittgenstein side by side. The subject heading "religion and religious belief" in Frongia and McGuinness, *Wittgenstein,* 398, covering the period from 1914 to 1987, lists no less than 126 books and articles on some aspect of Wittgenstein's relationship to religion, and the index of names features a good many references to figures like St. Augustine, St. Thomas Aquinas, and Kierkegaard. Calvin, however, is not mentioned. Searching for abstracts or titles of articles combining the terms "Calvin" and "Wittgenstein" on 16 March 2009 in JSTOR and the American Theological Library Association's religion database online yielded a single result: an article by Morse, "Raising God's Eyebrows," 39-49, which turns out to focus on Karl Barth. Full-text searches yield many more results, but only because they include references to Calvin College or to authors like Calvin Normore and Michael Calvin McGee. In order to compensate, however slightly, for the distance separating scholarship on Calvin from scholarship on Wittgenstein, I will take advantage of the footnotes to quote both Calvin and Wittgenstein at some length. I realize that experts on either side of the divide will be distraught by the degree to which quotations taken out of context from a limited range of sources can mislead unwary readers on the other side. I hope they will forgive me for having found no better way of making up for failing to do what I cannot do here and do not plan to do later, which is, to turn this chapter into a book.

Respect for the Word

ventional wisdom finds that there is some kind of gap or boundary or veil between myself and the external world. Unlike my thoughts and feelings, the external world is therefore not immediately present to my self. That is the reason *why* the knowledge I have of the external world is not as certain as the knowledge I derive from introspection.

Second, knowledge of the external world therefore requires some means with which to cross the boundary that lies between it and my self. Those means have been called many different names: ideas, sensations, immediate sense data, mental representations, and so on. But whatever the differences between the names, their basic function is the same: they provide an intermediary third between my self and the external world. Without that intermediary, my self would have no knowledge of the external world.

Third, my knowledge of the external world is therefore only indirect. Regardless of how well my ideas or my sensations succeed in representing the external world to me, they do not abolish the distinction between that world and its representation. What I actually know, conventional wisdom maintains, is therefore not the external world itself but only its representation. I study the phenomena as they appear to me. Reality as such is placed beyond my ken.

Fourth, my knowledge of what goes on in the minds of other people is even more indirect. The immediate knowledge that other people have of their own thoughts and feelings is utterly concealed from me. I know about the way they experience *their* thoughts and feelings only by analogy with my experience of *my* thoughts and feelings. That makes it possible to wonder if they even have the same thoughts and feelings that I have, or if they merely use the same words for completely different experiences. Conventional wisdom treats this question as both valid and impossible to answer. It is valid because I know about the selves of others only from their words. It is impossible to answer because their real thoughts and feelings are known only to themselves.

Fifth, it follows that language is merely an artificial system of more-or-less arbitrary signs whose meaning depends upon the things they signify. A chair is a chair, whether I call it *chair* or *Stuhl* or *cathedra* or *sedes*. And my thoughts and feelings are whatever my thoughts and feelings happen to be, regardless of the words in which they are expressed. Language merely serves as a channel for the communication *of* ideas, a system of signs referring *to* the material world, a symbolic structure of signification *about* reality. Its workings need to be explained in terms of the underlying realities to which it refers and from which it takes its meaning.

Conventional wisdom thus treats language as an epiphenomenon. What is basic about language is nothing in language itself. Basic is the underlying reality. Reality can of course be conceived in many different ways. The most familiar ways are three: dualism, which divides reality into ideas (mental, cultural, abstract) and matter (physical, natural, concrete); materialism, which views ideas as an effect of matter; and idealism, which views matter as a reflection of ideas. These three basic possibilities have given rise to many conflicts and permutations. But notwithstanding the differences between them, dualism, materialism, and idealism are in principle agreed on this: however the problems they raise may eventually be solved, they cannot possibly by solved by studying the language in which we talk about reality. They must be solved by reference to reality itself.

This, then, is conventional wisdom.[3] It tells us that the self is both privileged and lonely. The self is privileged because there is nothing as certain as the knowledge the self has of its own thoughts and feelings. The self is lonely because it has no equally certain knowledge of the external world. Its knowledge of the external world is only indirect. It is simply indirect for the physical world, because the self knows the external world only by means of mental representations. It is doubly indirect for other minds, because the self knows about them only by analogy with itself. Conventional wisdom concludes that language is a marvelous but arbitrary invention that allows the self to modify but not transcend its state of isolation.

I am confident that Calvin would have found it difficult to agree with any of this. The points of disagreement are so obvious that it will be enough for now merely to list the most important. In the first place, Calvin believes that human beings stand in dire need of salvation because they lack the very thing that conventional wisdom regards as their

---

3. Readers will notice that what I call conventional wisdom has obvious parallels in the thought of Descartes, Locke, Hume, Kant, and, more broadly speaking, in the main strands of modern philosophy. I have refrained from documenting those parallels because it would distract from the point, which is conceptual, not historical, at least not in the usual sense of "historical." Readers may also wonder just what gives me the right to describe conventional wisdom as I do. That is a question I cannot answer here.

most salient property: self-knowledge. As far as Calvin is concerned, whatever knowledge the self can have of itself is not only uncertain but downright impossible without true knowledge of God; and what is worse, true knowledge of God is impossible to obtain without true knowledge of self.[4] This may seem to be a point of mere epistemology. But it is something altogether different. It constitutes a paradox that goes to the foundations of what it means to be a human being. It is the first point Calvin makes in the *Institutes of the Christian Religion*: the reason *why* man stands in need of salvation, the beginning from which everything else follows and on which in some sense everything else depends.[5]

In the second place, the knowledge of God that Calvin regards as a necessary condition for true self-knowledge is not to be had from

---

4. Battles, *Institutes*, 35–37 (I.i.1): "Without knowledge of self there is no knowledge of God," and 37–38 (I.i.2): "Without knowledge of God there is no knowledge of self." Calvin's opening words are as follows: "Nearly all the wisdom we possess, that is to say, true and sound wisdom, consists of two parts: the knowledge of God and of ourselves. But, while joined by many bonds, which one precedes and brings forth the other is not easy to discern" (Battles, *Institutes*, 35). On 37–38 he clarifies this: "It is certain that man never achieves a clear knowledge of himself unless he has first looked upon God's face, and then descends from contemplating him to scrutinize himself. For we always seem to ourselves righteous and upright and wise and holy—this pride is innate in all of us—unless by clear proofs we stand convinced of our own unrighteousness, foulness, folly, and impurity. Moreover, we are not thus convinced if we look merely to ourselves and not also to the Lord, who is the sole standard by which this judgment must be measured. For, because all of us are inclined by nature to hypocrisy, a kind of empty image of righteousness in place of righteousness itself abundantly satisfies us." For a first approach to Calvin see McGrath, *A Life of John Calvin*; and Muller, *The Unaccommodated Calvin*. On the question of images in particular, see Zachman, *Image and Word*.

5. Book 1 of the *Institutes* thus deals with "The Knowledge of God the Creator," book 2 with "The Knowledge of God the Redeemer," book 3 with "The Way in Which We Receive the Grace of Christ," and book 4 with "The External Means or Aids by Which God Invites Us into the Society of Christ and Holds Us Therein." As the editors point out at the beginning of book 1, 35 n. 1, "The word 'knowledge' in the title, chosen rather than 'being' or 'existence' of God, emphasizes the centrality of revelation in both the structure and the content of Calvin's theology. Similarly, the term 'Creator,' subsuming the doctrines of Trinity, Creation, and Providence, stresses God's revealing work or acts rather than God in himself. The latter is more prominent in Scholastic doctrines of God, both medieval and later 'Calvinist.' Despite the titles of Books I and II, Calvin's epistemology is not fully developed in the *Institutes* until Book III, 'The Way in Which We Receive the Grace of Christ.'" Cf. especially the meaning of knowledge in faith, III.ii passim.

introspection or observation or sense impressions, let alone from their mental representations. It is to be had from but one single place, and that of course is Scripture.[6] Scripture, in a famous metaphor, serves as a kind of spectacles with whose help human beings can see clearly what they cannot discern so long as they look only into themselves or at the signs of God's presence in the created universe.[7] Scripture authenticates itself.[8] The certainty of knowledge therefore depends on Scripture, not on the self. Only Scripture offers the knowledge leading to salvation.

Language, therefore, is anything but a system of more-or-less arbitrary signs whose workings need to be explained in terms of the underlying realities to which it refers and from which it takes its meaning. It is the other way around: the underlying realities need to be explained in terms of language. For language is the means by which God created the world in the first place, and by which he reveals the saving truth to man. It is not an invention at all, not even an invention of God. Language is in and of itself divine and uncreated, the eternal Word, the Word spoken

---

6. Battles, *Institutes*, 69–71 (I.vi.1): "God bestows the actual knowledge of himself upon us only in Scripture."

7. Ibid.: "Just as old bleary-eyed men and those with weak vision, if you thrust before them a most beautiful volume, even if they recognize it to be some sort of writing, yet can scarcely construe two words, but with the aid of spectacles will begin to read distinctly; so Scripture, gathering up the otherwise confused knowledge of God in our minds, having dispersed our dullness, clearly shows us the true God. This, therefore, is a special gift, where God, to instruct the church, not merely uses mute teachers but also opens his own most hallowed lips. Not only does he teach the elect to look upon a god, but also shows himself as the God upon whom they are to look. He has from the beginning maintained this plan for his church, so that besides these common proofs he also put forth his Word, which is a more direct and more certain mark whereby he is to be recognized."

8. Ibid., 80–81 (I.vii.5): "Scripture bears its own authentication," esp. 80: "Let this point therefore stand: that those whom the Holy Spirit has inwardly taught truly rest upon Scripture, and that Scripture indeed is self-authenticated; hence, it is not right to subject it to proof and reasoning. And the certainty it deserves with us, it attains by the testimony of the Spirit. For even if it wins reverence for itself by its own majesty, it seriously affects us only when it is sealed upon our hearts through the Spirit. Therefore, illumined by his power, we believe neither by our own nor by anyone else's judgment that Scripture is from God; but above human judgment we affirm with utter certainty (just as if we were gazing upon the majesty of God himself) that it has flowed to us from the very mouth of God by the ministry of men. We seek no proofs, no marks of genuineness upon which our judgment may lean; but we subject our judgment and wit to it as to a thing far beyond any guesswork! This we do, not as persons accustomed to seize upon some unknown thing, which, under closer scrutiny, displeases them, but fully conscious that we hold the unassailable truth!"

Respect for the Word

by God, the Son of God the Father, the second Person of the Trinity.[9] If Scripture is the set of spectacles with through which to learn about God, the Word confirmed by the Spirit is the image of God himself.[10] Human language, however confused it may have become since the tower of Babel, is inconceivable apart from that foundation.

So Calvin's disagreement with conventional wisdom is obvious enough. But it is not so obvious what to make of that disagreement. One could of course say that Calvin was concerned with salvation, that his mind was on the supernatural, and that his domain was Christian faith. One could, in other words, draw a sharp line between faith and reason, and put Calvin on one side of that line. If one did so, one would find oneself in excellent intellectual company.[11] But one would also

---

9. Ibid., 129–30 (I.xiii.7): "The deity of the Word," and 130–31 (I.xiii.8): "The eternity of the Word," esp. 129: "'Word' means the everlasting Wisdom, residing with God, from which both all oracles and prophecies go forth. For as Peter testifies, the ancient prophets spoke by the Spirit of Christ just as much as the apostles did [1 Pet 1:10–11; cf. 2 Pet 1:21], and all who thereafter ministered the heavenly doctrine. Indeed, because Christ had not yet been manifested, it is necessary to understand the Word as begotten of the Father before time [cf. Ecclus. 24:14]. But if that Spirit, whose organs were the prophets, was the Spirit of the Word, we infer without any doubt that he was truly God. And Moses clearly teaches this in the creation of the universe, setting forth this Word as intermediary. For why does he expressly tell us that God in his individual acts of creation spoke, Let this or that be done [Gen. 1] unless so that the unsearchable glory of God may shine forth in his image? It would be easy for censorious babblers to get around this, saying that the Word is to be understood as a bidding and a command. But the apostles are better interpreters, who teach that the world was made through the Son, and that he upholds all things by his powerful word [Heb 1:2–3]. For here we see the Word understood as the order or mandate of the Son, who is himself the eternal and essential Word of the Father."

10. Ibid., 95–96 (I.ix.3): "Word and Spirit belong inseparably together"; esp. 95: "By a kind of mutual bond the Lord has joined together the certainty of his Word and of his Spirit so that the perfect religion of the Word may abide in our minds when the Spirit, who causes us to contemplate God's face, shines; and that we in turn may embrace the Spirit with no fear of being deceived when we recognize him in his own image, namely, in the Word."

11. I cannot think of any major modern thinker known for having engaged with Calvin as a rational intellectual worth taking seriously. Enlightenment thinkers are largely defined by breaking intellectual ground outside the limits of the confessions. Rousseau owes an obvious debt to Calvinism but writes in opposition to it. Marx, Durkheim, Troeltsch, and Weber, even at their most sympathetic to religion, stand at a critical distance from it. The only plausible exceptions may be thinkers like Schleiermacher, Barth, or Niebuhr, who are themselves primarily regarded as religious thinkers.

banish Calvin from the realm of reason and consign him to the realm of irrationality. One would turn him either into an object of purely historical interest, worthy of having his thoughts recorded but not of having them taken seriously in their own right; or into a theologian worth being taken seriously only by other theologians, by Calvinists, or by people willing to abandon reason for the sake of something unintelligible called religious faith. One would, in other words, beg the question *why* Calvin disagreed with conventional wisdom.

That is one of the main reasons why I think it is useful to take a closer look at Wittgenstein.[12] For Wittgenstein disagreed with conventional wisdom just as sharply as Calvin did. But of course he did not do so because he was a theologian, let alone a Calvinist. The form of reasoning he developed in the *Philosophical Investigations* is utterly modern and just about as far removed from the *Institutes of the Christian Religion* as could be imagined. That combination of a shared hostility to conventional wisdom and utterly different forms of reasoning presents a golden opportunity to grasp Calvin's meaning without putting him on one side of a line dividing faith from reason. It thus promises a means of rescuing Calvin from the historical and theological ghetto in which his rejection of images is difficult to understand as anything other than a kind of primitive spiritual taboo with a significance limited to a certain historical period and credible only for the members of a certain religious tribe; it allows Calvin's caution about images to stand as a particularly salient manifestation of a perfectly reasonable disagreement with the condition of humanity proposed by conventional wisdom.

In order to make good on that promise, I should begin by pointing out that there is at least one kind of image on which Wittgenstein launched as ferocious an assault as any iconoclast ever did on images of God or the Holy Trinity, namely, the mental representations that conventional wisdom regards as the necessary means by which we learn

12. On Wittgenstein in general see the biography by Monk, *Ludwig Wittgenstein*; and the introduction by McGinn, *Routledge Philosophy Guidebook to Wittgenstein*. Serious readers of the *Philosophical Investigations* will want to consult Baker and Hacker, *An Analytical Commentary*, a major scholarly accomplishment distinguished by equal degrees of thoroughness and lucidity but, like everything else in Wittgenstein scholarship, far from uncontroversial. For readers interested in looking more closely at the scholarship on Wittgenstein's place in theology and the philosophy of religion, one may recommend Kerr, *Theology after Wittgenstein*; Crosson, *The Autonomy of Religious Belief*; and Phillips and von de Ruhr, *Religion and Wittgenstein's Legacy*.

about the external world. His assault is all the more remarkable in that earlier in his life, in the *Tractatus Logico-Philosophicus*, Wittgenstein himself had offered perhaps the most elegant attempt any philosopher ever made to prove the truth of what is often called the picture theory of propositions: the theory that knowledge consists of propositions modeling reality like pictures of the reality they represent. Readers of Wittgenstein disagree about the meaning of the picture theory of propositions and about whether he actually endorsed it or merely advanced it tongue in cheek, as it were, in order to demonstrate its absurdity.[13] But no one doubts that he broke with it in the *Philosophical Investigations*. Throughout the *Philosophical Investigations*, he attacked the notion that our knowledge of the external world consists of mental representations and ridiculed introspection as a method for discovering their nature and function. He argued that most of the time there are no mental representations to be found at all, and when there are, they are beside the point.

Two objections Wittgenstein raised to the picture theory of propositions may be worth special mention. One is this: How could a picture possibly represent negation? How could it possibly explain our ability to tell that something is *not* the case? I have no trouble understanding what it means to say, "this table does *not* have five legs." But what intermediary form of representation could represent the nonexistence of those five legs to me? Whatever image you may conjure up in order to fulfill that purpose would have to represent *something*. It could not possibly represent *nothing*.[14]

The other objection is that the supposition of a picture's representing reality to me leads to an infinite regress. If my mind has no immediate access to reality but only access mediated by a picture representing the reality, how can it have immediate access to the picture? Would it

13. For a collection of essays laying out the terms of the debate, see Crary and Read, *The New Wittgenstein*.

14. Wittgenstein, *Philosophical Investigations*, henceforth cited as PI, § 429: "The agreement, the harmony, of thought and reality consists in this: if I say falsely that something is *red*, then, for all that, it isn't *red*. And when I want to explain the word 'red' to someone, in the sentence 'That is not red,' I do it by pointing to something red." PI § 443: "'The red which you imagine is surely not the same (not the same thing) as the red which you see in front of you; so how can you say that it is what you imagined?'—But haven't we an analogous case with the propositions 'Here is a red patch' and 'Here there isn't a red patch'? The word 'red' occurs in both; so this word cannot indicate the presence of something red."

not rather need a further intermediary image to mediate between the picture and myself, at least in order to distinguish representations of reality from mere illusions? Would it not need a means of representing the representation? And if there were such a means, would it then not need yet another means to represent this new representation of the representation of reality? And so on.

A powerful line of modern and postmodern thought takes this argument as proof that we can have no knowledge of reality at all.[15] According to this line of thought, our knowledge consists entirely of representations. It never makes contact with reality itself. We therefore live in something like an infinite hall of mirrors from which there is no possible escape. The signs are all we have. We can interpret them in many different ways, and we can even interpret the interpretations. But none of that allows us to cross over from interpretation to reality.

Given the frequency with which Wittgenstein has been enlisted in support of this line of thinking, it is important to stress that he repudiated it.[16] If he drew attention to the infinite regress entailed by the picture theory of propositions, he did not do so in order to prove that knowledge was impossible but, quite the contrary, in order to prove that the picture theory of propositions was absurd. He drew a cardinal distinction between interpretation and understanding. He acknowledged that every sentence can be subjected to infinitely many different interpretations, even a sentence as simple as "This table has four legs." But he insisted that the very possibility of offering any one of those interpretations presupposes understanding, and that understanding is

---

15. The literature supporting that line of thought is huge. In a basic sense it may be said to include most of phenomenology, structuralism, and poststructuralism—if not all of modern philosophy ever since Kant declared things in themselves to lie beyond the boundaries of knowledge. Among its most influential recent supporters one may count Roland Barthes, Michel Foucault, Jacques Derrida, and Richard Rorty. For an approach to the underlying issues and the current state of theoretical affairs in the study of history, see Pippin, *Modernism as a Philosophical Problem*; Bonnell and Hunt, *Beyond the Cultural Turn*; Jenkins, *The Postmodern History Reader*; and Sewell, *Logics of History*.

16. For influential accounts casting Wittgenstein as a relativist who destroyed the possibility of talking about reality, see Gellner, "A Wittgensteinian Philosophy," 65–102; Bloor, *Wittgenstein*; Rorty, *Contingency, Irony, and Solidarity*; and Rorty, *Objectivity, Relativism, and Truth*. For two pointed rebuttals, see Stone, "Wittgenstein on Deconstruction," 83–117, and Crary, "Wittgenstein's Philosophy," 118–45.

categorically different from interpretation.[17] When we say, "This table has four legs," we neither talk nor think about representations of the table. We talk about the table and its four legs. To understand the sentence "This table has four legs" is to talk about the table and its four legs. No intermediary is required.[18] To take the sentence "This table has four legs" as referring to a representation of the table rather than to the table itself is not to understand the sentence.[19]

Wittgenstein's hostility to the idea that knowledge of the external world requires mental representations of the external world vaguely resembles Calvin's hostility to the idea that knowledge of God requires images of God. Both Calvin and Wittgenstein clearly regarded the use of representations as a means of access to a fundamental but otherwise inaccessible reality as fraught with danger. But this resemblance is hardly enough to establish any substantial agreement. It rather raises a series of questions: What kind of danger did they have in mind? What could have excited their hostility to a degree so much greater than would appear to be warranted by a purely intellectual failing? What was the target of their anger? What was the cause of their concern? In order to answer those questions it will be instructive to consider two different

---

17. PI §201: "This was our paradox: no course of action could be determined by a rule, because every course of action can be made out to accord with the rule. The answer was: if everything can be made out to accord with the rule, then it can also be made out to conflict with it. And so there would be neither accord nor conflict here. It can be seen that there is a misunderstanding here from the mere fact that in the course of our argument we give one interpretation after another; as if each one contented us at least for a moment, until we thought of yet another standing behind it. What this shews is that there is a way of grasping a rule which is *not* an *interpretation*, but which is exhibited in what we call 'obeying the rule' and 'going against it' in actual cases. Hence there is an inclination to say: every action according to the rule is an interpretation. But we ought to restrict the term 'interpretation' to the substitution of one expression of the rule for another."

18. PI §94: "'A proposition is a queer thing!' Here we have in germ the subliming of our whole account of logic. The tendency to assume a pure intermediary between the propositional *signs* and the facts. Or even to try to purify, to sublime, the signs themselves.—For our forms of expression prevent us in all sorts of ways from seeing that nothing out of the ordinary is involved, by sending us in pursuit of chimeras."

19. Ibid., §95: "'Thought must be something unique.' When we say, and *mean*, that such-and-such is the case, we—and our meaning—do not stop anywhere short of the fact; but we mean: *this—is—so*. But this paradox (which has the form of a truism) can also be expressed in this way: *Thought* can be of what is *not* the case" (italics original).

but closely related arguments Wittgenstein made about the nature and extent of human self-knowledge.

One of these arguments focuses on statements like "I am in pain," which is to say, statements in the first-person present indicative about the speaker's own state of mind. The argument is that such statements amount neither to a description of that mental state nor to a claim to knowledge. They rather are expressions, avowals, or confessions of the speaker's feeling, sensation, or belief. They can of course serve as foundations on which to erect claims to knowledge. But this is not what they are in and of themselves. For Wittgenstein, the difference between *being in* pain and *knowing* pain is fundamental. Not to recognize that difference can only lead to confusion.

This is precisely the confusion at the heart of conventional wisdom. Conventional wisdom insists not only that statements in the first-person present indicative about the speaker's own mental state not only constitute a claim to knowledge, but also that the particular kind of knowledge to which they lay claim is more certain than any other claims. Now, Wittgenstein grants the certainty of those statements. Of course I can be positively certain that I have the feelings I express. Conventional wisdom is right that here there is no room for doubt. But conventional wisdom is wrong about the reason *why* there is no room for doubt. The reason is not that I know my thoughts and feelings particularly well. It is that I *have* them. I merely seem to know for certain. In fact, I do not know at all. To construe the relationship I have to a pain that I feel in terms of the relationship I have to things that I know is therefore to utterly misconstrue my feeling. If it were otherwise, then one should at least be able to imagine a case in which I do *not* know about a pain I have. In such a case it would make sense to say, "It's possible that I'm in pain, but I cannot be certain until I have examined myself." But that does not make sense: one cannot be in pain without feeling it. Hence the opposite does not make sense either: If I determine that I am in pain based not on my sensations but rather on my detached examination of myself, then I could say, "I have no doubt that I'm in pain because my knowledge of my own pain is absolutely certain." But what I say is neither true nor false because my feeling pain is not separate from the experience of pain. What I say is nonsense—the kind of nonsense we reject whenever someone doubts an expression of our feelings and we reply, presumably with some degree of irritation, "What do you mean, 'do I know'? I'm talking about my feelings here. What gives you the right to doubt what I am feeling?" To use the nonsense we reject as a foundation on which to postulate that I know my own thoughts and feelings better than anything else is to make an elementary mistake.[20]

The opposite is closer to the truth: It is much easier for me to know the thoughts and feelings of other people than my own. I know by listening to their words, by watching their behavior, and by looking at their bodies, especially their hands, their faces, and their eyes. "The human body is the best picture of the human soul," Wittgenstein wrote.[21] Of course I can go wrong. But that does not prove that I cannot instead be right. I know the thoughts and feelings of other people just as reliably as I know other things about the world. I can be wrong about those too. When I see someone groaning and writhing on the ground just after he has fallen from a window on the fifth floor, I know this person is in pain with as much certainty as anything is possible to know. To think otherwise is to ignore the ties of feeling and understanding uniting human beings with each other and to condemn them to the loneliness of solipsism.

It is quite different with my own thoughts and feelings. I can begin to know these only as soon as I no longer have them, perhaps because they have slid into the past or because I have somehow detached myself from them. All I can do until that moment is follow them wherever they may lead. They are not even really mine. They come to me unbidden and not infrequently unwanted. In that regard Wittgenstein was in agreement with what I take to be one of the basic points of psychoanalysis. Like a psychoanalyst, he was concerned to delve beneath the

---

20. Ibid., §244: "'So you are saying that the word "pain" really means crying?'—On the contrary: the verbal expression of pain replaces crying and does not describe it." PI §245: "For how can I go so far as to try to use language to get between pain and its expression?" PI §246: "In what sense are my sensations *private*?—Well, only I can know whether I am really in pain; another person can only surmise it.—In one way this is wrong, and in another nonsense. If we are using the word 'to know' as it is normally used (and how else are we to use it?), then other people very often know when I am in pain.—Yes, but all the same not with the certainty with which I know it myself!—It can't be said of me at all (except perhaps as a joke) that I *know* I am in pain. What is it supposed to mean—except perhaps that I *am* in pain? Other people cannot be said to learn of my sensations *only* from my behaviour,—for *I* cannot be said to learn of them. I *have* them. The truth is: it makes sense to say about other people that they doubt whether I am in pain; but not to say it about myself."

21. Ibid., part II, section iv, 178.

appearance of what merely looks like knowledge I have of myself, but what is in fact an expression of my feeling or belief. And like a psychoanalyst, he did so, not in order to ascertain any reality supposedly underlying the feeling, but in order to relieve the pain of human beings' mistakenly confusing their thoughts and feelings with knowledge of themselves and so suffering the consequences of their mistake.

The second argument turns on what has come to be known as Moore's paradox, because G. E. Moore, Wittgenstein's friend and predecessor at Cambridge, was the first to draw attention to its importance. It consists of an important variation on statements in the first-person present indicative involving the speaker's own state of mind, namely, statements that do lay a certain claim to knowledge. The paradox is this: I cannot meaningfully say, "I believe it is raining and it is not raining." I can of course say the words, but I cannot say them in the conviction that they are true.

Why is this a paradox? Because the sentence that I cannot meaningfully say may very well be true. It is perfectly conceivable that I believe it is raining when in fact it is not raining. There is no objective reason why such might not be the case. To the contrary, this is precisely the sort of thing that happens on a daily basis to every human being: believing something to be true that is in fact false. Nor is there any logical reason to make the sentence incoherent.[22] "I believe it is raining" is a contingent proposition. "It is not raining" is also a contingent proposition. There is no logical obstacle to combining the two contingent propositions into a composite proposition linked by the operator *and*: "I believe it is raining *and* it is not raining." Both parts of the composite may very well be true. Neither contradicts the other. If both are true, the whole sentence is true. And yet I cannot state that truth without spouting nonsense. As Wittgenstein put it, "One can mistrust one's own senses, but not one's own belief. If there were a verb meaning 'to believe falsely,' it would not have any significant first person present

---

22. There *is* a logical reason if "logic" includes what Wittgenstein called "grammar." To have shown that logic must include grammar is perhaps Wittgenstein's most fundamental philosophical accomplishment. But in order to avoid confusing the reader I shall use "logic" and "logical" to refer to laws of reasoning whose validity is traditionally thought to require no attention to grammar, such as above all the law of the excluded middle.

indicative."²³ An expression of belief in the first-person present indicative, it seems, can only express belief in truth.

This is all the more remarkable in that it applies only to the *first-person present* indicative. It does of course not apply to the subjunctive. I can very well say, "I believe it is raining, but it might not be raining." There is no conflict between my present belief and my awareness of my fallibility as a general matter. Yet Moore's paradox does also not apply to statements in the *third*-person present indicative. One can very well say, "He believes it is raining, and it is not raining." There is no obstacle to someone else's pointing out that something I believe to be true is in fact false. I just cannot do it for myself. And still more striking, I cannot do it for myself only at the moment at which I am holding the erroneous belief. Later on, when time has passed, and I have recognized my error, I can speak about my *past* error without falling into paradox, as if it were no longer really mine but that of some other person. I can say, "Yesterday morning I believed it was raining, and actually it was not raining at all." Nothing prevents me from speaking meaningfully about my own errors so long as they lie safely in the past. The only thing I cannot do is to avow my present error.²⁴ My present error is in principle impossible for me to acknowledge, not in and of itself, but for me.

The reason for Moore's paradox obviously consists in a grammatical distinction between statements in the first person and statements in the third person or in the past tense. But even though the paradox may be obvious, it is easy to misconstrue.²⁵ Let me therefore repeat: the reason why I cannot say, "I believe it is raining and it is not raining," is neither physical nor logical. It is not a matter of some personal bias that could be corrected by an effort of will, by a more determined applica-

---

23. PI, part II, section x, 190.

24. Hence the apparent simplicity of the difference between the tenses of "I believe" and "I believed" is thoroughly deceptive. It shows the difference between past and present, but it conceals the difference between a belief I can disavow and a belief I cannot disavow. "Don't look at it as a matter of course, but as a most remarkable thing, that the verbs 'believe', 'wish', 'will' display all the inflexions possessed by 'cut', 'chew', 'run.'"(PI part II, section x, 190).

25. "Moore stirred up a philosophical wasps' nest with his paradox; and the only reason the wasps did not duly fly out was that they were too listless" (Wittgenstein, *Culture and Value*, 76e). In the meantime, a whole body of scholarship has grown up around Moore's paradox; see Green and Williams, *Moore's Paradox*. Even so one wonders if the wasps have become more animated than Wittgenstein thought they were.

tion of scientific discipline, or by an improvement in my education. It cannot be eliminated by any conceivable improvement in the mechanical engineering of my brain or by administering drugs. It has no material cause. But neither is it the result of a logical contradiction. Nothing really prohibits anyone from acknowledging its truth if it is true. Only I cannot acknowledge its truth. And the reason lies in a grammatical distinction.

That puts Wittgenstein in stark opposition to conventional wisdom about the nature of human beings, their place in the universe, and their relationship to one another.[26] According to conventional wisdom, the starting point in any effort to determine who we are, what we can know, and what we ought to do consists in the distinction between myself and the external world. But conventional wisdom states that beginning in the third person. "I" do not show up in that beginning, except in the guise of "my self." This is not insignificant. Note how comfortably the language of *self* and *world* flows from the tongue. Note how much easier it is to speak about my misguided subjectivity than to say, "I have been wrong." It is easier because it conceals the naked truth that *self* means "I" so well that I no longer need to be afraid of being shamed by Moore's paradox. Transforming the first-person "I" into the third-person "self" puts me at a distance from the beliefs I hold and thus absolves me of responsibility for holding them. It turns what "I believe" into "my beliefs" or "my ideas"—ideas that I seem free to keep or drop as I please. It collapses the difference between the first person and the third person into the language of objects conducted entirely in the third person. It seems to endow me with the power to abstract from the first person and treat my self as though it were a certain kind of thing—a thing whose nature I can analyze objectively by means of introspection, a thinking thing, *res cogitans*, whose difference from other things, *res extensae*, chiefly consists in that it happens to be thinking and happens to be mine.

Replacing "I" with "my self" looks like a minor twist in language, a tiny sleight of speech. But the significance of that sleight exceeds its trifling size by a considerable measure. It constitutes a license for crossing a sacred line. Crossing that line is to replace the lead of language with fictions designed to show us how the world might be if only we could take a stand outside the ground that language has prepared for us. But

---

26. This and the following paragraph owe a great deal to Tugendhat, *Self-Consciousness and Self-Determination*. Cf. Winch, "The Expression of Belief," 7–23.

the entire enterprise is misconceived.[27] It assumes that the distinction between myself and the external world is like the difference between two different kinds of things—between an inner world of mind and an external world of matter—as opposed to two different grammatical persons. It begs the fundamental question: what is the relationship between these persons? Instead of taking up that question, it assumes that a description of "my self" in the third person is sufficient for an adequate understanding of myself and my relationship to the world. Once this assumption has been made, there is no turning back.[28]

Wittgenstein's objections to the picture theory of propositions thus go far beyond mere questions of epistemology. If one accepts the arguments about human self-knowledge that I have just sketched, language is nothing like a system of more-or-less arbitrary signs representing supposedly more fundamental logical and scientific truths on which it is based and by reference to which it needs to be explained. There is no underlying reality to which we could refer in order to explain why language distinguishes between the first person and the third person. The idea of such an underlying reality is a mirage, a fiction of a misguided imagination that puts false images of the truth in the place of language. Language, as it were, stands on its own two feet. It is the ground of our existence, the given that we must accept in order to be able to live our lives as human beings. Agreement in language, as Wittgenstein put it in

27. PI §413: "Here we have a case of introspection, not unlike that from which William James got the idea that the 'self' consisted mainly of 'peculiar motions in the head and between the head and the throat'. And James' introspection shewed, not the meaning of the word 'self' (so far as it means something like 'person', 'human being', 'he himself', 'I myself'), nor an analysis of such a thing, but the state of a philosopher's attention when he says the word 'self' to himself and tries to analyse its meaning. (And a good deal could be learned from this.)"

28. Ibid., §339: "Thinking is not an incorporeal process which lends life and sense to speaking, and which it would be possible to detach from speaking, rather as the Devil took the shadow of Schlemiehl from the ground.—But how 'not an incorporeal process'? Am I acquainted with incorporeal processes, then, only thinking is not one of them? No; I called the expression 'an incorporeal process' to my aid in my embarrassment when I was trying to explain the meaning of the word 'thinking' in a primitive way. One might say 'Thinking is an incorporeal process', however, if one were using this to distinguish the grammar of the word 'think' from that of, say, the word 'eat'. Only that makes the difference between the meanings look *too slight*. (It is like saying: numerals are actual, and numbers non-actual, objects.) An unsuitable type of expression is a sure means of remaining in a state of confusion. It as it were bars the way out."

a famous line, is nothing like agreement in opinions; it rather is agreement in a form of life.[29] Language tells us what the essence of things is.[30] It lays foundations that logic must presuppose before it can even begin to do its work of discriminating true from false.[31] Language—not logic, not physics, not metaphysics, but language—fixes the terms of our relationship to the world, to other people, and to ourselves at the most fundamental level. It is language that prevents us from acknowledging our present error while permitting us to see the errors of our neighbors plainly as day. Language guarantees that expressions of our beliefs and feelings are matters neither of knowledge nor of observation. Language is the reason for our shame and humiliation whenever we are forced to admit that we were wrong. Whenever our belief is shown to rest on an illusion, such that it turns out to be *mere* belief; whenever our expectations are deceived; whenever our memories are shown to be mistaken; whenever, in short, we are compelled to renounce a belief that we once held in the first-person present indicative, we are divided into parts, sacrificed, so to speak, on the altar (or, if you prefer, crucified on the cross) on which our belief dies at the command of the third person, so that we may renew our ability to express our belief in the first person with full confidence, despite the possibility that this expression too may turn out to lead us into error and may have to be sacrificed.

That brings us to the heart of the matter—the point at which reading Wittgenstein and Calvin side by side opens an approach to the core of their thinking that would be difficult to find by reading either one in isolation from the other. I would put it like this: Calvin and Wittgenstein share a basic understanding of what it means to be a human being. For both of them a human being comprises two separate persons: the feeling, believing, thinking, and remembering person that avows its feelings, beliefs, thoughts, and memories in the first-person

---

29. Ibid., §23: "The *speaking* of a language is part of an activity, or of a form of life." PI §241: "'So you are saying that human agreement decides what is true and what is false?'—It is what human beings *say* that is true and false; and they agree in the *language* they use. That is not agreement in opinions but in form of life." PI IIxi, 226: "What has to be accepted, the given, is—so one could say—*forms of life*."

30. Ibid., §371: "*Essence* is expressed by grammar." PI §373: "Grammar tells what kind of object anything is. (Theology as grammar.)"

31. Ibid., §242: "If language is to be a means of communication there must be agreement not only in definitions but also (queer as this may sound) in judgments. This seems to abolish logic, but does not do so."

present indicative but has no knowledge of itself; and the objectively existing person that is seen, examined, known, described, and judged primarily by others, only with difficulty by itself, and not at all in the first-person present indicative. For both Calvin and Wittgenstein the difference between these persons is asymmetrical. For both it is a matter neither of logic nor of physics nor of metaphysics but of what Calvin called the Word and what Wittgenstein called language. It does not permit one person to be substituted for the other, and it cannot be represented by images, because it is itself the ground on which the meaning of those images depends. Attempts to overcome the asymmetry of persons by images or by any other means of representation can therefore only take one of two equally destructive forms: eliminating the first person in the name of the third, or the third person in the name of the first. Eliminating the first person means suppressing, denying, and exterminating expressions of feeling and belief in the name of logic, science, nature, history, and whatever else "one knows" to be the case. Eliminating the third person means suppressing, denying, and exterminating observation, proof, and knowledge in the name of mere feeling and belief. The former establishes the tyranny of reason over feeling and believing, the latter, of feeling and believing over reason. Both are destructive of humanity. For language makes a human being what it is: a creature internally divided, never fully present to itself, and impossible to reduce to coherence without annihilating one of the two persons, which is to say, without killing the human being. That is the danger Calvin and Wittgenstein had in mind. That is the reason why Calvin believed that man stands in need of salvation and why Wittgenstein believed that "the philosopher's treatment of a question is like the treatment of an illness."[32] That is the link between Calvin's hostility to the idea that knowledge of God requires images of God and Wittgenstein's hostility to the idea that knowledge of the external world requires mental representations of the external world.

It follows that the sort of autonomy or sovereignty promised to human beings by conventional wisdom is spurious. Coherence does not lie within the grasp of human beings except in death. The truth is that human beings, by virtue of being human, are vulnerable to a special kind of suffering that arises from the impossibility of reducing the

---

32. Ibid., §255.

first person to coherence with the third—the impossibility of seeing the beam in your own eye as clearly as the mote in the eye of your neighbor, of loving your neighbor as yourself, and above all of knowing what you are doing. Every belief and feeling passes, and in passing dies a certain kind of death, not because it has passed, but because in passing it turns from what is felt, remembered, and believed into what can be known as no first-person present statement can. Every passing moment thus furnishes an opportunity for feeling and belief to conflict with what is known to be the case. The possibility of such a conflict has to be endured. It is not a problem, much less a problem that could conceivably be solved. It rather is what makes a human being human.

Reading Calvin and Wittgenstein side by side thus puts them both into a different light. Neither was first and foremost concerned with mere avowals of belief (in isolation from the truth) or with mere truths of logic, history, or science (in isolation from belief). Both rather were preoccupied with the relationship between the two. Calvin was emphatic that faith rests on knowledge and is incompatible both with ignorance and with blind submission to authority.[33] Wittgenstein was equally emphatic that religious faith is radically different from mere opinion.[34] Both recognized the asymmetry between the persons as

33. Battles, *Institutes*, 545 (III.ii.2): "Faith rests not on ignorance, but on knowledge. And this is, indeed, knowledge not only of God but of the divine will. We do not obtain salvation either because we are prepared to embrace as true whatever the church has prescribed, or because we turn over to it the task of inquiring and knowing. But we do so when we know that God is our merciful Father, because of reconciliation effected through Christ [2 Cor. 5:18-19], and that Christ has been given to us as righteousness, sanctification, and life. By this knowledge, I say, not by submission of our feeling, do we obtain entry into the Kingdom of heaven." Battles, *Institutes*, 551 (III.ii.7): "Now we shall possess a right definition of faith if we call it a firm and certain knowledge of God's benevolence toward us, founded upon the truth of the freely given promise in Christ, both revealed to our minds and sealed upon our hearts through the Holy Spirit."

34. Wittgenstein, *Culture and Value*, 64e: "It strikes me that a religious belief could only be something like a passionate commitment to a system of reference. Hence, although it's *belief*, it's really a way of living, or a way of assessing life. It's passionately seizing hold of *this* interpretation. Instruction in a religious faith, therefore, would have to take the form of a portrayal, a description, of that system of reference, while at the same time being an appeal to conscience. And this combination would have to result in the pupil himself, of his own accord, passionately taking hold of the system of reference. It would be as though someone were first to let me see the hopelessness of my situation and then show me the means of rescue until, of my own accord, or not at any rate led to it by my *instructor*, I ran to it and grasped it." I am grateful to Linda

fundamental to humanity and as a paradox—the paradox identified by G. E. Moore and stated by Calvin at the beginning of the *Institutes*.[35] Both denied that they were seeking to develop novel theories. On the contrary, they insisted that the kind of truth at which they aimed lay open to public view, freely available to every human being—something of which one might have said, as Vincent of Lérins did say in antiquity, that it "has been believed everywhere, at all times, and by all," had it not been for the temptations that keep leading human beings to seek the truth where it cannot be found.[36] They thought of themselves, not as creators or inventors, but as teachers trying to show their students how to avoid misunderstanding.[37] Both regarded the spell cast by misleading

---

Zerilli for drawing my attention to this passage.

35. See n. 4, above.

36. Battles, *Institutes*, "John Calvin to the Reader, 1559," 4: "I have had no other purpose than to benefit the church by maintaining the pure doctrine of godliness." Battles, *Institutes*, 80 (I.vii.5): "We seek no proofs, no marks of genuineness upon which our judgment may lean; but we subject our judgment and wit to it as to a thing far beyond any guesswork! This we do, not as persons accustomed to seize upon some unknown thing, which, under closer scrutiny, displeases them, but fully conscious that we hold the unassailable truth!" PI §89: "It is, rather, of the essence of our investigation that we do not seek to learn anything *new* by it. We want to *understand* something that is already in plain view. For *this* is what we seem in some sense not to understand." PI §124: "Philosophy may in no way interfere with the actual use of language; it can in the end only describe it. For it cannot give it any foundation either. It leaves everything as it is." PI §126: "Philosophy simply puts everything before us, and neither explains nor deduces anything.—Since everything lies open to view there is nothing to explain. For what is hidden, for example, is of no interest to us." PI §435: "If it is asked: 'How do sentences manage to represent?'—the answer might be: 'Don't you know? You certainly see it, when you use them.' For nothing is concealed. How do sentences do it?—Don't you know? For nothing is hidden." For Vincent of Lérins see *Duo Commonitoria*, MPL 50:640: "In ipsa item Catholica Ecclesia magnopere curandum est ut id teneamus quod ubique, quod semper, quod ab omnibus creditum est." Cf. Wittgenstein's observation in PI §128: "If it were possible to advance *theses* in philosophy, it would never be possible to debate them, because everyone would agree to them."

37. Battles, *Institutes*, "John Calvin to the Reader, 1559," 4: "It has been my purpose in this labor to prepare and instruct candidates in sacred theology for the reading of the divine Word, in order that they may be able both to have easy access to it and to advance in it without stumbling. For I believe I have so embraced the sum of religion in all its parts, and have arranged it in such an order, that if anyone rightly grasps it, it will not be difficult for him to determine what he ought especially to seek in Scripture, and to what end he ought to relate its contents." PI §90: "Our investigation is therefore a grammatical one. Such an investigation sheds light on our problem by clearing misunderstandings away." Wittgenstein, *Culture and Value*, 18e: "Language sets everyone the same traps; it is an immense network of easily accessible wrong turnings. And

John Calvin, Myth and Reality

images over the human mind as the chief obstacle to overcome.[38] Both attacked the pride that leads human beings to rebel against the lessons they are taught by language and to replace them with superstitions of their own invention.[39] Both thought that victory over superstition con-

---

so we watch one man after another walking down the same paths and we know in advance where he will branch off, where walk straight on without noticing the side turning, etc. etc. What I have to do then is erect signposts at all the junctions where there are wrong turnings so as to help people past the danger points."

38. Battles, *Institutes*, 109–10 (I.xi.9): "Any use of images leads to idolatry"; esp. 109: "Now it appears that men do not rush forth into the cult of images before they have been imbued with some opinion too crass—not indeed that they regard them as gods, but because they imagine that some power of divinity dwells there. Therefore when you prostrate yourself in veneration, representing to yourself in an image either a god or a creature, you are already ensnared in some superstition. For this reason, the Lord forbade not only the erection of statues constructed to represent himself, but also the consecration of any inscriptions and stones that would invite adoration [Ex. 20:25]." PI §112: "A simile that has been absorbed into the forms of our language produces a false appearance, and this disquiets us. 'But *this* isn't how it is!'—we say. 'Yet *this* is how it has to *be*!'" PI §115: "A *picture* held us captive. And we could not get outside it, for it lay in our language and language seemed to repeat it to us inexorably."

39. Battles, *Institutes*, 47–8 (I.iv.1), "Superstition," esp. 47: "Indeed, vanity joined with pride can be detected in the fact that, in seeking God, miserable men do not rise above themselves as they should, but measure him by the yardstick of their own carnal stupidity, and neglect sound investigation; thus out of curiosity they fly off into empty speculations. They do not therefore comprehend God as he offers himself, but imagine him as they have fashioned him in their own presumption. When this gulf opens, in whatever direction they move their feet, they cannot but plunge headlong into ruin." *Institutes*, 99–100 (I.xi.1), "We are forbidden every pictorial representation of God," esp. 100: "God himself is the sole and proper witness of himself . . . Therefore in the law, after having claimed for himself alone the glory of deity, when he would teach what worship he approves or repudiates, God soon adds, 'You shall not make for yourself a graven image, nor any likeness' [Ex. 20:4]. By these words he restrains our waywardness from trying to represent him by any visible image, and briefly enumerates all those forms by which superstition long ago began to turn his truth into falsehood." *Institutes*, 107–9 (I.xi.8): "The origin of images: man's desire for a tangible deity"; esp. 108: "Man's mind, full as it is of pride and boldness, dares to imagine a god according to its own capacity; as it sluggishly plods, indeed is overwhelmed with the crassest ignorance, it conceives an unreality and an empty appearance as God." PI §109: "Philosophy is a battle against the bewitchment of our intelligence by means of language." PI §110: "'Language (or thought) is something unique'—this proves to be a superstition (*not* a mistake!), itself produced by grammatical illusions. And now the impressiveness retreats to these illusions, to the problems." PI §118: "Where does our investigation get its importance from, since it seems only to destroy everything interesting, that is, all that is great and important? (As it were all the buildings, leaving behind only bits of stone and rubble.) What we are destroying is nothing but houses of cards and we are clearing up the ground of language on which they stand."

sisted of a fundamental turn away from the allure of images—the kind of turn to which Calvin referred as repentance, and that Wittgenstein described as "turning our whole examination round the fixed point of our real need."[40]

I do not mean to belittle the differences between Calvin and Wittgenstein. Language is not simply identical with the Word, and grammar is not identical with Scripture. The self-authentication of Scripture in Calvin's thought is not to be confused with the autonomy of grammar in Wittgenstein's thought. Wittgenstein leaves more room for pictures in religion than Calvin could have countenanced.[41] The God of the Hebrew Bible, who says, not coincidentally in the first person, "I am who I am," differs from the Word of the New Testament that is said to have become incarnate in Christ and promised eternal life to his followers—and both differ from the language whose philosophical

---

Wittgenstein, *Culture and Value*, 72e: "Religious faith and superstition are quite different. One of them results from *fear* and is a sort of false science. The other is a trusting."

40. Battles, *Institutes*, 597, 601: "On this account, in my judgment, repentance can thus be well defined: it is the true turning of our life to God, a turning that arises from a pure and earnest fear of him; and it consists in the mortification of the flesh and of the old man, and in the vivification of the Spirit . . . Therefore, in a word, I interpret repentance as regeneration, whose sole end is to restore in us the image of God that had been disfigured and all but obliterated through Adam's transgression." PI § 108: "The *preconceived idea* of crystalline purity can only be removed by turning our whole examination round. (One might say: the axis of reference of our examination must be rotated, but about the fixed point of our real need)." PI §133: "The real discovery is the one that makes me capable of stopping doing philosophy when I want to.—The one that gives philosophy peace, so that it is no longer tormented by questions which bring *itself* in question." PI §309: "What is your aim in philosophy?—To shew the fly the way out of the fly-bottle." It may be useful to point out that "repentance" was coined in Latin to render the Greek μετάνοια, meaning "change of mind."

41. PI IIiv, 178: "Religion teaches that the soul can exist when the body has disintegrated. Now do I understand this teaching?—Of course I understand it—I can imagine plenty of things in connexion with it. And haven't pictures of these things been painted? And why should such a picture be only an imperfect rendering of the spoken doctrine? Why should it not do the *same* service as the words? And it is the service which is the point." For more detail see Winch, "Wittgenstein," 64–80. Cf. Battles, *Institutes*, 12 (I.xi.): "The functions and limits of art"; 112: "Therefore it remains that only those things are to be sculptured or painted which the eyes are capable of seeing: let not God's majesty, which is far above the perception of the eyes, be debased through unseemly representations. Within this class some are histories and events, some are images and forms of bodies without any depicting of past events. The former have some use in teaching or admonition; as for the latter, I do not see what they can afford other than pleasure."

John Calvin, Myth and Reality

study is supposed to remind us of what we have always known. There are striking parallels between the "incommunicable" quality that Calvin summoned in order to explain how one and the same God can be divided into three different persons and the grammatical asymmetry that Wittgenstein identified as crucial to grasping the nature of a human being.[42] It would be enlightening to pursue those parallels and quite in keeping with Wittgenstein's endeavor. Wittgenstein was deeply preoccupied with religion. He once asserted "I cannot help seeing every problem from a religious point of view."[43] But in the very same sentence he also asserted that "I am not a religious man," and in 1946 he wrote, "I cannot kneel to pray because it's as though my knees were stiff. I am afraid of dissolution (my own dissolution), should I become soft."[44] Nowhere in Wittgenstein's thought will readers find an equivalent to Calvin's belief in a personal God whose providential action guides the world at every step of the way from creation to the final judgment. Precisely because Calvin and Wittgenstein agreed that human beings cannot be reduced to logical coherence without violence to their nature, it would be a travesty to claim that their thinking is united by some underlying essence establishing some kind of definite identity between the two. "I'll teach you differences" is a line from *King Lear* that Wittgenstein regarded as a suitable motto for his approach to philosophy.[45] Those differences are not to be ignored.

I do believe that Wittgenstein and Calvin were united in tracing the gravest threat to human integrity, not to human fallibility, but, quite the contrary, to the desire to emancipate humanity from fallibility. That desire finds its most pointed expression in the attempt to seek knowledge of reality from representations of reality. On the surface, representations of God may seem to have little to do with those mental representations of the external world that lie at the heart of modern epistemology. In reality, both promise human beings a means of detaching themselves from their own belief, achieving control over their fal-

---

42. Battles, *Institutes*, 128 (I.xiii.6): "The meaning of the most important conception"; esp. 128: 'Person,' therefore, I call a 'subsistence' in God's essence, which, while related to the others, is distinguished by an incommunicable quality. By the term 'subsistence' we would understand something different from 'essence.'"

43. Malcolm, *Wittgenstein*, 1; cf. Bouwsma, *Wittgenstein*.

44. Malcolm, *Wittgenstein*, 1, 22; cf. Wittgenstein, *Culture and Value*, 56e.

45. Rhees, *Ludwig Wittgenstein*, 171.

libility, and thereby delivering themselves from the necessity of sacrifice demanded by the asymmetry of persons. But that promise is treacherous. It is the serpent's promise that "your eyes shall be opened, and ye shall be as gods, knowing good and evil."[46] Belief cannot consist of my attachment to any kind of object, mental or otherwise—not even to an object called a representation of reality. Belief can only be expressed in the first-person present indicative, "I believe." The first-person present indicative leaves no room for distinguishing myself from my belief—no room for holding any truth that I do not believe. It requires that I do in fact believe what I call my belief. If I do no believing in the first-person present indicative, then I do not believe at all. And if I say what I do not believe, then I disqualify myself from speaking. Thus the picture theory of propositions and what Calvin called idolatry both lead from the desire to avoid sacrifice, via the invention of images designed to carry the burden of my fallibility, into exile from speech. "So in the end when one is doing philosophy one gets to the point where one would like just to emit an inarticulate sound."[47]

Two conclusions seem to me to follow from the line of reasoning I have laid out above. One is that Calvin's hostility to images is poorly understood if it is cast as nothing but an expression of religious faith or mindless obedience to a divine command for which nothing that looks like an intelligible reason can be adduced. Of course it was an expression of religious faith and of obedience to a divine command, but no more irrational or mindless than it is to follow any kind of rule, religious or otherwise.[48] It went hand in hand with a perfectly intelligible understanding of humanity. On that understanding, human beings may not be imagined as consisting of a self that knows nothing better than itself but is divided from the external world. Human beings are rather to be taken as composed of separate persons, and the difference between these persons is to be taken as something that is given in language and that no picture on its own account can represent. Only language makes it possible for us to speak in different persons. That is the reason why the Word deserves respect. Not to respect the Word is

---

46. Gen 3:5 (KJV).

47. PI §261.

48. Ibid., §218: "When I obey a rule, I do not choose. I obey the rule *blindly*" (italics original).

to do violence to human nature. That is the reason why images must not be substituted for the Word.

The second conclusion is that what I have called conventional wisdom must be regarded as an instance of what Calvin called idolatry. Conventional wisdom about the self and its privileged but lonely position in the universe merely seems to rest on more-or-less self-evident truths that lie at the foundation of all knowledge. In fact it is an artifice invented to shelter human pride from the humiliating recognition that language does not allow me to detach myself from my erroneous belief. It substitutes the self—what nowadays is often designated "my identity"—for the asymmetry of persons. That may seem more persuasive than the wooden, graven, painted things the ancients used to represent the place of human beings in the world. But it marks a break from language quite like the break that Calvin charged to idolatry. The price for making such a break consists of treating myself as though I were a thing, or more precisely, two different kinds of thing: a body and a mind. The price may well seem small. But it entails a deep confusion that saps our ability to speak intelligibly to one another, to recognize each other as fellow human beings, to distinguish truth from illusion, and to trust our judgment in the face of opposition. It would be rash to jump to the conclusion that Descartes and his followers are responsible for the ills of the modern world. But one need not at all invoke the wrath of God or threaten the punishments of hell to recognize the danger that lack of respect for the asymmetry of persons and resistance to the sacrifice that it demands lead to tyranny and human desolation. One merely needs to read Wittgenstein and Calvin side by side.

11

God's Gracious Provision
Calvin and His Heirs on Political Order

DAVID T. KOYZIS

Remarkably, despite the fact that Calvin was not and never claimed to be a political philosopher, and despite his never holding political office, he concludes his magnum opus, *The Institutes of the Christian Religion*, with a treatment of governmental authority![1] This tells us immediately that, for Calvin, concern for political affairs is not of mere incidental significance to the Christian life. True, government cannot save us, but it nevertheless plays a significant role in God's providential ordering of the world. So essential is government to human flourishing that Calvin famously asserts that "its function among men is no less than that of bread, water, sun, and air; indeed, its place of honour is far more excellent."[2] For Calvin government is no mere necessary evil; it is nothing less than God's gracious provision for a complete and obedient human life *coram Deo*—before the face of God.

---

1. Battles, *Institutes*, IV.xx. It is perhaps noteworthy that in his treatment of Calvin, Bouwsma reverses this order, treating society and government *before* the institutional church; Bouwsma, *John Calvin*, 191–229.

2. Battles, *Institutes*, 1488 (IV.xx.3).

Modernity and the Political

Although Calvin was not a political theorist as such, he and his heirs powerfully contributed to the development of a genuinely *political* theory, while the main secular currents of the modern age, even as they took up political theory in a more intentional fashion, have nevertheless been antipolitical at best. We shall begin with the latter statement first and then proceed to the former.

In the last century several political theorists noted that much of the Western tradition had little use for the political enterprise, viewing it as ancillary to something else, perhaps economics, technique or, worst of all, as an ideological vision of the future society to be implemented through coercive means. Fifty years ago Sheldon S. Wolin coined the term *"the political,"* idiosyncratically making a noun of an adjective and affirming the importance of a particular kind of life in community that is irreplaceable by any other kind, especially by the smaller, more intimate communities of civil society on which people have increasingly—and improperly—focused their political energies.[3] Hannah Arendt sought to affirm the integrity of the political realm of action and speech against those who would reduce it to economics on the one hand or to a finished product dreamt up in the realm of thought on the other.[4] Similarly, Sir Bernard Crick defended politics against its technological, ideological, and even democratic detractors, defining politics as the peaceful conciliation of diversity within a particular unit of rule.[5]

What these figures share is the considered judgment that the modern age has been characterized by an antipolitical prejudice. Following Leo Strauss, the principal traditions within modernity can be divided into roughly three: those following John Locke, Jean-Jacques Rousseau, and Friedrich Nietzsche; corresponding respectively to the moderate Enlightenment, the radical Enlightenment, and what has come to be called postmodern historicism.[6] Despite their differences, all view political authority as deriving its validity from something fundamentally nonpolitical. Locke, who would have such a strong influence on the American founding, believed that "Government has no other end but

---

3. Wolin, *Politics and Vision*.
4. Arendt, *The Human Condition*.
5. Crick, *In Defence of Politics*.
6. See Strauss, "What Is Political Philosophy?" 9–55.

the preservation of Property,"⁷ perhaps the strongest statement to appear in his *Second Treatise* to the effect that politics is ancillary to what C. B. MacPherson has called possessive individualism.⁸ In Rousseau, government is little more than a hired agent of the general will, charged not so much with doing justice as with implementing that which has been legislated by the sovereign assembly.

Karl Marx stands in the Rousseauan line, arguing that the state, far from being an impartial arbiter of the struggles within civil society (*bürgerliche Gesellschaft*), is nothing more than an instrument of class oppression fueled by an age-old struggle between the owners of productive means and their workers. If this is so, he is convinced that the forthcoming classless society will eliminate the need for government, at least in the sense in which it now exists. Marx and Engels believe that the state will then "lose its political character,"⁹ while Engels goes one step further in averring that the state will die out or wither away.¹⁰ If politics calls for reconciling diverse interests, there can be no place for it in a society where the interest of the working class will have triumphed over class oppression. Ironically the heirs of both Locke and Marx agree that economics drives politics, though they differ as to whether or not this is a good thing.

The radical historicism of Nietzsche's heirs picks up where Marx leaves off, agreeing that all human activities, including politics, are impelled by self-interest, but a self-interest tethered to a collective identity determined by one's place in an oppressive power relationship that cuts across the whole of society. Politics is thus inescapably reflective of the interests of the wielders of power, whether these be Westerners, males, heterosexuals, Caucasians, or some other group perceived to be dominant. Truth claims can never be taken at face value but are subjected to a hermeneutic of suspicion calling for a probing analysis of the collective interests of those in power. In this context, politics itself tends to be reduced to a struggle between oppressed and oppressor. There is no uniquely political contribution that government makes to human life. While Nietzsche's heirs do not generally envision an eschatological end

---

7. Locke, *Second Treatise of Civil Government*, VII, §94.
8. MacPherson, *Political Theory*.
9. Marx and Engels, *Manifesto of the Communist Party*, II.
10. Engels, *Socialism*, III; cf. Lenin, *The State and Revolution*.

to this oppressive situation, they nevertheless do see the need for the oppressed to fight back continually to defend and advance their own interest, while not necessarily claiming that such action is in accord with what others might label natural justice.[11]

The quarrels among these "waves"[12] of modernity ought not to be underestimated, but neither should they be overstated. John Fonte has argued that the current culture war, at least in the United States, has its roots in the clash between the disciples of Alexis de Tocqueville and Antonio Gramsci: between the proponents of civil society and the adherents of "absolute historicism."[13] What is missing in both schools is a robust appreciation for the distinctive role of the state in doing public justice, something that makes it irreplaceable either by the pluriform communities of civil society or by totalizing identity groups, as celebrated respectively by Tocquevilleans and Gramscians.

Calvin and the Political

Ever since Max Weber posited a connection between the Calvinist Reformation and the rise of capitalism, it has become a commonplace that Protestantism contributed to the development of modernity.[14] This is a half-truth at best. Its accuracy is most manifest in the process of secularization, which meant that modernity would take on a distinctive flavor in those countries, such as England, Scotland, the Netherlands, Switzerland, and the United States, which had known the historical influence of Calvinism. However, it is also true that while in its secularized form Calvinism would assume an individualistic spirit, it would be difficult to attribute this spirit to Calvin himself as expressed in his voluminous writings. While Locke, for example, might be seen to reflect Calvin's influence in some measure, there are other figures heir to an alternative lineage that did not accept the spiritual assumptions of modernity but stood closer to Calvin's own reformational spirit. It

---

11. Nevertheless, at least Jacques Derrida believes that justice is undeconstructible, i.e., exempt from the historicism that relativizes virtually everything else. See Derrida, "The Force of Law," 14–15.

12. This is Leo Strauss's term.

13. Fonte, "Why There Is a Culture War."

14. Weber, *The Protestant Ethic*; cf. Tawney, *Religion and the Rise of Capitalism*; Fanfani, *Catholicism, Protestantism and Capitalism*.

is this group that not only remained true to the Reformed Christian confession but also, nearly uniquely, affirmed the integrity of political community and governmental authority within it.[15]

We turn first to Calvin himself. We noted above his glowing approval of civil government, his citing its necessity to human flourishing, his even likening it to "bread, water, sun and air," all of which are required for life itself. Among other things, it is responsible "to cherish and protect the outward worship of God, to defend sound doctrine of piety and the position of the church, to adjust our life to the society of men, to form our social behaviour to civil righteousness, to reconcile us with one another, and to promote general peace and tranquility" (Battles, *Institutes*, IV.xx.2). Within government the office of magistrate is invested by God with great dignity and divine authority; the magistrate acts as God's representative, serving him in this capacity. Magistrates are nothing other than "ministers of God" and "vicars of God," possessing a "holy ministry" (IV.xx.3, 6, 7). Although these terms have often been associated more with ecclesiastical than with political office, Calvin nevertheless freely uses them for the latter, echoing Paul's reference to political authority as God's *servant* (διάκονος) and, in the plural, as *ministers* of God (λειτουργοί, Rom 13:4, 6).[16]

In addition to affirming that civil government is ordained by God, Calvin's political thought is characterized by seven additional themes. First, its possession and use of coercive power is entirely legitimate and should not be taken to exclude Christians from its exercise (IV.xx.7). Second, there is a legitimate diversity in forms of government, though Calvin does affirm the superiority of some combination of aristocracy and democracy, or what the classical political philosophers called the mixed constitution (IV.xx.8). Third, he believes that magistrates prop-

---

15. So important is the place of government within the larger Calvinist tradition that H. Henry Meeter devoted somewhat more than half of *The Basic Ideas of Calvinism* to politics and the state. As if this were not enough, the revised sixth edition of the book contains two additional chapters on the subject by Paul A. Marshall.

16. The parallels between Reformed church polity and civil political order are evident to Meeter, who writes, "If then in the most sacred institution on earth, the church, the government of which the Calvinist patterned after the Bible, the people were given governmental authority and lay members even had the right of control— thus the Calvinist argued—why not in political institutions as well? For the Calvinist, the government of the church became in practice a model for state formation" (*Basic Ideas*, 94).

erly concern themselves with both tables of the law, i.e., not only with those norms governing human relations but also with those governing the right worship of God (IV.xx.9).[17] Fourth, he recognizes in government the right to wage war against external aggression (IV.xx.11–12). Fifth, governments have the right to collect taxes (IV.xx.13). Sixth, obedience is due even bad magistrates (IV.xx.23–26). Seventh, however, in a polity properly ordered by law the various magistrates ought to check each other so as to prevent any one of them from becoming a tyrant (IV. xx.30–31).

This is not just an eclectic list of themes; taken together they constitute a powerful affirmation of constitutional government that would come to have an impact, initially in those countries where Calvin's influence was greatest, but later throughout the globe, especially in Commonwealth countries and in the United States.[18] It would have an influence even on the development of international law through the Dutch jurist Huig de Groot, better known to the world as Hugo Grotius.[19] This support for constitutional government was not, of course, original with Calvin, having antecedents in the medieval era. Yet it was Calvin and his followers who argued, with unparalleled effectiveness, that obedience to God and his law has political implications, which are not simply peripheral to the faith. In fact, virtually all the sixteenth- and seventeenth-century Reformed confessions address the need for civil government, thereby making this issue a confessional matter. To deny the proper role of political authority is to flirt with heresy, as indicated in Calvin's rejection of the Anabaptists.

The one element of Calvin's political thought to which virtually everyone now would take exception is his belief that government should take responsibility for upholding the right worship of God, something that found its way into subsequent Reformed confessions such as the unaltered Belgic Confession and the Westminster standards. While this would seem to call for political authority to overextend its competence, we do well to remember, not only that Calvin was a man of his times

17. See Hesselink, *Calvin's Concept of the Law*.

18. Abraham Kuyper, in an 1874 essay, goes so far as to label Calvinism the "Source and Stronghold of Our Constitutional Liberties" (Bratt, *Abraham Kuyper*, 279–322).

19. See Grotius, *De iure belli ac pacis*. Though Grotius was on the side of the Remonstrants in the controversy leading up to the Synod of Dort (1618-1619), he certainly carried on the tradition of political reflection characterizing Reformed Christianity in the broadest sense.

(which comes perilously close to straying into cliché territory), but that for Calvin justice requires it. If government sees that justice be done to mere human beings, it should be even more solicitous to ensure that God receive the worship he is due. Nevertheless, it is true that many of Calvin's successors broke with him on this point, eventually embracing full religious freedom, not simply out of pragmatism, but out of principle.[20]

Johannes Althusius

The first explicitly *political* theorist in the Calvinist movement was Johann Althaus, better known as Johannes Althusius, who has also been labeled the first federalist, due to his influence in the shaping of theories in modern constitutional federalism.[21] Largely unknown and unappreciated after his death until Otto von Gierke revived interest in him in the late nineteenth century,[22] Althusius distinguishes between the efficient and final causes of political association, arguing that the former is "consent and agreement among the communicating citizens" while the latter is "the enjoyment of a comfortable, useful, and happy life, and of the common welfare," and "also the conservation of a human society that aims at a life in which [one] can worship God quietly and without error."[23]

Although he is sometimes thought to have anticipated the rise of social-contract and popular-sovereignty theories,[24] Althusius conceives of the commonwealth as composed of a variety of symbiotic associations joined together by the bonds of universal symbiotic communion under the rule of law (IX). While the "right of the realm" belongs to associated members of the realm, these members are not individual citizens, as liberal and democratic theories would have it, but the cities, provinces and regions (IX, 62) that make it up and might be said to stand

---

20. For a brief history of the development of religious freedom in Calvinist thought and practice, see Koyzis, "Persuaded, Not Commanded."

21. See Benoist, "The First Federalist," 2–34.

22. Von Gierke, *Development of Political Theory*, especially part 1.

23. Althusius, *Politics*, I, in Carney, *Politics of Johannes Althusius*, 19. Subsequent references are placed in parentheses in the text.

24. Von Gierke implausibly connects Althusius with Rousseau's idea of popular sovereignty, despite the latter's abhorrence of partial societies within the body politic.

between the commonwealth and the individual subjects. Althusius, in other words, affirmed what has come to be known as civil society, while taking care to recognize the crucial place of political community (or *consociatio publica*) in human social life.

Following Calvin and the classic political philosophers, Althusius too favors a mixed constitution whose elements are carefully balanced so as to produce just governance. Here is where the seventeenth-century Reformed thinker is least similar to Rousseau, Gierke's conclusion to the contrary notwithstanding. Whereas Rousseau expresses hostility to partial communal bodies that might divide the general will and deflect governors and people alike from their public duties, Althusius's world is a socially variegated one, composed of a multiplicity of associations and corporations, each pursuing its own welfare while contributing to the greater good of the whole.

These partial societies have a twofold character, working to keep government within constitutional limits and thus to prevent tyranny. The first form of society is external to government: the *consociatio simplex et privata*, which brings together its members for purposes peculiar to the group itself. Such forms of association include the family and the collegium, the former of which is a natural and the latter a civil association wherein "three or more men of the same trade, training, or profession are united for the purpose of holding in common such things they jointly profess as duty, way of life, or craft" (IV, 28–29). These are roughly comparable to the medieval guilds as well as to the modern professional associations and trade unions.

The second form of society is internal to government, dividing sovereignty for political purposes, arguably anticipating the works of Montesquieu and the theory and practice of the American founders in the eighteenth century. These partial societies include provinces and cities, each of which is a self-governing part of the whole body politic. Within the central or federal government a further distinction is made between the chief magistrate and the lower magistrates, or Ephors, who are empowered to check the former and thus prevent tyranny. A political constitution thus constrains government from both without and within.

Groen and Kuyper

The pluriformity of the social order championed by Althusius would come to be eclipsed in the mainstream of Western political theory, which was preoccupied with locating a temporal source of sovereignty within society as an alternative to the Christian belief in the sovereignty of God. Thomas Hobbes famously referred to his omnicompetent sovereign as a "mortal god,"[25] a revealing expression that nicely encapsulates the mood of the era. The totalitarian régimes of the twentieth century can be said to have had their spiritual origins in these earlier political monisms. At the end of the eighteenth century the French Revolution would crystalize these trends, as the monarchical absolutism of the Bourbon monarchs was supplanted, not by constitutional government, but by the absolutism of the popular will, or, more accurately, of self-appointed élites claiming to give voice to that will.

In the postrevolutionary nineteenth century a number of Christians, both Catholic and Protestant, undertook to counter the influence of these monistic trends by reaffirming societal pluriformity while at the same time affirming the positive task of political authority. In the Netherlands, Guillaume Groen van Prinster (1801–1876), an archivist for the royal House of Orange who founded and led what is arguably the first European Christian democratic movement, expressed concern over the state centralization that was impacting even his own country. In his own words, "Centralization always begins by destroying the rights of provinces and municipalities and, if forced to be consistent, ends by tolerating in fact no right or activity or existence except under its supervision and control, as a benign favour. It has no place for autonomy, for independence within one's own sphere."[26]

Although the early Groen fell under the influence of the restorationist sentiments that were so strong throughout Europe after 1815, his singular contribution was to affirm that every government, whether monarchical or republican, must be constrained by the existence of institutions external to itself, whose distinctive status it is obligated to recognize and protect. Groen further understood that the ideologies spawned by the revolution, while claiming to follow the popular will, deprecated the very orders and estates that actually empowered

---

25. Hobbes, *Leviathan*, XIII.
26. Groen van Prinsterer, "Unbelief and Revolution," 48.

the people vis-à-vis the state. Echoing St. Paul in Romans 13, Groen averred that a "civil power is God's *lieutenant* and God's *minister*,"[27] properly submitting to his supreme power.

Unfortunately, Groen proved unwilling, at least in his major work, to affirm the public legal character of monarchical constitutions, instead viewing them as "patrimonial principalities" rooted in something close to private ownership of property.[28] It thus fell to Groen's successor, Abraham Kuyper (1837-1920), to extricate this movement from the grip of a backwards-looking orientation and to affirm the place of the state as a unique community of government and citizens led by the principle of public justice. He did so by articulating the principle of *soevereiniteit in eigen kring*, which is translated as "sovereignty in its own sphere," or simply "sphere sovereignty."[29]

Affirming that God is the ultimate sovereign over his creation, Kuyper asserts that, by his grace, he has chosen to confer a share of this sovereignty on his human image bearers, "so that on earth one never directly encounters God Himself in visible things but always sees his sovereign authority exercised in *human* office."[30] These offices are pluriform in nature; there is no one earthly agent to whom God has delegated the whole of his sovereignty in undivided fashion. Rather, much as the natural world is characterized by a brilliant diversity of creaturely kinds, so is the human social world, with authority being dispersed among a variety of responsible agents. Thus earthly authorities "possess the power to compel obedience only in a limited sphere, a sphere bordered by other spheres in which another is sovereign."[31] This stands in stark contrast to the ancient Caesar, who fancied himself a god and believed himself to be the source of all authority within the Roman *imperium*. With the coming of Jesus, however, all sovereignty finds its ultimate focus in the "sinless Messiah," who "directly denies and challenges all absolute Sovereignty among *sinful* men on earth, and does so by dividing life into *separate spheres*, each with its own

---

27. Ibid., 52.

28. See Groen's Lecture VI in ibid., 120-51.

29. See Kuyper, "Sphere Sovereignty," the inaugural address he delivered in 1880 at the opening of the Free University of Amsterdam, in Bratt, *Abraham Kuyper*, 461-90.

30. Bratt, *Abraham Kuyper*, 466 (italics original).

31. Ibid.

sovereignty."[32] What are these spheres? They differ slightly with each telling, but Kuyper typically lists the domains of nature, "of the personal, of the household, of science, of social and ecclesiastical life, each of which obeys its own laws of life, each subject to its own chief."[33] This yields a "rich, multifaceted multiformity of human life."[34]

The state has its own "special sphere" within this pluriformity of authorities, with the mandate to "provide for sound mutual interaction among the various spheres" and to "keep them within just limits."[35] Personal life has its own sphere, which the state is obligated to defend from the tyrannical encroachment of group life. Though the state is not *ontically* higher than the other spheres, Kuyper admits that in one sense it does indeed rise "high above them by its right to command and compel." Yet the state properly refrains from interfering in the internal life of those spheres, which follow their own law under God. The authority possessed by these spheres issues immediately from God himself and not mediately through the state, which simply *recognizes* its antecedent status and in no sense can be said to *confer* it.

It should be noted that by acknowledging that the state's authority ultimately comes from God, Kuyper is freed from the necessity of having to locate a temporal or creaturely source of that authority and is thus better able to account for the distinctive *political* task of the state. By contrast, liberalism in its various forms collapses political community into a private contract among sovereign individuals who retain the right to alter the terms of the contract if it no longer meets their self-defined needs. If all communities are effectively voluntary associations, to be joined and quit at will, then there is nothing fundamentally distinctive about *any* of these. This Kuyper cannot accept, believing as he does in the divinely mandated pluriformity of human society.

Nevertheless, Kuyper does admit that because of the absence of any power above the state capable of compelling it to do justice, the state will tend to expand its own sphere of authority, potentially at the expense of the others. "Do not forget," Kuyper warns us, "that every

---

32. Ibid., 467.
33. Ibid.
34. Ibid., 467–68.
35. Ibid., 468.

State power tends to look upon all liberty with a suspicious eye."[36] The state is, in effect, "the sphere of spheres" and, whether out of sheer power hunger or out of a legitimate pursuit of the common good, it will tend by its nature to "draw the iron band as tightly around the staves as the crimp of those staves allows," in a metaphor oddly appropriate for a man whose surname bespeaks his ancestors' barrel-making profession.[37]

Given this reality, the only effective way to obstruct this potential expansiveness is for the other societal spheres to maintain their own vitality over time and to be vigilant in the defense of their own liberties. In short, sphere sovereignty is the sole antidote to state sovereignty.

Kuyper's Successors

We should not, of course, pretend that Kuyper's life and thought represent the major Calvinistic influence on especially English-speaking democracies. For example, no one can ignore the impact played by Jonathan Edwards (1703-1758) on the development of American Calvinism, in both its Congregational and Presbyterian forms.[38] Yet, while some observers believe that Edwards's influence contributed after his death to the development of the nascent American republic, and others believe that Edwards's beliefs themselves had political implications,[39] Edwards was nevertheless a theologian and not a political thinker as such. Consequently, his political legacy was more indirect than direct.

A century and a half later, political scientist Woodrow Wilson (1856-1924) was a devout Reformed Christian who had a high sense of the political calling and, with his election to the United States presidency in 1912, of his own place within the divine plan of history. Nevertheless, his practical political legacy was less enduring that he would have liked, as the United States Senate turned down his Covenant of the League of Nations, and his scholarly writings in the field of political science did

---

36. Ibid., 472.
37. Ibid., 473.
38. See George M. Marsden's magisterial biography, *Jonathan Edwards: A Life*.
39. See McDermott, *One Holy and Happy Society*.

not obviously offer an explicitly biblical and Christian understanding of the state.[40]

The latter decades of the twentieth century found especially evangelical Christians becoming more conscious than their recent forebears had been of their political responsibilities and were seeking resources within their own traditions that would enable them to fulfill these. Having been largely detached from their confessional moorings by the revivalism of the nineteenth century, the liberalism of the early twentieth century and the separatist fundamentalism of the same era, these evangelicals turned in one of three directions: first, towards a renewed Anabaptist tradition, in which the overtly dualistic ethic of the Schleitheim Confession (1527) had been supplanted by one revolving around an active and holistic peacemaking agenda; second, towards the Thomistic approach of traditional Roman Catholicism, with its notion of subsidiarity as foundational for making sense of the pluriformity of the social order; or third, towards the heirs of Calvin, as represented especially by the Dutch tradition with its strong emphasis on the cultural mandate (Genesis 1:26-28), within which politics was accorded an important though hardly all-encompassing place.

The difficulty with the Anabaptist approach, as exemplified by the likes of John Howard Yoder and Stanley Hauerwas, is that it does not offer a normative theory of the state as a differentiated political community with a positive mandate to do public justice. The Schleitheim Confession holds that "the sword is ordained to be used by the worldly magistrates." It properly "punishes and puts to death the wicked, and guards and protects the good," yet its ordination by God lies "outside the perfection of Christ." Thus "it is not appropriate for a Christian to serve as a magistrate" (article 6). While traditional Anabaptists were content to leave the power of the sword in the hands of the magistrate, more recent Anabaptists have sought to cut through this dualism by urging government to abandon its ways by forswearing the sword as much as possible. Short of this, government becomes at best an obstacle to peace and reconciliation among people, and Christian peacemaking will be best practiced by trying to work around it rather than by means of it. Justice is still sought, but it remains unclear what role, if any, the state might normatively play in implementing it.

40. See Magee, *What the World Should Be,* for an account of the role Wilson's Presbyterian Christianity played in his political career.

Although many evangelicals have been attracted to Catholic social teachings, as articulated by popes from Leo XIII through John Paul II, and although there have been some high-profile conversions to Rome in recent decades, these can hardly be said to represent a mass movement in that direction. Nevertheless, the impressive edifice of such teachings, as manifest in more than a century-long series of social encyclicals, offers a formidable effort to cut through the distorting influence of the secular ideologies that have so marked—and marred—the political landscape of the past two centuries or more. For those seeking a coherent effort to grapple with the realities of social and political life rooted in the great tradition extending from Augustine through Thomas Aquinas up to Jacques Maritain (1882–1973)[41] and Yves René Simon (1903–1961)[42] in the twentieth century, this particular Catholic approach has undeniable appeal. The principle of subsidiarity in particular offers a powerful defense of the institutions of civil society against an overweening state.

Yet subsidiarity is perhaps better understood as a sound principle of federalism rooted in prudential considerations rather than as a theoretical articulation of the normative task of the state. For example, already at the end of the eighteenth century the Ninth and Tenth Amendments to the United States Constitution could be seen to embody subsidiarity in so far as they reserve all powers not explicitly assigned to the Congress of the United States (article I, section 8) "to the states respectively, or to the people" (amendment 10). More recently, the treaties of the European Union, under more direct, if unacknowledged, influence of Catholic social teachings, enshrine the principle of subsidiarity as key to the ongoing relationships between the institutions of the Union and the several member states. Subsidiarity assumes that the state seeks the common good but it is less than fully clear what makes this good a distinctively *political* good. All communities, after all, can be said to pursue a common good *for that community*. Here perhaps we must look beyond subsidiarity to locate a basis for a genuinely political theory.

This brings us to the third tradition to which many North American evangelicals have looked for guidance, viz., the Reformed or Calvinist tradition. In fact, *Time Magazine* has recently called atten-

---

41. See Maritain, *Man and the State*; and Maritain, *The Person and the Common Good*.

42. See Simon, *Philosophy of Democratic Government*; and Simon, *A General Theory of Authority*.

tion to "The New Calvinism" as number 3 of their "10 Ideas Changing the World Right Now."[43] Nicholas Wolterstorff has called Calvinism a "world-formative" religion,[44] while H. Richard Niebuhr, more than half a century ago, placed Calvin and his heirs in the forefront of efforts to transform the larger culture for the cause of Christ.[45]

In this neocalvinist revival, the heirs of Kuyper have played a substantial role in developing a healthy appreciation, not only of the multiple institutions of civil society, but of the state's unique task of pursuing public justice. The Dutch Christian legal philosopher Herman Dooyeweerd (1894-1977) has been a seminal influence on a number of thinkers, through the pedagogical and practical efforts of philosopher H. Evan Runner (1916-2002)[46] of Calvin College, political theorist Bernard Zylstra (1934-1986)[47] of Toronto's Institute for Christian Studies, economist Bob Goudzwaard[48] of Amsterdam's Free University, James W. Skillen[49] of the Center for Public Justice, and Paul Marshall[50] of the Hudson Institute.

Following in the tradition of Kuyper, Dooyeweerd's singular contribution has been to analyze what he calls the structural principle of the state, primarily by distinguishing between the *things* of God's creation and the *ways* in which they function, also known as aspects or modalities.[51] Recognizing that everything has a jural side to it—for example, the computer on which I typed this essay is, among other things, an object of ownership by my employer—there is nevertheless a sense in which the jural side of reality is uppermost in any effort to make sense of the state as political community and the role of govern-

---

43. Van Biema, "Ten Ideas."

44. Wolterstorff, *Until Justice and Peace Embrace*, 3-22.

45. Niebuhr, *Christ and Culture*, 217-18.

46. Runner did not publish widely, but his principal publication on the subject of politics is *Scriptural Religion and Political Task*, which began life as a series of lectures first delivered in 1961.

47. Zylstra, *From Pluralism to Collectivism*.

48. Goudzwaard, *Capitalism and Progress*; and Goudzwaard, *Globalization and the Kingdom of God*.

49. Skillen, *The Scattered Voice*; and Skillen, *In Pursuit of Justice*.

50. Marshall, *Their Blood Cries Out*; and Marshall, *God and the Constitution*.

51. See Dooyeweerd, *A New Critique*, especially vol. 3, where he treats the various social spheres, including the state.

ment within that community. This enables us better to make sense of the place of justice within the state. If justice is a thing—a concept or even an ideal—that is either present or absent, then we may be tempted, like St. Augustine was, to define the commonwealth apart from it, since, after all, the old Roman republic denied God the worship due him and thus to that extent lacked justice.

Yet if the state's jural side means that whatever else it does, it must always weigh in the balance the pluriform interests domiciled within its jurisdiction (which is precisely what sphere sovereignty entails), then even political realists such as Hans Morgenthau cannot so easily shunt it aside, given their own emphasis on the desirability of maintaining a *balance* of powers both domestically and internationally. Justice is not an entity that can be excluded from consideration; it is always present in some fashion. *Injustice*, then, is not the absence of justice, but the perversion or miscarriage of justice, i.e., a failure to get the balance right. But that balancing role is always present in every state, from the parliamentary democracies of the Western world to the nepotistic oligarchies of the Middle East to the outright despotisms of parts of Africa and Asia. It is this emphasis on the distinctive, normative task of the state that has characterized those working with Dooyeweerd's political theory since he began to articulate it in the 1930s.

The foregoing evidence should suffice to indicate that Calvinist political theory and practice are still a vital enterprise five centuries after Calvin's birth. While there are, to be sure, many noncalvinists—political scientists and practitioners alike—who have a healthy appreciation for the unique role of political order and community in human life, the most influential of the twentieth century's secular ideologies, viz., liberalism and Marxism, have viewed the state respectively as product of social contract and as oppressor of the proletariat. In both cases the state has no intrinsic nature or task; it is merely the hired agent of either the voting citizenry or the bourgeoisie. Moreover, as evangelical Christians have looked more deeply into the Christian tradition for something that would facilitate their living out the kingdom of God within the political realm, it should not surprise us to find that very many have latched onto Calvin and his heirs, who, though not without their flaws, have nevertheless been a powerful catalyst to deep and sustained reflection on the place of political authority and political community in God's world.

12

The Doctrine of Scripture in the Calvinist Churches in Korea

JAY J. SHIM

In this chapter I would like to shed some light on the theological debates concerning the doctrine of Scripture from the 1930s to the 1950s that had a long-lasting impact on the foundation of the Presbyterian churches in Korea. The debates were primarily between Dr. Hyungryong Park (1897-1978) and Dr. Jaejoon Kim (1901-1987). Their differences regarding the nature of scriptural authority were so closely tied to fundamental matters of the Christian faith that their division eventually caused a major split in the Korean church in 1953.

One result of this disagreement and the split that ensued was that Park became the father of Calvinistic orthodoxy in the conservative Presbyterian churches of Korea, namely, in the Hapdong and Kosin denominations, which belong to the Yejang (Jesus Presbyterian) Church.[1]

---

1. Harvie M. Conn, professor of missiology at Westminster Theological Seminary, recognized Park as a representative theologian of Korean conservative theology, cited in Kim, "Theology of Hyungryong Park," 233. All the sources used in this chapter are in Korean, and the titles, references, and citations from them are in an English translation made by the present author.

John Calvin, Myth and Reality

With the split Kim and his colleagues formed a new denomination, the Kijang (Christ Presbyterian) Church. The split of the Presbyterian Church signals up to the present day the conflict between orthodox theology and modernist theology in the Calvinist churches of Korea. The debate on scriptural authority is very much alive today within Korean Calvinist churches, in that scholars on both sides are still passionately engaging the issue, and the doctrinal standards that were laid at that time are still used as a litmus test for denominational standards. Most who are engaged in this debate, be they from Park's church[2] or Kim's church,[3] remain true to their founders' theological stances, although there are a good number of unbiased reviews of the debate.

Theology is never done in a vacuum: theological topics are always interrelated with and contextualized by a given historical situation. The dispute over the doctrine of Scripture during the 1930s–50s in Korea also reflects complex interactions with such diverse and significant matters as the nature of orthodox theology, the nature of higher criticism, the engagement of social and political issues, and the struggle for ecclesiastical authority. In this chapter I will focus on theological issues related to scriptural authority as debated by the two theological giants of the day, with special attention given to themes that determined the directions of the polemics. I will seek to show that the orthodox Calvinistic doctrine of Scripture has been shaped in Korea by Hyungryong Park in his polemics with Jaejoon Kim, that their followers still advocate their doctrines, and that these bitter polemics have caused a false dichotomy in the Calvinist church[es] of Korea.

Before discussing the actual teachings of Hyungryong Park and Jaejoon Kim, I need to address the terms with which they have been stigmatized. It is well known that Park classified Jaejoon Kim as a lib-

2. Park, *The Life and Thought*; Chang, *Theological Study*; Kim, "Hyungryong Park's Doctrine of Scripture," 67–107; Park, "Hyungryong Park," 48–66; Choi, "Hyungryong Park," 158–86; Choi, "Theological Exclusivism," 200–20; Lee, "Disputes on doctrine of Scripture." 79–106; Jung, "Revisiting the Reformed faith," 1–9; Kim, "Jooksan Hyungryong Park," 10–47; Lee, "Significance of Dr. Hyungryong Park," 186–209; Ham, "A Study of the Dispute."

3. Park, *Is Korean Presbyterian Doctrine of Scripture Calvinist?*; Yeon, "A Study of Calvinist Theology"; Shim, "Study of theological thought," 7–30; Lee, "Comparative study"; Kang, "Study of the theological thought"; Seo, "Reflection of Dr. Jaejoon Kim," 4–9; Kim, "Life and thought of Jang-gong Jaejoon Kim." Online: http://cafe.naver.com/chcom.cafe?iframe_url=/ArticleRead.nhn%3Farticleid=29/.

eral theologian, and that Kim in turn judged Park as lacking piety, due to his alleged denial of the facts of Scripture, namely, the living voice of God through Christ. Although these accusatory labels have stuck, they fail to do justice to their respective theologies.

Neither Park nor Kim was a fully established fundamentalist or liberal theologian at the beginning of his theological career, but both did shape their theologies in the process of the polemics. An unfortunate tendency within the Korean Presbyterian church at that time was to argue with a black-and-white dichotomy and lack of detailed analysis. This was due in part to the checkered history of the period as well as to the personalities involved. Both Park and Kim were born at the turn of the last century, when the Chosun dynasty was in its demise and the influence of Japanese imperialism was growing fast in the Korean Peninsula. They both lived through the harsh persecution during the Japanese occupation, the glorious but chaotic years of national independence, the years of the Korean War, the experience of a church split, as well as many years of political and social uneasiness. Leisure time or respite, which might have led them to deeper theological reflection, was at a premium; instead, the reality of the church demanded that they provide leadership. Consequently, the polemics further aggravated their theological disagreements and eventually polarized their theological trends and exacerbated the tensions in the church.

Let me begin by making this point clear: Dr. Jaejoon Kim did not deny the doctrine of the virgin birth of Christ. While orthodox reviews frequently cite his study of *Immanuel* based on Isaiah to demonstrate that Kim is a liberal theologian, Kim did not deny that the Holy Spirit caused the virgin birth of Jesus. The thesis of his article was to demonstrate, using the tools of criticism, that the Hebrew word *elma* might have meant either "virgin" or "young married woman," and that Isaiah himself might not have had a clear understanding of the term, but that, looking retrospectively after the virgin birth of Jesus, the words of Isaiah evidence the wisdom of God. Kim also did not deny the miracles recorded in the gospels. He said that as long as one accepts the greatest miracle in Jesus, in whom the natural and supernatural meet, it is not so important whether or not one literally believes the miracles in the Bible. Kim's statement should not be used as evidence of his denial of miracles. In fact, Kim clearly believed in the bodily resurrection of Christ as an historical event. Dongmin Chang, a modern reviewer

Dr. Hyungryong Park	History of Korea	Dr. Jaejoon Kim
	Mid 19th century: Protestant Christianity introduced to Korea	
1897 born in Korea		
	1907 Great Revival at Pyongyang	1901 born in Korea
1920 graduated from Soongsil College, Korea 1923 graduated from Kumnong University, China	1910–1945 Japanese Occupation	
1926 gr. Princeton Seminary, New Jersey, with B. Th. and M. Th		1925 moved to Japan to study theology
1931 became professor of systematic theology at Pyongyang Seminary		1929 graduated from Princeton and Western Seminaries with STB and STM degrees
1932 graduated from Southern Baptist Seminary, Kentucky, with PhD degree		
		1940 established Chosun Seminary (now Hansin University)
	1950–1953 Korean War	
1978 died		1987 died

from the orthodox side, concludes that in his confessional stance on the doctrines of Christ, redemption, justification, and believers' final resurrection, Kim was much closer to traditional evangelical theology than the classical European liberals.[4]

Kim's historical context also shows he was not educated in liberal theology. Kim was born in a non-Christian family and was raised in the Confucian tradition in his youth and worked at a secular position before becoming a Christian. After his conversion he attended for a long time a conservative church that was influenced by a revival movement. Liberal theology as understood in the nineteenth-century European

4. Chang, *Theological Study*, 124–25, 164–66; see also Sangkyu Lee, "Significance," 195–98.

context was neither a major part of theological education nor relevant to the cultural situation of the Korean church at that time. His first contact with the theologies of Karl Barth and Emil Brunner—they are not liberal theologies—was in Japan, after his initial theological education in Korea, and before he moved to Princeton Seminary. Kim indeed was convinced of the benefits of higher criticism, but he did not use it theologically to reduce biblical authority. His theological mind was not shaped by secular nineteenth-century liberalism. He simply found in it a way of enriching his own way of interpreting Scripture. Similarly, he found in Barth's theology an alternative theological approach that could serve as an antidote to the problems he perceived in the Korean church, namely, orthodox dogmatism and the misuse of ecclesiastical authority centering on the leadership of the missionaries. This historical background shows that Kim was quite different from the liberal mind that flourished in the European context in the nineteenth century.[5]

Significant is that Chang provides for a fresh review of Park and Kim; he highlights two reasons why Kim has notoriously been known as a liberal theologian. First, Kim's theology has reductionistically been reviewed on the basis of solely his doctrine of Scripture, with a special emphasis on his denial of verbal inspiration and his arguments for the existence of errors in the Scripture. Second, the unique dispute with Park over the doctrine of Scripture was wrought in the Korean context and has long been reviewed with the same underlying schema as the American dispute between modernism and fundamentalism during the 1920s. So the other determining factors of the Korean context were neglected, and the discussion of the dispute focused on the issue of Kim's modernism.[6]

Hyungryong Park, on the other hand, introduced his theology with diverse designations such as *Calvinism*, *Reformed theology*, and *orthodox* and *fundamentalist theology*. He indeed appealed to the fundamentalist theologians and used their terms, which he acquired in the United States. But a close reading of his work shows that he was not, at least at the beginning of his theological career, part of the sectarian, anticultural, or anti-intellectual types of fundamentalism. Park's understanding of fundamentalism was quite naïve in that he identified it with

---

5. Chang, *Theological Study*, 167–69.
6. Ibid., 168.

Christianity itself and at other times with the orthodox theology of the traditional church.

Kim's and Park's harsh criticism of each other polarized their theological trends and aggravated the ecclesiastical situation of the Korean church. In the end, Park condemned Kim's theology as heretical because of his denial of the verbal inspiration of Scripture. Kim, in turn, judged Park's orthodox theology and ecclesiastical conservatism as a more human-centered heresy disguised by the mask of orthodoxy.

Kim's Doctrine of Scripture

Kim criticized the orthodox doctrine of Scripture as being a product of an "impious attitude of theology," a product of "fossilized Pharisees," and even a product of "being possessed of a spirit" to the point of losing self-consciousness—borrowing a term from a superstitious practice in Korea. He said that orthodox theology read into Scripture a mechanical inspiration theory in order to establish the verbal infallibility of Scripture. This impious attitude not only distorted the truth of theology, but also denied the self-consciousness of the biblical authors.

Kim began his doctrine of Scripture with a statement borrowed from Bowne's *Christian Revelation*: "We will not determine the nature of Scripture by a theory of inspiration but by the fact of Scripture." By the "fact of Scripture" Kim seemed to have two issues in mind. First, by explaining the theory of organic inspiration, without naming it, he emphasized the biblical authors' self-consciousness in the recording of the Word: "The Holy Spirit did not suppress the functions of the authors in their classification of the pre-existing literature, arranging them, and selecting from them." Prophets were conscious of the subject-object relationship when they said "the Word of the Lord came to me." Kim also said that "God did not put the ready-made Word into the mind of the authors without their knowledge, but God first inspired them with his Spirit, had them recognize the meaning of the Word, and had them record what they recognized in their own personality and character." In the second aspect of the "fact of Scripture," Kim separated the Word of God and the expressed form of human language. The Word of God is absolutely infallible, but the forms of expression by nature are limited by their historical situations. Consequently, "God did not mean to maintain ultimate infallibility in the historical, scientific, and chronological record of the Scripture. He left such record to the level of knowledge of each historical period." This point is relevant to the fundamental issue of Park's orthodox theology, namely, whether the Bible has errors in it. According to Kim, "God did not expect verbal infallibility of such records since the message of salvation in Scripture does not depend on the imperfect record of linguistic, historical, or scientific facts." Kim fully agreed with the divine authority of Scripture, but his understanding of scriptural authority did not depend on verbal infallibility. He said, "Let's recognize the fact of Scripture . . . In fact, there are linguistic, scientific, and historical errors in the record of Scripture. Though they are not great errors, errors are errors."[7]

Then Kim moved to the issue of the purpose of Scripture. Citing John 5:39, he said that "the purpose of recording Scripture is to receive eternal life and eternal life is to witness about Jesus. Scripture is neither a scientific textbook nor an introduction to philosophy." When one reads the Word in Scripture with a prayerful heart, then he comes to meet Jesus in the work of the Holy Spirit. "In Jesus is found the whole personified Word of God. In Jesus both Old and New Testaments are truly the Word of God. The Word of God is not to be limited to literature or forms, but as the power of God it works in us." With this neo-orthodox doctrine of Scripture Kim said, "Scripture is the infallible rule in both faith and practice."[8]

Kim published six articles on the doctrine of Scripture and on exegesis of the Old Testament, and in none of these articles did he deny the divine inspiration of Scripture or the traditional confessions of Reformed theology. In his exegesis of Job 19:25, which was often cited by the orthodox to prove his liberal stance of Scripture, Kim in fact argued that it is a mistake to try to extract a completed doctrine of *sheol* or of the immortality of the soul from this passage. He never denied the traditional doctrine of the soul's immortality. What he denied was a dogmatic misuse of the Scripture.[9]

Scripture is "a witness of God's soteriological activity in the form of historical record." A witness recorded in human languages may include words that are embedded in the historical and cultural particularity of

---

7. Jaejoon Kim, "Verbal Inspiration," 1–3.
8. Ibid., 3–5.
9. Chang, *Theological Study*, 173.

history. Then, Scripture may include historical or scientific errors. But he quickly added that such errors should not damage the divine authority or truthfulness of Scripture. His understanding of the divine authority of Scripture is based not on the infallibility of the letters of Scripture but on the soteriological function of the living voice of God, that is, on God's unfailing acts of salvation through Scripture. Kim eventually argued against Park that soteriological infallibility cannot be compatible with verbal infallibility. As a result of the separation between the Word itself and its form, Kim welcomed higher criticism and believed such use of criticism would prevent the theological discipline from distorting the nature of scriptural texts with preconceived dogmas. More positively, biblical criticism would ensure that the reader would find a clearer sense of Scripture since it shows the texts within the given contexts.[10]

The emphasis on the context of theology for reading Scripture was intricately related to the historical situation in Korea during Kim's lifetime. With such an understanding of Scripture, Kim was concerned about the historical consciousness of divine action within the Korean historical setting—the period from the last phase of Japanese imperialism through the Korean War to the chaotic years of the 1970s. Kim related the divine providential care for Israel throughout her checkered history to the Korean situation. He believed that God had been intervening in the history of Korea and had called the Korean church to proclaim that the same God is saving the people from the dark situations in Korea. As a consequence, the kingdom of God that lives in a tangible historical setting, the restoration of human dignity, and the democratization of the country were all serious theological matters for Kim.[11]

Kim also had a concern for the ecclesiastical situation. During the 1920s and 1930s the Korean church's organization, ministry, and theological education were highly centralized under the leadership of the missionaries. Within this context, Park and Kim, who were both raised within conservative theological settings, had different ideas about the life of the church. While Park was concerned about the doctrinal purity of the church, being faithful to the teaching of the missionaries, Kim recognized the historical consciousness of God's saving work in the

10. Yeon, "A Study of Calvinist Theology," 130.
11. Ibid., 130–31.

Korean context, and he envisioned reforming the dogmatic exclusivism of the church. In this way, Kim's doctrine of Scripture was inevitably shaped by historical consciousness and eventually related to the emphasis on the reforming character of Calvinism.

Park's Orthodox Doctrine of Scripture

Park's theological stance was heavily shaped by the old Princeton theologians.[12] He considered the Calvinist church, especially its English Presbyterian expression, to be the most complete and perfect theological system because it most fully interprets Scripture and thus follows its teaching.[13] Given his strongly orthodox Calvinist convictions, Park claimed that the true theology is not to be re-created, but only to be transferred from one generation to another. The orthodox theology in Korea, he said, was received from the missionaries, and his task was to defend it against the challenges of liberalism and to transfer it to the next generation in its pure form. Park was an orthodox and conservative theologian in the purest sense. Park identified his orthodox theology with fundamentalism, a term he borrowed from his American experience, using Machen's *Christianity and Liberalism* as an authority. "Fundamentalism is nothing but orthodoxy and orthodox Christianity. Fundamentalism reflects such faith that believes the historical orthodox truth of Christianity and thus it must be a legitimate definition of it to say that Fundamentalism is Christianity itself."[14]

Park began his masterpiece on theology, *Theological Critique*, with an apology of the orthodox confession.[15] He set theological orthodoxy on an absolute basis: "True orthodoxy must be one . . . The ultimate authority that determines the eternal religious truth must be an absolute and unchangeable authority of the epistemological type . . . It is found

---

12. Park's theological method and prolegomena were shaped during his study at Princeton mostly by Charles Hodge, B. B. Warfield, and Gresham Machen, but his systematic theology was heavily dependent on Louis Berkhof's *Systematic Theology*. His teaching on the systematic loci was in fact a rearrangement of Berkhof. See Chang, *Theological Study*, 61–88; Kim, "Theology of Hyungryong Park," 235–36; Cha, "Principle of Hyungryong Park's Theology," 407–10; Choi, "Hyungryong Park," 167, 176–77.

13. Park, *Works*, 14:164–66.

14. Ibid., 13:280–81.

15. The *Theological Critique* is published at the beginning of Park's *Works*, vol. 8.

only in the Scripture that was recorded by heavenly inspiration. Only the religious statements that are purely based on it are to be considered part of the orthodox faith."[16] He moved on, saying, "The orthodox theology advocates a supernatural view of Scripture that takes the Old and New Testaments to be the Word of God that came to us through heavenly inspiration and thus Scripture is the ultimate rule for Christian faith and practice."[17] Any teaching that deviates from this orthodoxy must be judged as nonorthodox and thus heretical.[18] The ultimate authority of Scripture expressed in the equation of Scripture with the Word of God is the beginning and fundamental basis of his theology.

Though Park discussed the organic inspiration of Scripture in other places, he claimed an absolute authority of religious truth incontestably based on the divine origin of Scripture. Therefore, his theology tended to emphasize the divine element of Scripture and minimize or even deny the diversity of interpretation of Scripture. Park in fact identified his orthodox doctrine of Scripture as the only correct way of interpreting Scripture, based on the argument that it was the only way of reading it since it was given by divine inspiration.

This absolute sense of orthodoxy led him to use interchangeably such terms as "classical liberalism," as reflected by Schleiermacher, Ritschl, and Harnack on the one hand, and the "neo-orthodoxy" of Karl Barth on the other. To Park's orthodox point of view, a whole continuum of views belongs to the one category that denies the divine and infallible authority of Scripture and reconstructs theology on a human basis. Park considered them all "liberal" from this point of view.[19] When Park explained the orthodox view of Scripture against the "liberal" view of it, he made a sharp contrast between the way of knowing God through the absolutely reliable Word of Scripture and the way of knowing God through human experience. He did not allow any middle ground between the two. He criticized the neo-orthodox understanding of Scripture by saying that its christocentric view of Scripture was only a disguise to hide their humanism since they use tools of criticism.[20]

16. Ibid., 8:23–24.
17. Ibid., 8:26.
18. Ibid., 8:28.
19. Ibid., 8:28–41; Chang, *Theological Study*, 159.
20. Park, *Works*, 8:36–37.

For his doctrine of verbal and plenary inspiration of Scripture, Park appealed to the old Princeton theologians, such as Charles and A. A. Hodge and B. B. Warfield, and he appealed to Louis Berkhof for the theory of organic inspiration. He also used Luther and Calvin for his doctrine. He contended that "divine inspiration extends to all parts of Scripture so that it covers both every thought and every word of Scripture." From the definition of biblical inspiration Park moved to defend his position against a common criticism that his was a circular argument, and that it has relevance only to the original manuscript. Then he argued for the necessity of the doctrine of inerrancy as a consequence of verbal, plenary inspiration. Park was fully convinced that such doctrine is the demand of Scripture itself, and he claimed the doctrine as an absolute necessity for Christian faith: "Revelation becomes non-revelation if it is not inerrantly communicated and it becomes non-communication if it is not inerrantly recorded."[21]

Next, Park dealt with the issue of whether or not Scripture contains error. Against various "liberal" theologians, such as Jaejoon Kim and Harry Emerson Fosdick of Union Theological Seminary, he argued, first of all, that Scripture is not a scientific text, and, second, that there are no scientific, chronological, or moral errors in it: "The descriptions of natural movements in Scripture are not recorded to provide scientific explanations of nature, but are recorded as parts of processes to provide us with spiritual teaching. In such cases Scripture uses common or poetic language. When we face such descriptions in the Scripture, we should not expect them to be scientific." Park admitted the existence of some passages in Scripture that are difficult to explain with the present scientific and historical knowledge, but he categorically denied them to be proven errors of any kind.[22]

These words of Park did not put him in a defensive position against the authority of science. Rather, he boldly claimed that the truth of Scripture is compatible with scientific truth. A fuller compatibility will be achieved when science further develops and becomes able to explain those difficult passages of Scripture. Park even claimed that some of the biblical descriptions of physical phenomena such as in Job 26:7, Ps 135:7, Eccl 1:7, and Isa 40:22 are actually advanced beyond the

---

21. Ibid., 1:329–48.
22. Ibid., 8:39.

scientific knowledge of the days of the biblical authors. He emphasized the divine origin of Scripture with these examples. Park explained those alleged historical errors in the Scripture either as scribal errors or as arising from a deficiency of historical knowledge. He was convinced that historical and archeological findings would prove the truth of the Bible.[23] In these statements Park recognized human aspects of the biblical record, such as the biblical authors' limited scientific knowledge and their diverse ways of description, but for him the human aspects are fully under divine control in the recording of Scripture.

A claim for verbal inerrancy is a natural consequence of Park's claim for the absolute authority of Scripture. If orthodoxy is a single phenomenon, and it is based on Scripture, Scripture must be the ultimate authority for all Christian faith and practice. Scripture must be true both in itself and in our understanding of it. Then there must be one true way of interpreting it.

This exclusive view of Scripture was Park's basic perspective when reading Kim's doctrine of Scripture. During the 1930s through 1950s Park did not distinguish between scriptural inspiration and biblical hermeneutics. More precisely, Park did not recognize the possibility of diverse principles of biblical interpretation. He regarded all other interpretations besides his orthodox way, which was probably a more literal interpretation than others, as interpretations that deny the divine inspiration of Scripture. This rigid tendency is well expressed in his harsh criticism of Kim's doctrine of Scripture, by which Kim advocated a freer interpretation of Scripture since it is not a fixed doctrine but a living voice of God for given contexts. In the polemics with Park, Kim also did not develop the relationship between biblical inspiration and hermeneutics; he argued for the possibility of errors in the texts of Scripture and for the use of higher criticism and denied verbal inspiration.

Modern Reviewers

The disputes between Park and Kim on the doctrine of Scripture were basically wrought on the doctrinal level and thus left limited advice on the implications of such doctrines for the practice of reading. In light of this, it is interesting to see how recent scholars of both sides comment

---

23. Ibid., 8:39–40; see also ibid., 1:349–64.

The Doctrine of Scripture in the Calvinist Churches in Korea

on the dispute. Jichan Kim, an Old Testament scholar at Chongshin Theological Seminary, which has been the fortress of Park's orthodox theology, passionately advocates Park's verbal inspiration. Jichan Kim argues that Jaejoon Kim misunderstood Park's doctrine of verbal infallibility and placed a false dichotomy between knowing God through the personal relationship with Christ and knowing God through the verbally infallible text. Jaejoon Kim distinguishes between the letters of Scripture and the voice of God in his statement that to hold the orthodox doctrine of verbal infallibility is "to believe the letters that are materialized instead of Christ who is the subject of revelation." Jichan Kim is quite right in pointing out that Kim's false dichotomy was made for the sake of argument, for Park never separated the letters of Scripture from Christ in his doctrine of Scripture.[24] Park simply claimed that the Scripture has been inspired even down to the letters of the text. With this, he dealt with the issue of how the letters lead us to the voice, or thought, of God. Park wrote, appealing to Charles Hodge: "The doctrine of verbal inspiration . . . comes with both clear biblical and inferential evidence. Inspiration was designed with the purpose of communicating clearly the thoughts of divine revelation, and without proper use of words it's not possible to express the thoughts clearly. Thoughts are in words. They cannot be separated. If such words as sacrifices, atonement, compensation, reconciliation, and justification by blood do not have divine authority, the doctrines based on them shall lose divine authority."[25]

Jichan Kim suggests his own understanding of verbal inspiration in the line of Park's doctrine:

> Verbal inspiration is such a concept that is related to the forms and functions of words. It recounts how nouns, verbs, prepositions, and definite articles are used in a sentence. Verbal inspiration describes that the Holy Spirit inspired the human authors so that they could communicate the detailed meanings of the divine truth using their own linguistic and grammatical forms and literary styles. How can one better describe this phenomenon than with the term verbal inspiration? It is so, indeed, if we do not take the word "verbal" mechanically . . . Regarding Jaejoon Kim's theory of inspiration in terms of Christ who meets

24. Jichan Kim, "Hyungryong Park's Doctrine of Scripture," 82–83.
25. Park, *Works*, 1:320.

us in his person . . . the question we have to ask is how we meet such a Christ. Only those who have scrutinized the structures and meanings of the words and sentences of the biblical text are entitled to discuss the thoughts of the text.[26]

Jichan Kim argues for the same orthodox doctrine of verbal infallibility that Park did in the past, though not based on the dogmatic concepts of revelation and perfect divine attributes as Park did, but based on the function of the text of Scripture. For him, the doctrine of verbal infallibility is not simply a dogmatic assertion or a measuring stick to judge one's orthodoxy. Rather, it more importantly provides principles for reading the text of Scripture.

Park and Kim collided on the most significant issue between the two, namely, whether there is error in the Bible. Jaejoon Kim criticized Park by saying that it is a distortion of the facts and a sign of impiety to deny the presence of errors in the Bible. Park in return condemned Kim for his denial of the fundamental truth of divine revelation. While they agreed that Scripture is not a scientific text, they parted sharply on the issue of error. Park argued that since it is not a scientific text, it is not legitimate to attempt to prove or even to discuss scientific errors in its text, and he claimed that there is no error whatsoever in it. For Park, the issue of error in the Bible was a fundamental issue. He quickly admitted that there are some difficult texts to explain now in terms of scientific knowledge, but they are only difficult texts, not errors.

Jaejoon Kim, on the other hand, contended that since Scripture is not a scientific text, that is, since it was not scientifically written, it is possible to have errors, and that in fact this is the case. The errors, however, never pose a problem for Kim, since the authority of Scripture does not depend on the letters, the form, but on its function as a witness to Christ. This is the fact of Scripture, he said. Knowing God is not by the letters but by the personal meeting with Christ. Kim was confident about the positive role of higher criticism to help find the meaning of the text. Kim did not seem to attempt to diminish the authority of Scripture along the lines of liberal theology, as Park criticized. Kim even seemed to share the same goal as Park: to define the nature of the authority of Scripture for the church of their homeland. But Park and Kim clashed bitterly on where the authority lies.

26. Jichan Kim, "Hyungryong Park's Doctrine of Scripture," 85.

Jaejoon Kim criticized Park for his literal interpretation of Scripture. Contrary to Kim's criticism, Jichan Kim points out that Park never read the Bible literally when he argued for verbal infallibility. Though Park warned against spiritual interpretation and the use of higher criticism, for fear of altering the natural sense of Scripture, he admitted the implications of organic inspiration in the interpretation of the text. In fact, asserts Jichan Kim, it was Jaejoon Kim who read the text literally when he claimed to find errors in the Bible. Jaejoon Kim claimed there is a scientific error in the description of the creation account. He wrote: "The Bible reads that the earth is floating over the water, heaven is fixed on the poles, and there is *sheol* under the earth and all dead souls move there. Isn't this description an example of a scientific error?"[27]

Jaejoon Kim supported the idea of the organic inspiration of the Bible, and thus he accepted a certain divine authority of the text. However, his polemical stance against Park's orthodoxy, which was increasingly intensified by his use of literary criticism, forced Kim to challenge the orthodox foundation that the biblical text is free from errors of any kind. When Kim claimed he found errors in the biblical text, he did so only by compromising his idea of organic inspiration. The alleged errors were found when he read the text literally from his modern, scientific point of view, not from the biblical authors' cultural point of view. That literal reading was exactly the method of reading the text with which he criticized Park's orthodox theology.[28]

Another reviewer of the debate is Kyuhong Yeon, and at the center of his modern argument for Jaejoon Kim's doctrine of Scripture, which heavily appeals to Calvin's *Institutes*, is the neo-orthodox distinction between Christ as the Word himself and the subject of revelation, on the one hand, and Scripture as a tool to witness to him, on the other hand. Since Scripture witnesses to the divine truth revealed in Christ, Scripture is not truth itself. Thus, inspiration of Scripture belongs to the Word, Christ himself, and not to the letters of Scripture. While the letters by themselves are letters that kill, they work the wonders of God with the inner witness of the Holy Spirit.[29]

27. Cited in Jichan Kim, "Hyungryong Park's Doctrine of Scripture," 89.

28. Jaejoon Kim, "Verbal inspiration," 1–3; Jichan Kim, "Hyungryong Park's Doctrine of Scripture," 89.

29. Yeon, "A Study of Calvinist Theology," 152–55.

It is noteworthy that Yeon, seventy years later, shares the same fear as Kim. They are afraid to equate the Word of God and Scripture since, they think, the equation allegedly presupposes a mechanical theory of inspiration and would lead to dogmatism and rigid ecclesiastical authority and would eventually deny the freedom to interpret the text. Thus, they make a sharp distinction between the soteriological aspect of the authority of Scripture and the doctrine of verbal inspiration. The former describes the function of Scripture as a tool the Holy Spirit uses to witness to Jesus Christ. Then the infallibility of Scripture can be explained in terms of the infallible meaning or teaching of the message of Scripture. Yeon explains the latter, that is, the doctrine of verbal inspiration, as the product of the Holy Spirit's dictation and thus as the storehouse of eternally fixed propositional truths. In this way, Yeon poses the dichotomy and argues that church must choose one or the other.

This is a false dichotomy. First, Park never based the divine authority of Scripture on the dictation theory of inspiration. Though his theology tended to be generally fundamentalist and propositional, he fully advocated the organic theory of inspiration. Second, it is a wrongly posed dichotomy because the doctrine of verbal inspiration may be compatible with the soteriological emphasis of scriptural authority. As long as the verbal inspiration takes Christ as the center of divine revelation by the inner witness of the Holy Spirit, there is no dichotomy. No one on the orthodox side would deny this compatibility. Indeed, the doctrine of verbal inspiration does not necessarily imply or lead to natural or rationalist theology.

The burden is on Kim and Yeon to demonstrate that the verbal inspiration and verbal infallibility of Scripture are invalid, either biblically or theologically. That's why both argued for the presence of errors in the Bible. However, Kim's argument for such errors causes another problem, as mentioned earlier. For the errors in the Bible are recognized only when he reads the text out of the context of organic inspiration which he so strongly advocated.

Kim's doctrine of Scripture should be understood within the Korean historical context of his day. It might have been the misuse of dogmatic orthodoxy and not the orthodox confession itself that Kim was actually criticizing, for the immediate context of Kim's doctrine of Scripture was his recognition of the imperialistic dogmatism of the missionaries and their orthodox exclusivism. Kim charged Park with "slavishly" following the missionaries without thinking critically. Kim lamented the abuse of ecclesiastical authority and a dogmatism that displaces the freedom of conscience and dynamic faith, and he believed these losses were damaging the church of Korea.[30] Kim tried to provide a sound theology with the living voice of God, using the tools of biblical criticism, for a people who were under oppression, but the contribution he made has been misunderstood and neglected by his opponents.

Park was more concerned about doctrinal purity during the initial and challenging years of the church in Korea. Diverse theological traditions that had been shaped and developed over a long period of time in the West were introduced to the Korean church within a short period of time. Without the luxury of extensive theological study, leaders of the Korean church were compelled to preach, teach, and educate younger generation of the church. Park used the theological system, terms, and conflicts of the West to analyze theological thoughts, judge the unorthodox, and organize the orthodox theological system of his church. He understood all of the challenges found in his contemporary church to be altered forms of the rationalist and liberal theologies of the West. In this way he himself might have been confused about the diverse theological trends and have bequeathed confusion and a misconception of the terms to the coming generations of his church. His view of reading theology was the conflict between liberalism and fundamentalism. At the center of this conflict, he believed, was the doctrine of Scripture.

---

30. Choi, "Theological Exclusivism," 211–12; see also Park, "Hyungryong Park," 59–60; Shim, "A Study of Theological Thought," 13.

Bibliography

Unpublished Sources

Den Haag, Koninklijke Bibliotheek: Hs KA XLVIII.
Nîmes: Archives du Gard: 42 J 27, Registre du consistoire de l'église chrestienne de la ville du Nismes, (1578–83).
Paris: La Bibliothèque de la Société de l'Histoire du Protestantisme Français: MS 566/ 1, Synodes provinciaux du Bas-Languedoc (1561–1595).

Works Written before 1800

Alesius, Alexander. *Expositio Prioris Epistolae ad Timotheum*. S.l., 1550.
Ambrosiaster qui dicitur commentarius in Epistulas Paulinas: Pars Tertia. . . ad Timotheum. Edited by H. J. Vogels. Corpus Scriptorum Ecclesiasticorum Latinorum 81/2. Vienna: Hoelder-Pichler-Tempsky, 1968.
Antwoordt op de malitieuse calumnie der contra-remonstranten in de Vereenighde Nederlanden. S.l, 1620.
Aquinas, Thomas, Saint. *Summa theologiae cura fratrum in eiusdem ordinis*. 5 vols. Madrid: Biblioteca de Autores Cristianos, 1962–1965.
Augustine, Saint. *Letters 100–155*. Edited by Boniface Ramsey. Translated and notes by Roland Teske. The Works of Saint Augustine. Hyde Park, NY: New City, 2003.
Aymon, Jean, editor. *Actes Ecclesiastiques et civiles de tous les synodes nationaux des eglises reformées de France*. 2 vols. The Hague, 1710.
Basil, Saint. *Opera D. Basilii magni Caesariae Cappadociae episcopi omnia, recens versa, sive ad Graecos archetypos ita collata per Wolfgangum Musculum Dusanum, ut aliam omnino faciem sumpsis se videantur*. Basel: Herwagen, 1545.
Biblia Latina cum glossa ordinaria. Facsimile edition of Adolph Rusch of Strassburg 1480/81. Edited by Karlfried Froehlich and M. T. Gibson. Brepols: Turnhout, 1992.
Bibliotheca Reformatoria Neerlandica. Vol. 7. Edited by S. Cramer and F. Pijper. 's-Gravenhage: Martinus Nijhoff, 1910.
Borrhaus, Martin. *In sacram Josuae, Judicum, Ruthae, Samuelis, & Regum Historiam* Basel: Oporinus, 1557.

Bibliography

Brandt, Caspar. *The Life of James Arminius, D.D.* Translated by John Guthrie, introduction by T. O. Summers. Nashville: Stevenson and Owen, 1857.

Brandt, Gerard. *The History of the Reformation and Other Ecclesiastical Transactions in and about the Low-Countries, from the Beginning of the Eighth Century, Down to the Famous Synod of Dordt, inclusive.* vol 3. London: Printed by T. Wood, for John Nicks, 1722.

Bugenhagen, Johannes. *Annotationes ab ipso iam emissae in Deuteronomium, in Samuelem prophetam* . . . Basel: Petri, 1524.

———. *Annotationes . . . in decem epistolas Pauli* . . . Basel: Petri, 1525.

Bullinger, Heinrich. *De testamento seu foedere Dei unico & aeterno brevis expositio.* Zurich: Froschauer, 1534.

———. *In omnes apostolicas epistolas divi videlicet Pauli et VII canonicas, commentarii.* Zurich: Froschauer, 1537.

Cajetan (Tommaso de Vio). *Epistolae Pauli et aliorum Apostolorum. . . iuxta sensum literalem enarratae.* Venice, 1531.

———. *In omnes authenticos Veteris Testamenti historiales libros commentarii.* Rome: Antonius Bladius, 1533.

Calckman, Jan Jansz. *Antidotum, tegen-gift vant gebruyck of on-gebruyck vant orgel inde kercken der Vereenighde Nederlanden.* 's-Gravenhage: Aert van Meurs, 1641.

Calvin, John. *The Bondage and Liberation of the Will: A Defense of the Orthodox Doctrine of Human Choice against Pighius.* Edited by Anthony N. S. Lane. Translated by G. I. Davis. Texts and Studies in Reformation and Post-Reformation Thought 2. Grand Rapids: Baker, 1996.

———. *Commentaries on the Epistles to Timothy, Titus, and Philemon.* Edited by W. Pringle. Edinburgh: Calvin Translation Society, 1856.

———. *Commentaries on the First Book of Moses called Genesis.* Edited by J. King. 2 vols. Edinburgh: Calvin Translation Society, 1847–1850.

———. *Commentaries on the Prophet Ezekiel.* Edited by T. Myers. Edinburgh: Calvin Translation Society, 1850.

———. *Commentaries on the Prophet Jeremiah and the Lamentations.* Edited by J. Owen. Edinburgh: Calvin Translation Society, 1850.

———. *Commentary on the Book of Psalms.* Translated by James Anderson. 5 vols. Grand Rapids: Baker, 1979.

———. *Commentary on the Book of the Prophet Isaiah.* Edited by W. Pringle. Edinburgh: Calvin Translation Society, 1852–1853.

———. *Commentaries on the Catholic Epistles by John Calvin.* Edited by J. Owen. Edinburgh: Calvin Translation Society, 1850.

———. *The First and Second Epistles of Paul to the Corinthians and the Epistles to Timothy, Titus and Philemon.* Translated by T. A. Smail. Edinburgh: St. Andrews, 1964.

———. *La Forme des Prières et chantz ecclesiastiques, avec la maniere d'administrer les sacramens, & consacrer le marriage: selon la coustume de l'Eglise ancienne.* [Geneva:] 1542.

———. *Institutes of the Christian Religion.* Edited by John T. McNeill, translated by Ford Lewis Battles. 2 vols. Library of Christian Classics, 20–21. Philadelphia: Westminster, 1960.

———. *Institution of the Christian Religion 1536.* Edited and translated by F. L. Battles. Atlanta: John Knox, 1975.

---. *Jean Calvin. Institution de la religion chrétienne. Edition Critique.* Edited by Olivier Millet. Textes littéraires français 598. Geneva: Droz, 2008.
---. *Opera quae supersunt omnia.* Edited by Wilhelm Baum, et al. Corpus Reformatorum 29–87. Braunschweig: Schwetschke, 1863–1900.
---. *Opera Selecta.* Edited by P. Barth, et al. 5 vols. Munich: Kaiser, 1926–1959.
---. *Selected Works of John Calvin: Tracts and Letters.* Edited by H. Beveridge and Jules Bonnet. 7 vols. Edinburgh: Calvin Translation Society, 1844–1858. Reprint, Grand Rapids: Baker, 1983.
---. *Sermon où il est montré quelle doit être la modestie des femmes en leurs habillements.* Caen, 1561.
---. *Sermons of Maister John Calvin upon the Booke of Iob.* Translated by Arthur Golding. London, 1574.
---. *La Vraie façon de réformer l'Eglise chrétienne et d'apaiser les différends qui sont en elle.* Edited by Eric Fuchs. Paris: Labor et Fides, 1957.
Carney, Frederick S., abridger and translator. *The Politics of Johannes Althusius.* Beacon Series in the Sociology of Politics and Religion. Boston: Beacon, 1964.
Catechesis continens explicationem simplicem, et breuem, Decalogi: Symboli Apostolici: orationis Dominicae: Doctrinae de poenitentia: et sacramentis. Contexta ex Corpore Doctrinae Christianae... Leipzig, 1571.
Chrestienne instruction touchant la pompe et excez des hommes débordez et femmes dissolues en la curiosité de leurs parures et attifemens d'habits qu'ils portent, contravenans à la doctrine de Dieu, et a toute modestie Chrestienne. S.l., 1551.
Christelijcke waerschouwinghen teghen de principaelste lasteringhen ende leughenen Calvini. Antwerp: Hieronymus Verdussen, 1609.
Chrysostom, John. *Old Testament Homilies.* Vol. 1, *Homilies on Hannah, David and Saul.* Translated and Introduction by Robert C. Hill. Brookline, MA: Holy Cross Orthodox Press, 2003.
Coornhert, Dirck Volckertsz. *Dierck Volckertsz Coornherts Wercken. Waer van eenige noyt voor desen gedruckt zyn.* Amsterdam: Colom, 1630.
---. *Synodus vander conscientien vryheyt, eerste deel.* Haarlem: Ketel, 1582.
---. *Een corte confutatie of wederlegghinge: gheschreven teghen een ketters boecxken, ghenaemt, corte belijdinghe des gheloofs.* Louvain: Boogaerts, 1567.
Coster, Franciscus. *Antwoorde... veur het eerste deel van sijn hand-boeck ghenaemt Schild der Catholijcken: teghen Franciscum Gomarum Calvinisch Leeraer inde Schole van Leyden. Wt het Latijn in onse Neder-landsche spraecke overgheset.* Antwerp: Moerentorf, 1604.
Cruciger, Caspar. *In Epistolae Pauli ad Timotheum.* Strasbourg, 1540.
Danckaerts, Sebastiaan. *Cattechismus Attau Adjaran Derri Agamma Christaon.* 's-Gravenhage: Hillebrant Jacobsz van Wouw, 1623.
Daneau, Lambert. *Deux Traitez de Florent Tertullian, docteur tres-ancien, et voisin du temps des apostres, environ CLXX ans apres l'incarnation de Iesus Christ l'un des parures et ornemens: l'autre des habits et accoustremens des femmes Chrestiennes. Plus un traité de sainct Cyprian evesque de Carthage, touchant la discipline et les habits des filles.* Geneva, 1580.
---. *Traite de l'estat honneste des Chrestiens en leur accoustrement.* Geneva, 1580.
de Sales, François. *Introduction to the Devout Life* (3/25). Edited and translated by W. H. Hutchings. London: Longmans, 1913.

Bibliography

Denis, the Carthusian. *Opera omnia in unum corpus digesta* . . . Montreuil-sur-Mer: Carthusians of St. Mary of Prato, 1896–1913.

Duncanus, Martinus. *Catholijcke catechismus, met wederlegginghe van der Heydelbersche ofte ghereformeerde catechismus met vraghe ende antwoort.* Antwerp: Verdussen, 1594.

Erasmus, Desiderius. *Desiderii Erasmi Roterodami Opera Omnia.* Edited by Jean Le Clerc. Leiden: 1703–6. London: Gregg, 1962.

Eusebius of Caesarea. *Church History.* A Select Library of the Nicene and Post-Nicene Fathers, 2 ser., 1. New York: Christian Literature Company, 1890.

Francis, de Sales, Saint. *Introduction to the Devout Life.* Edited and translated by W. H. Hutchings. London: Longmans, 1913.

Frossard, Ch-L., editor. *Recueil de reglements extraits des actes des synodes provinciaux tenu dans la province du Bas-Languedoc de 1568 à 1623.* Paris: Grassart, 1885.

Gomarus, Franciscus. *Disputationem theologicarum decima-quarta, de libero arbitrio.* Leiden: J. Patius, 1603.

Grotius, Hugo. *De iure belli ac pacis libri tres.* Paris, 1625.

Harmonia Confessionvm Fidei, orthodoxarum & reformatarum ecclesiarum. Geneva: Santandreanus, 1581.

Hartknoch, Christoph. *Preussische Kirchen-Historia.*.. Frankfurt: Beckenstein, 1686.

Hessels, J. H. *Ecclesiae Londino-Batavae Archivvm.* 4 vols. Cambridge: Typis Academiae, sumptibus Ecclesiae Londino Batavae, 1887–1897.

Heurnius, Justus. *Jang Ampat Evangelia Derri Tuan Kita Jesv Christi, daan Berboatan Derri Jang Apostolic Bersacti, Bersallin Dallam Bassa Malayo.* Oxford: H. Hall, 1677.

———. *Vocabularium; Ofte Worden-Boek Nae Ordre van den Alphabeth, in't Duytsch en Maleisch.* Amsterdam: VOC, 1650.

Hobbes, Thomas. *Leviathan.* New York: Dutton, 1950.

Hugh of St. Cher. *Opera omnia.* Venice: Pezzana, 1703.

Hughes, Philip Edgcumbe, editor. *The Register of the Company of Pastors of Geneva in the Time of Calvin.* Grand Rapids: Eerdmans, 1966.

Ioannes Calvinus. Vreedt, bitter, vals. Antwerp: Mesens, 1619.

Iperen, Josua van. *Kerkelijke historie van het psalm-gezang der christenen, van de dagen der apostelen af, tot op onzen tegenwoordigen tyd toe; en inzonderheid van onze verbeterde Nederduitsche psalmberyminge.* Amsterdam: Loveringh en Allart, 1778.

Jansenius van Hulst, Cornelius. *Een corte confutatie of wederlegghinghe: gheschreven teghen een ketters boecxken, ghenaemt, corte belijdinghe des gheloofs: dwelck over al in Nederlandt ghestroydt wordt.* Louvain: Boogaerts, 1567.

Jewel, John. *A Defence of the Apologie of the Church of England, conteining an answer to a certaine booke lately set forth by M. Harding.* London: Norton, 1611.

John of Damascus, Saint. *De fide orthodoxa.* A Select Library of the Nicene and Post-Nicene Fathers, 2 ser., 9. New York: Christian Literature Company, 1899.

Kingdon, Robert M., et al., editors. *Registers of the Consistory of Geneva in the Time of Calvin.* Vol. 1: *1542–1544.* Translated by M. Wallace McDonald. Grand Rapids: Eerdmans, 2000.

Knuttel, W. P. C. *Acta der particuliere synoden van Zuid-Holland, 1621–1700.* 's-Gravenhage: Nijhoff, 1908.

Lasco, Johannes a. *Joannis a Lasco Opera tam edita quam inedita.* Edited by Abraham Kuyper. 3 parts in 2 vols. Amsterdam: Muller, 1866.

Bibliography

Leigh, Edward. *A Systeme or Body of Divinity: consisting of ten books wherein the fundamentals and main grounds of religion are opened.* 2nd ed. London: A. M. for William Lee, 1662.

Limborch, Philippus van, and Christiaan Hartsoeker, editors. *Praestantium ac eruditorum virorum epistolae ecclesiasticae et theologicae, quarum longe major pars scripta est a Jac. Arminio, editio secunda, ab innumeris mendis repurgata, & altera parte auctior.* Amsterdam: Wetstenius, 1684.

Locke, John. *Second Treatise of Civil Government.* Amherst, NY: Prometheus, 1986.

Loyseleur de Villiers, Pierre. *Ratio ineundae Concordiae inter Ecclesias Reformatas. Siue Quibus modis occurri posit mirificis artibus, quibus Pontificij per quosdam imprudentes Theologos vniuersas Christi ecclesias potissimum autem & primum Germanicas pessundare conantur . . .* [s.l.] 1579.

Luis, de Granada. *A Memoriall of a Christian Life.* Translated by Richard Hopkins. London: Loyselet, 1599.

Luther, Martin. *Luther's Works.* Edited by Jaroslav Pelikan and Helmut T. Lehmann. 55 vols. St. Louis: Concordia, 1955–86.

———. *Werke. Kritische Gesamtausgabe.* Weimar: Böhlaus Nachfolger, 1883–1986.

Maccovius, Johannes. *Distinctiones et regulae theologicae et philosophicae.* Amsterdam: Elzevir, 1656.

Marlorat, Augustin. *A Catholike and ecclesiasticall exposition of the Holy Gospell after S. Matthew, gathered out of all the singular and approved divines.* London: Marsh, 1570.

———. *A Catholike . . . exposition of St. Marke and Luke.* 2 parts. London: Marsh, 1583.

Mayer, John. *A Commentarie upon the New Testament. Representing the divers expositions thereof, out of the workes of the most learned, both ancient Fathers, and moderne Writers.* 3 vols. London: Cotes and Haviland, 1631.

———. *A Commentary upon the Whole Old Testament; consisting of four parts, I The Pentateuch, or five Books of Moses. II The Historicall Part, from Joshua to Esther. III Job, Psalms, Proverbs, Ecclesiastes, and Solomons Song. IV All the Prophets, both great and Small,* 4 vols. London: R.L. and R.I., 1654.

Melanchthon, Philipp. *Opera quae supersunt omnia.* Edited by Karl Bretschneider, et al. Corpus Reformatorum 1–28. 1834–1860. New York: Johnson, 1963.

———. *Melanchthons Werke in Auswahl.* Vol. 6, *Bekenntnisse und kleine Lehrschriften.* Edited by Robert Stupperich. 7 bks. in 9 vols. Gütersloh: Mohn, 1955.

McKee, Elsie Anne, editor. *John Calvin: Writings on Pastoral Piety.* Classics of Western Spirituality. New York: Paulist, 2001.

Ménard, Léon. *Histoire civile, ecclésiastique et littéraire de la ville de Nîmes.* Paris, 1753. Reprint, Marseille: Lafitte, 1976.

Migne, J. P., editor. *Patrologiae cursus completus, Series Graeca.* 162 vols. Paris, 1857–1866.

———. *Patrologiae cursus completus, Series Latina.* 217 vols. Paris, 1844–1864.

Mörlin, Joachim. *Wider die Landlügen / der Heidelbergischen Theologen.* Eisleben: Petri, 1565.

Musculus, Wolfgang. *Loci communes sacrae theologiae.* Basel: Iohannes Herwagen, 1560; 3rd edition, 1573.

Olin, John C., editor. *A Reformation Debate: Sadoleto's Letter to the Genevans and Calvin's Reply; John Calvin and Jacopo Sadoleto.* New York: Fordham University Press, 2000.

Bibliography

Pellican, Conrad. *Commentaria Bibliorum. . . Tomus Secundus in quo continetur. . . Samuelis . . .* Zurich: Froschauer, 1533.

———. *In omnes apostolicas epistolas. . . commentarii.* Zurich: Froschauer, 1539.

Perkins, William. *The Whole Works of that famous and worthy minister of Christ.* 3 vols. London: Legatt, 1631.

Petronius, J. *Kettersche spinnecoppe.* Brussels: Velpius, 1598.

Polanus von Polansdorf, Amandus. *Syntagma theologiae christianae.* Editio absolutissima. Geneva: Albertus, 1617.

Poole, Matthew. *Synopsis criticorum aliorumque sacrae scripturae interpretum et commentatorum, summo studio et fide adornata.* 5 vols. London: Flesher & Roycroft, 1669–1676.

Postilla super total Bibliam. Facsimile of Strassburg 1492 edition. 4 vols. Frankfurt: Minerva, 1971.

Protocol. Dat is alle handelinge des gespreeks tot Embden in Oostvrieslant met den wederdooperen. Emden: Goossen Goebens, 1579.

Protocol. Dat is, de gantsche handelinge des ghesprecx ghehouden tot Leeuwarden in Vrieslandt, tusschen Ruardum Acronium dienaer des Godlijcken woordts ter eenre, ende Peeter van Ceulen dienaer by de Mennisten ofte Wederdooperen ter ander syden: Begonnen den 16. Augusti 1596 ende voleyndighet den 17. Novembris des selvighen jaers. Franeker: vanden Rade, 1597.

Ratelwachts Roep: recht, tegent boeck vanden schijnduechtsamen engel, ofte geest Cornelis van Hil, predikant gheweest zijnde tot Alckmaer. S.l., 1611.

Reitsma, J., and S. D. van Veen. *Acta der Provinciale en Particuliere Synoden, gehouden in de Noordelijke Nederlanden gedurende de jaren 1572–1620.* 8 vols. [Groningen: Wolters, 1892–1899].

Retortie ofte weder-steeck, gheheven met de smadelijcke sift by eenighe bittere calvinisten, ende calumniateurs in figuren af-ghebeeldet, ende met rijmen beduydet en uyt-geleyt. S.l., 1619.

Revius, Jacobus, and Wisse Alfred Pierre Smit. *Over-ysselsche sangen en dichten.* Amsterdam: Uitgeversmaatschappij Holland, 1935.

Rivetus, Andreas. *Critici sacri libri IV. In quibus expenduntur, confirmantur, defenduntur, vel rejiciuntur censurae doctorum tam orthodoxus quam pontificiis,* fourth edition. Geneva: Chouet, 1642.

Rutgers, F. L., editor. *Acta van de Nederlandsche synoden der zestiende eeuw.* 's-Gravenhage: Nijhoff, 1899. Dordrecht: van den Tol, 1980.

Scherp-sinnighe characteren. Antwerp: Lesteens, 1622.

Schoock, Martinus. *Exercitationes variae, de diversis materiis, quae hac editione nova tum locupletatae et vindicatae.* Trajecti ad Rhenum: à Zyll, 1663.

Scultetus, Abraham. *Medulla theologiae patrum: qui a temporibus apostolorum ad Consilium quuque Nicenum floruerunt methodo analytica & synthetica expressa.* Amberg: Forster, 1598.

Sendbrieff Der KirchenDiener, so in den Reformirten Kirchen der Niderlanden das wort Gottes Predigen. Geschrieben An die Autores oder Schreiber deß Bergischen Buchs, welches sie das Concordien Buch nennen. S.l., 1580.

Skolnitsky, Seth, editor. *Men, Women, and Order in the Church: Three Sermons by John Calvin.* Dallas: Presbyterian Heritage, 1992.

Speuij, Henderick Joostensz. *De Psalmen Davids, gestelt op het Tabulatuer van het Orghel.* Dordrecht: Verhaghen, 1610.

Bibliography

Toussaint van Boelaere, F. V., editor. *Twee XVIe eeuwsche dialogen.* Antwerp: De Nederlandsche Boekhandel, 1945.

Turretin, Francis. *Institutio theologiae elencticae.* 3 vols. Geneva: Samuel des Tournes, 1679–1685.

Val, Anthoine de. *Den spieghel der calvinisten, ende die wapenen der christenen, om die lutheranen ende nieuwe evangelisten van Geneven te wederstaen.* Antwerp: Tronaesius, 1567.

Valentyn, François. *Oud en Nieuw Oost-Indiën.* Dordrecht: Van Braam, 1724.

Vant swingelsche calff, off descriptie des swingelsche calff, waer inne bewesen wordt . . . dat die caluinisten predicanten Gods wordt . . . niet en hebben. Een oprechte patriot, ende een waerachtich lieffhebber des gherechte ende lysamighe wordt Christi Jesu. 's-Hertogenbosch: Scheffer, [1580].

Venatorius, Thomas. *In Divi Pauli Apostoli Priorem ad Timotheum epistolam distributiones XX.* Basel: Cratander, 1533.

Vente, Maarten, and C. C. Vlam, editors. *Documentaet archivalia ad historiam musicæ neerlandicæ. Bouwstenen voor een geschiedenis der toonkunst in de Nederlanden.* Amsterdam: Vereniging voor Nederlandse Muziekgeschiedenis, 1965.

Vermigli, Peter Martyr. *The Common Places of Peter Martyr.* Translated by Anthony Marten. London: Denham et al., 1583.

———. *In duos libros Samuelis . . . commentarii.* Zurich: Christoph Froschauer, 1564.

[Verstegen, Richard]. *Nederlantsche antiquiteiten.* Antwerp: Gaspar Bellerus, 1613.

———. *Oorspronck ende teghenwoordighen staet van de calvinische secte.* Antwerp: Bruneau, 1611.

Voetius, Gisbertus. *[Liber de] Politicae Ecclesiasticae.* Amsterdam: Joannis à Waesberge, 1663–1676.

Voor-looper van sommighe swaricheden ghemoveert ende vraechse wijse voorghestelt by ettelijcke oude, vrome, eenvoudighe, ende treffelijcke patriotten. 's Gravenhage 1620.

Waterworth, J., editor and translator. *The Canon and Decrees of the Sacred and Oecumenical Council of Trent.* London: Burns & Oates, 1848.

Wevers, Richard F. *Institutes of the Christian Religion of John Calvin 1539: Text and Concordance.* 4 vols. Grand Rapids: The Meeter Center for Calvin Studies at Calvin College and Seminary, 1988.

Wigand, Johannes. *Analysis exegeseos Sacramentariae, sparsae in sede Lvtheri. . . .* Königsberg: Daubmann, 1574.

———. *Cavsae, cvr in Coenae Dominicae Verbis το ρετον sit retinendvm . . .* Jena: Ritzenhan, 1571.

———. *Christliche Erinnerung Von der Bekentnis der Theologen in Meissen vom Abendmal Jetzt newlich außgangen. . . .* Königsberg: Daubman, 1574.

———. *Commonefactio de fravdibus qvorvndam sacramentariorum. Opposita scripto anonymo de ratione inevndae concordiae.* Wittenberg, 1579.

———. *De Sacramentarijsmo, Dogmata et Argvmenta ex qvatvor patriarchis sacramentariorum, Carlstadio. Zwinglio, Oecolampadio, Calvino potissimum, & quibusdem alijs . . . Item: De Schismate Sacramentario . . .* Leipzig: Dafner, 1585.

———. *Ex Sidonii Catechismo maiore seu Institutione de pietate. . .* Magdeburg, 1550.

———. *Synopsis. Oder Spiegel des römischen Antichrists durch den Geist des mundes Gottes offenbaret . . .* Jena, 1560.

Bibliography

———. *De vbiqvitate sev omnipraesentia Dei. In genere, in specie, in sua Ecclesia. Hvmanae naturae in persona Christi, in toto mundo. In Dominico. In Ecclesia, & in credentibus. Consideratio Methodica*. . . . Königsberg: Osterbergen, 1588.

———. *Verlegung aus Gottes wordt des Catechismi der Jhesuiten, Summa doctrinae Christianae genand*. Magdeburg, 1556.

———. *Vrsachen Warumb Christliche Oberkeit vnd Gemeine / die Sacramentirische Lehre vnd Lehrer nicht leiden sollen. Zur erinnerung vnd warnung verzeichnet*. Königsberg: Osterbergen, 1583.

———. *Warnung vor dem Catechismo D. Canisii, des grossen Jhesuwidders*. . . Jena, 1570.

[Wigand, Johannes, et al.] *Von den Fallstricken Etlicher newer Sacramentschwermer zu Wittenberg im newen Bekentnis listiglich verstecket die Welt damit zu beru[e]cken vn zuuerfu[e]ren. Erinnerung vnd Warnung Durch die Theologen zu Jhena*. Jena, 1572.

Witsius, Herman. *De oeconomia foederum Dei cum hominibus libri quattuor*. Second edition. Leeuwarden: J. Hagenaar, 1677.

The Zurich Letters, or the Correspondence of several English bishops and others, with some of the Helvetian Reformers, series 3, vol. 2. Cambridge: Cambridge University Press, 1847.

Zwingli, Ulrich. *Huldreich Zwinglis sämtliche Werke*. Edited by Emil Egli, et al. Corpus Reformatorum 88–101. Leipzig: Heinsius, 1905–1991.

———. *Ulrich Zwingli (1484-1531): Selected Works*. Edited by Samuel Macauley Jackson. Pennsylvania Paperback 49. Philadelphia: University of Pennsylvania Press, 1972.

Works Written after 1800

Ackermans, Gian. *Herders en Huurlingen. Bisschoppen en priesters in de Republiek (1663–1705). Cultuurgeschiedenis van de Republiek in de 17de eeuw*. Amsterdam: Prometeus/Bakker, 2003.

Anderson, Janice Capel. "Reading Tabitha: A Feminist Reception History." In *A Feminist Companion to the Acts of the Apostles*, edited by Amy-Jill Levine with Marianne Blickenstaff, 22–48. Feminist Companion to the New Testament and Early Christian Writings 9. New York: T. & T. Clark, 2004.

Andriessen, Jozef. *De Jezuïeten en het samenhorigheidsbesef der Nederlanden 1585–1648*. Antwerp: De Nederlandsche Boekhandel, 1957.

Arendt, Hannah. *The Human Condition*. Chicago: University of Chicago Press, 1958.

Aritonang, Jan Sihar, and Karel Steenbrik. *A History of Christianity in Indonesia*. Studies in Christian Mission 35. Leiden: Brill, 2008.

Arthur, Linda, editor. *Religion, Dress and the Body*. Dress, Body, Culture. Oxford: Berg, 1999.

Aughterson, Kate, editor. *Renaissance Woman: A Sourcebook; Constructions of Femininity in England*. London: Routledge, 1995.

Augustijn, Cornelis. "Die Reformierte Kirche in den Niederlanden und der Libertinismus in der zweiten Hälfte des 16. Jahrhunderts." In *Querdenken. Dissens und Toleranz im Wandel der Geschichte*, edited by Michael Erbe, 107–21. Mannheim: Palatium, 1996.

Bibliography

Backus, Irena. "The Fathers in Calvinist Orthodoxy: Patristic Scholarship." In *Reception of the Church Fathers in the West: From the Carolingians to the Maurists*, edited by Irena Backus, 2:839-66. 2 vols. Leiden: Brill, 1997.

———. *Lectures humanistes de Basile de Césarée. Traductions latines (1439-1618)*. Collection des études augustiniennes. Série Antiquité 125. Paris: Institut d'études augustiniennes, 1990.

———. *Life Writing in Reformation Europe: Lives of Reformers by Friends, Disciples and Foes*. St. Andrews Studies in Reformation History. Aldershot, UK: Ashgate, 2008.

Baker, Gordon P., and P. M. S. Hacker. *An Analytical Commentary on the "Philosophical Investigations."* 4 vols. Chicago: University of Chicago Press, 1980-1996.

Baker, J. Wayne. *Heinrich Bullinger and the Covenant: The Other Reformed Tradition*. Athens: Ohio University Press, 1980.

Balfoort, D. J. *Het muziekleven in Nederland in de 17de en 18de eeuw*. Amsterdam: P. N. van Kampen & Zoon, 1938.

Barth, Karl. *The Theology of John Calvin*. Translated by G. W. Bromiley. Grand Rapids: Eerdmans, 1995.

Battles, F. L. "Against Luxury and License in Geneva: A Forgotten Fragment of Calvin." *Interpretation* 19 (1965) 182-202.

Bauer, Susan Wise. *The Art of the Public Grovel: Sexual Sin and Public Confession in America*. Princeton: Princeton University Press, 2008.

Bavinck, Johann H. *Zending in Een Wereld in Nood*. Wageningen, Netherlands: Zomer & Keuning's Uitgeversmaatschapij, 1948.

Bayly, David and Tim. "Calvin: woman rulers are God's judgment . . ." *BaylyBlog: Out of our mind too*. . . . Online: http://www.baylyblog.com/2007/04/bullinger_knox_.html/.

———. "John Calvin on Deborah . . ." *BuylyBlog: Out of our mind too*. . . . Online: http://www.baylyblog.com/2007/04/john_calvin_on_.html#more/.

Beaty, Mary, and Benjamin W. Farley, translators. *Calvin's Ecclesiastical Advice*. Louisville: Westminster John Knox, 1991.

Benedict, Philip. *Christ's Churches Purely Reformed: A Social History of Calvinism*. New Haven: Yale University Press, 2002.

———. "Two Calvinisms." In *The Faith and Fortunes of France's Huguenots, 1600-85*, 208-28. Aldershot, UK: Ashgate, 2001.

Benoist, Alain de. "The First Federalist: Johannes Althusius." *Krisis* 22 (March 1999) 2-34.

Blaisdell, Charmarie Jenkins. "Calvin's and Loyola's Letters to Women." In *Calviniana: Ideas and Influence of Jean Calvin*, edited by Robert V. Schnucker, 235-53. Sixteenth Century Essays & Studies 10. Kirksville, MO: Sixteenth Century Journal Publishers, 1988.

———. "Calvin's Letters to Women: The Courting of Ladies in High Places." *Sixteenth Century Journal* 13 (1982) 67-84.

Bloor, David. *Wittgenstein: A Social Theory of Knowledge*. New York: Columbia University Press, 1983.

Boer, Wietse de. "Calvin and Borromeo: A Comparative Approach to Social Discipline." In *Early Modern Catholicism: Essays in Honour of John W. O'Malley, SJ*, edited by Kathleen M. Comerford and Hilmar M. Pabel, 84-96. Toronto: University of Toronto Press, 2001.

Bibliography

———. *The Conquest of the Soul: Confession, Discipline, and Public Order in Counter-Reformation Milan.* Studies in Medieval and Reformation Thought 84. Leiden: Brill, 2001.

———. "The Politics of the Soul: Confession in Counter-Reformation Milan." In *Penitence in the Age of Reformations*, edited by Katharine Jackson Lualdi and Anne T. Thayer, 116–33. St. Andrews Studies in Reformation History. Aldershot, UK: Ashgate, 2000.

Boetzelaer van Dubbeldam, Carel Wessel Theodorus, van, baron. *De Protestantsche Kerk in Nederlandsch-Indie: Haar Ontwikkeling van 1620–1939.* 'S-Gravenhage: Nijhoff, 1947.

Bonnell, Victoria E., and Lynn Avery Hunt, editors. *Beyond the Cultural Turn: New Directions in the Study of Society and Culture.* Studies on the History of Society and Culture 34. Berkeley: University of California Press, 1999.

Bouwsma, O. K. *Wittgenstein: Conversations, 1949–1951*, edited with an introduction by J. L. Craft and Ronald E. Hustwit. Indianapolis: Hackett, 1986.

Bouwsma, William J. *John Calvin: A Sixteenth-Century Portrait.* New York: Oxford University Press, 1988.

Bratt, James D., editor and translator. *Abraham Kuyper: A Centennial Anthology.* Grand Rapids: Eerdmans, 1998.

Brouwer, A. M. "Het Onstaan der Protestantsche Zending." In *De Zending in Oost en West: Verleden en Heden*, edited by H. D. J. Boissevain, vol. 1. 's-Gravenhage: Algemeene Boekhandel voor Inwendige en Uitwendige Zending, 1945.

Brown, Meg Lota, and Kari Boyd McBride. *Women's Roles in the Renaissance.* Women's Roles through History. Westport, CT: Greenwood, 2005.

Bruyn, C. A. L. Van Troostenburg de. *De Hervormde Kerk in Nederlandsch Oost-Indië onder de Oost-Indische Compagnie, 1602–1795.* Arnhem: Tjeenk Willink, 1884.

Buitendijk, W. J. C. *Het calvinisme in de spiegel van de zuidnederlandse literatuur der contra-reformatie.* Groningen-Batavia: Wolters, 1942.

Burnett, Amy Nelson. *The Yoke of Christ: Martin Bucer and Christian Discipline.* Sixteenth Century Essays & Studies 26. Kirksville, MO: Northeast Missouri State University, 1994.

Bussert, Joy M. K. *Battered Women: From a Theology of Suffering to an Ethic of Empowerment.* New York: Division for Mission in North America, Lutheran Church in America, 1986.

Callenbach, Jacobus Richardus. *Justus Heurnius: Eene Bijdrage to de Geschiedenis des Christendoms in Nederlandsch Oost-Indië.* Nijkerk: Callenbach, 1897.

Carlson, Dale, and Hannah Carlson. *Girls Are Equal Too: How to Survive; For Teenage Girls.* 2nd, rev. ed. Madison, CT: Bick, 1998.

Cha, Youngbae. "The Principle of Hyungryong Park's theology." In *The Life and Thought of Dr. Hyung Nong Park*, edited by Yong Kyu Park, 407–10. Seoul: Chongshin University Press, 1996. [in Korean]

Chang, Dongmin. *Theological Study of Hyungryong Park.* Seoul: Society of Korean Church History, 1998. [in Korean]

Chareyre, Philippe. "Le Consistoire de Nîmes, 1561–1685." 2 vols. PhD diss., Université Montpellier 3, 1987.

———. "'The Great Difficulties One Must Bear to Follow Jesus Christ': Morality at Sixteenth-Century Nîmes." In *Sin and the Calvinists: Morals Control and the*

Bibliography

Consistory in Reformed Tradition, edited by Raymond Mentzer, 63–96. Sixteenth Century Essays and Studies 32. Kirksville MO: Sixteenth Century Journal Publishers, 1994.
Choi, Ducksung. "Hyungryong Park and Reformed Orthodox Theology." In *Revisiting Reformed Theology of Hyungryong Park*, 158–86. Seoul: Society of Korean Reformed Theology, 2007. [in Korean]
Choi, Sungsoo. "Theological Exclusivism as Reflected in the Disputes between Hyungryong Park and Jaejoon Kim and Theological Criticism as Project of Korean Theology." *Christian Thoughts* 510 (2001) 200–220. [in Korean]
Choisy, Eugène. *Calvin et Servet: Le Monument Expiatoire de Champel.* Neuilly: Editions de "LaCause," n.d.
Christman, Robert. "Heretics in Luther's Homeland: The Controversy over Original Sin in Late Sixteenth-Century Mansfeld." PhD diss., University of Arizona, 2004.
———. "'I Can Indeed Respond': Lay Confessions of Faith in the Late Sixteenth-Century Central Germany." *Sixteenth Century Journal* 39 (2008) 1003–19.
Clanton, Dan. *The Good, the Bold, and the Beautiful: The Story of Susanna and its Renaissance Interpretations.* Library of Hebrew Bible/Old Testament Studies 430. T. & T. Clark Library of Biblical Studies. New York: T. & T. Clark, 2006.
Clarke, Rita-Lou. *Pastoral Care of Battered Women.* Philadelphia: Westminster, 1986.
Coolsma, S. *De Zendingseeuw voor Nederlandsch Oost-Indie.* Utrecht: Breijer, 1901.
Cooper-White, Pamela. *The Cry of Tamar: Violence against Women and the Church's Response.* Minneapolis: Fortress, 1995.
Cottret, Bernard. *Calvin: A Biography.* Translated by M. Wallace McDonald. Grand Rapids: Eerdmans, 2000.
Crary, Alice M., and Rupert J. Read, editors. *The New Wittgenstein.* London: Routledge, 2000.
Crary, Alice M. "Wittgenstein's Philosophy in Relation to Political Thought." In *The New Wittgenstien*, edited by Alice M. Crary and Rupert J. Read, 118–45. London: Routledge, 2000.
Crick, Bernard. *In Defence of Politics.* 5th ed. London: Continuum, 2000.
Crosson, Frederick J., editor. *The Autonomy of Religious Belief: A Critical Inquiry.* University of Notre Dame Studies in the Philosophy of Religion. Notre Dame: University of Notre Dame Press, 1981.
Curtis, Alan. "Henderick Speuy and the Earliest Printed Dutch Keyboard Music." *Tijdschrift van de Vereniging voor Nederlandse Muziekgeschiedenis* 19 (1962–1963) 143–62.
Datenbank des Projekts "Controversia et confessio. Quellenedition zur Bekenntnisbildung und Konfessionalisierung (1548–1580)." Online: http://www.litdb.evtheol.uni-mainz.de/datenbank/index_front.php/.
Davies, Horton. *Worship and Theology in England.* Vol. 1, *From Cranmer to Hooker.* Grand Rapids: Eerdmans, 1996.
Davies, Sarah. "Destroying the Devil's Bagpipe: Iconoclasm and the Fate of the Organ in Reformation Switzerland." Budapest: Institute for Musicology of the Hungarian Academy of Sciences, 2000.
Davis, Thomas J. "Images of Intolerance: John Calvin in Nineteenth-Century History Textbooks." *Church History* 65 (1996) 234–48.
———. "Rhetorical War and Reflex: Calvinism in Nineteenth-Century Popular Fiction and Twentieth-Century Criticism." *Calvin Theological Journal* 33 (1998) 443–56.

Bibliography

De Jong, Peter Y. "Early Reformed Missions in the East Indies." *Mid-America Journal of Theology* 6 (1990) 33–74.

De Jonge, Christiaan. *Apa Itu Calvinisme.* Jakarta: BPK Gunung Mulia, 1998.

Derrida, Jacques. "The Force of Law: The Mystical Foundation of Authority." In *Deconstruction and the Possibility of Justice*, edited by Drucilla Cornell, et al., 3–67. New York: Routledge, 1992.

Deursen, Arie Theodorus van. *Bavianen en slijkgeuzen. Kerk en kerkvolk ten tijde van Maurits en Oldenbarnevelt.* Franeker: Van Wijnen, 1991.

Dingel, Irene. *Concordia Controversa: Die öffentlichen Diskussionen um das lutherische Konkordienwerk am Ende des 16. Jahrhunderts.* Quellen und Forschungen zur Reformationsgeschichte 63. Gütersloh: Gütersloh, 1996.

———. "Historische Einleitung." In *Die Debatte um die Wittenberger Abendmahlslehre und Christologie (1570–1574)*, edited by Irene Dingel, 3–15. Controversia et confessio: Theologische Kontroversen 1548–1577/80, Kritische Auswahledition 8. Göttingen: Vandenhoeck & Ruprecht, 2008.

———. " Johannes Wigand." In *TRE* 36:33–38.

———. "Die Torgauer Artikel (1574) als Vermittlungsversuch zwischen der Theologie Luthers und der Melanchthons." In *Praxis Pietatis: Beiträge zu Theologie und Frömmigkeit in der Frühen Neuzeit. Wolfgang Sommer zum 60. Geburtstag*, edited by Hans-Jörg Nieden and Marcel Nieden, 119–34. Stuttgart: Kohlhammer, 1999.

Dooyeweerd, H. *A New Critique of Theoretical Thought.* 4 volumes. Amsterdam: Paris, 1953–1958.

Douglass, Jane Dempsey. "Women and the Continental Reformation." In *Religion and Sexism: Images of Woman in the Jewish and Christian Traditions*, edited by Rosemary Radford Reuther, 292–318. New York: Simon & Schuster, 1974.

———. *Women, Freedom, and Calvin.* Annie Kinkead Wakefield Lectures 1983. Philadelphia: Westminster, 1985.

Dufour, Alain. "Das Religionsgespräch von Poissy: Hoffnungen der Reformierten und der 'Moyenneurs.'" In *Die Religionsgespräche der Reformationszeit*, edited by Gerhard Müller, 117–26. Schriften des Vereins für Reformationsgeschichte 191. Gütersloh: Mohn, 1980.

Eitner, Robert, and Hermann Wilhelm Springer. *Biographisch-bibliographisches Quellen-lexikon der Musiker und Musikgelehrten der christlichen Zeitrechnung bis zur Mitte des neunzehnten Jahrhunderts.* 11 vols. Leipzig: Breitkopf & Haertel, 1900–1904.

End, Th. van den. *Ragi Carita.* 2 vols. Jakarta: BPK Gunung Mulia, 2006.

———. "Transfer of Reformed Identity on the Missionfield in Indonesia." In *Changing Partnership of Missionary and Ecumenical Movements: Essays in Honour of Marc Spindler*, edited by Lenny Lagerwerf, et al., 113–30. IIMO Research Publication 42. Leiden-Utrecht: Interuniversity Institute for Missiological and Ecumenical Research,

Engel, Mary Potter. "Historical Theology and Violence against Women: Unearthing a Popular Tradition of Just Battery." In *Revisioning the Past: Prospects in Historical Theology*, edited by Mary Potter Engel and Walter E. Wyman, Jr., 51–75. Minneapolis: Fortress, 1992.

Engels, Friedrich. *Socialism: Utopian and Scientific.* Translated by Edward Aveling. Social Science Series 56. London: Sonnenschein, 1892.

Fanfani, Amintore. *Catholicism, Protestantism and Capitalism.* Sheed & Ward, 1935.

Bibliography

Farthing, John L. "*De coniugio spirituali*: Jerome Zanchi on Ephesians 5:22-23." *Sixteenth Century Journal* 24 (1993) 621-52.

Findlay, Alison. *A Feminist Perspective on Renaissance Drama*. Oxford: Blackwell, 1999.

Fonte, John. "Why There is a Culture War: Gramsci and Tocqueville in America." *Policy Review* 104 (December 2000 & January 2001) 15-31. Online: http://www.hoover.org/publications/policyreview/3484376.html/.

Fortune, Marie M. "Religious Issues and Violence against Women." In *Sourcebook on Violence against Women*, edited by Claire M. Renzetti, et al., 371-86. Thousand Oaks, CA: Sage, 2001.

Franks, Robert S. *The Work of Christ: A Historical Study of Christian Doctrine*. Nelson's Library of Theology. London: Nelson, 1962.

Frijhoff, Willem. "Votive Boats or Secular Models? An Approach to the Question of the Figurative Ships in the Dutch Protestant Churches." In *Embodied Belief: Ten Essays on Religious Culture in Dutch History*, edited by Joris van Eijnatten and Fred van Lieburg, 215-34. ReLiC: Studies in Dutch Religious History 1. Hilversum: Uitgeverij Verloren, 2002.

Frongia, Guido, and Brian McGuinness. *Wittgenstein: A Bibliographical Guide*. Oxford: Blackwell, 1990.

Gallatin, Marie-Lucile de. "Les ordonnances somptuaires à Genève au xvie siècle." *Mémoires et documents publiés par la Société d'Histoire et d'Archéologie de Genève* 36 (1938) 193-275.

Garrisson-Estèbe, Janine. *Protestants du Midi, 1559-1598*. Le Midi et son histoire. Toulouse: Privat, 1980.

Gelderen, Martin van. "De Nederlandse Opstand (1555-1610): van 'vrijheden' naar 'oude vrijheid' en de 'vrijheid der conscientien'." In *Vrijheid: Een geschiedenis van de vijftiende tot de twintigste eeuw*, edited by E. O. G. Haitsma Mulier and W. R. E. Velema, 27-52. Reeks Nederlandse begripsgeschiedenis 2. Amsterdam: Amsterdam University Press, 1999.

Gellner, Ernest. "A Wittgensteinian Philosophy of (or against) the Social Sciences." In *Spectacles & Predicaments: Essays in Social Theory*, 65-102. Cambridge: Cambridge University Press, 1979.

Gierke, Otto von. *The Development of Political Theory*. Translated by Bernard Freyd. New York: Norton, 1939.

Goovaerts, Alphonse Jean Marie André. *Histoire et bibliographie de la typographie musicale dans les Pays-Bas*. Antwerp: Kockx, 1880.

Gordon, Bruce. *Calvin*. New Haven: Yale University Press, 2009.

Gorski, Philip S. "Calvinism and State Formation in Early Modern Europe." In *State/Culture: State-Formation after the Cultural Turn*, edited by George Steinmetz, 147-81. The Wilder House Series in Politics, History, and Culture. Ithaca: Cornell University Press, 1999.

Goudzwaard, Bob. *Capitalism and Progress: A Diagnosis of Western Society*. Translated and edited by Josina Van Nuis Zylstra. Toronto: Wedge Publishing Foundation, 1979.

———. *Globalization and the Kingdom of God*. Washington, DC: Center for Public Justice, 2001.

Graham, Michael. "Social Discipline in Scotland, 1560-1610." In *Sin and the Calvinists. Morals Control and the Consistory in Reformed Tradition*, edited by Raymond

Bibliography

Mentzer, 129-57. Sixteenth Century Essays & Studies 32. Kirksville, MO: Sixteenth Century Journal Publishers, 1994.

Green, Mitchell S., and John Williams, editors. *Moore's Paradox: New Essays on Belief, Rationality, and the First Person.* Oxford: Clarendon, 2007.

Groen van Prinsterer, Guillaume. "Unbelief and Revolution." In *Groen van Prinsterer's Lectures on Unbelief and Revolution,* edited by Harry Van Dyke. Jordan Station, ON: Wedge Publishing Foundation, 1989.

Grosse, Christian. *L'Excommunication de Philibert Berthelier: Histoire d'un conflit d'identité aux premiers temps de la Réforme genevoise.* Geneva: Société d'Histoire et d'Archeologie de Genève, 1995.

Grundmann, Herbert. "Der Typus des Ketzers in mittelalterlicher Anschauung." In *Ausgewählte Aufsätze,* 1:313-27. 3 vols. Schriften der Monumenta Germaniae Historica 25. Stuttgart: Hiersemann, 1976.

Guggenheim, Ann. "The Calvinist Notables of Nîmes during the Era of the Religious Wars." *Sixteenth Century Journal* 3 (1972) 80-96.

Ham, Youngok. "A Study of the Dispute over the Doctrine of Scripture in Korean Church History," PhD diss., Chongshin University, 1991. [in Korean]

Hamilton, Alastair. "Max Weber's *Protestant Ethic and the Spirit of Capitalism*." In *The Cambridge Companion to Weber,* edited by Stephen P. Turner, 151-71. New York: Cambridge University Press, 2000.

Heckel, Matthew C. "'His Spear through My Side into Luther': Calvin's Relationship to Luther's Doctrine of the Will." PhD dissertation, Concordia Theological Seminary, 2005.

Heppe, Heinrich. *Reformed Dogmatics Set Out and Illustrated from the Sources.* Foreword by Karl Barth. Revised and edited by Ernst Bizer. Translated by G. T. Thomson. Grand Rapids: Baker, 1978.

Hesselink, I. John. *Calvin's Concept of the Law.* PTMS 30. Allison Park, PA: Pickwick Publications, 1992.

Hoekema, Alle G. "Kyai Ibrahim Tunggul Wulung (1800-1885): 'Een Javaanse Apollos.'" *Netherlands Theologisch Tijdschrift* 33 (1979) 89-110.

Hoëvell, Wolter Robert baron van, editor. *Tijdschrift voor Nederlandsch Indië.* Zalt-Bommel: Joh. Noman en zoon, 1867.

Hollander, Anne. *Seeing through Clothes.* Berkeley: University of California Press, 1993.

Holt, Mack P. "The Social History of the Reformation: Recent Trends and Future Agendas." *Journal of Social History* 37 (2003) 133-44.

Jakob, Friedrich. *Der Orgelbau im Kanton Zürich: Von seinen Anfängen bis zur Mitte des 19. Jahrhunderts.* 2 vols. Publikationen der Schweizerischen Musikforschenden Gesellschaft, 2nd ser., 18. Bern: Haupt, 1969-1971.

Janssen, H. Q. *Catalogus van het Oud-Synodaal Archief.* 's-Gravenhage, 1878.

Jenkins, Keith, editor. *The Postmodern History Reader.* London: Routledge, 1997.

Jones, R. Tudur. "Union with Christ: The Existential Nerve of Puritan Piety." *Tyndale Bulletin* 41 (1990) 186-208.

Jung, Ilwoong. "Revisiting the Reformed Faith of Hyungryong Park." In *Papers of Korean Reformed Theology* 21, 1-9. Seoul: Society of Korean Reformed Theology, 2007. [in Korean]

Kang, Shinsok. "A Study of the Theological Thought of Janggong Jaejoon Kim," PhD diss., Hansin University, 1983. [in Korean]

Bibliography

Kapic, Kelly M. *Communion with God: The Divine and Human in the Theology of John Owen*. Grand Rapids: Baker Academic, 2007.

Karant-Nunn, Susan C. "Changing One's Mind: Transformations in Reformation History from a Germanist's Perspective." *Renaissance Quarterly* 58 (2005) 1101–27.

Kaufmann, Thomas. *Universität und lutherische Konfessionalisierung: Die Rostocker Theologieprofessoren und ihr Beitrag zur theologischen Bildung und kirchlichen Gestaltung im Herzogtum Mecklenburg zwischen 1550 und 1675*. Quellen und Forschungen zur Reformationsgeschichte 66. Gütersloh: Gütersloher, 1997.

Kerr, Fergus. *Theology after Wittgenstein*. 2nd ed. London: SPCK, 1997.

Kim, Jaejoon. "Verbal Inspiration and Biblical Inerrancy." *Crusades* (March 1950) 1–3. [in Korean]

Kim, Jichan. "Hyungryong Park's Doctrine of Scripture and the Korean Presbyterian church as reflected in his disputes against Jaejoon Kim." *Korean Reformed Theology* 21 (2007) 67–107. [in Korean]

Kim, John E. "Theology of Hyungryong Park." In *The Life and Thought of Dr. Hyung Nong Park*, edited by Yong Kyu Park, 233–55. Seoul: Chongshin University Press, 1996. [in Korean]

Kim, Kyungjae. "Life and Thought of Jang-gong Jaejoon Kim." Online: http://cafe.naver.com/chcom.cafe?iframe_url=/ArticleRead.nhn%3Farticleid=29/. [in Korean]

Kim, Younghan. "Jooksan Hyungryong Park and Korean Reformed Theology." In *Papers of Korean Reformed Theology* 21 (2007) 10–47. [in Korean]

Kingdon, Robert M. *Adultery and Divorce in Calvin's Geneva*. Harvard Historical Studies 118. Cambridge: Harvard University Press, 1995.

———. "Efforts to Control Hate in Calvin's Geneva." In *Calvin Studies IX: Papers Presented at the Ninth Colloquium on Calvin Studies*, edited by John H. Leith and Robert A. Johnson, 113–22. Davidson, NC: Davidson College and Davidson College Presbyterian Church, 1998.

———. "Social Control and Political Control in Calvin's Geneva." In *Die Reformation in Deutschland und Europa: Interpretationen und Debatten*, edited by Hans R. Guggisberg, et al., 521–32. Archiv für Reformationsgeschichte Sonderband. Gütersloh: Mohn, 1993.

Kist, N. C. "Het kerkelijke orgel-gebruik bijzonder in Nederland: Een historisch onderzoek." *Archief voor Kerkelijke geschiedenis inzonderheid van Nederland* 10 (1840) 193–304.

Klueting, Harm. "Reformierte Konfessionalisierung in West- und Ostmitteleuropa." In *Konfessionsbildung und Konfessionskultur in Siebenbürgen in der Frühen Neuzeit*, edited by Volker Leppin and Ulrich Wien, 25–56. Quellen und Studien zur Geschichte des östlichen Europa 66. Stuttgart: Steiner, 2005.

Knedlik, Manfred. "Praetorius, Peter." In *Biographisch-Bibliographisches Kirchenlexikon* 24: 1183–84. 31 vols. Nordhausen: Bautz, 2005.

Kohnle, Armin. "Konfliktbereinigung und Gewaltprävention: Die europäischen Religionsfrieden in der frühen Neuzeit." In *Das Friedenspotenzial von Religion*, edited by Irene Dingel and Christiane Tietz, 1–19. Veröffentlichungen des Instituts für Europäische Geschichte Mainz. Abteilung für Abendländische Religionsgeschichte 78. Göttingen: Vandenhoeck & Ruprecht, 2009.

Kolb, Robert. "The Braunschweig Resolution. The Corpus Doctrinae Prutenicum of Joachim Mörlin and Martin Chemnitz as an Instrument of Wittenberg Theology."

Bibliography

In *Confessionalization in Europe, 1555–1700: Essays in Honor and Memory of Bodo Nischan*, edited by John M. Headley, et al., 67–89. Aldershot: Ashgate, 2004.
Koyzis, David C. "Persuaded, Not Commanded: Neo-Calvinism, *Dignitatis Humanae*, and Religious Liberty." In *Catholicism and Religious Freedom: Contemporary Reflections on Vatican II's Declaration on Religious Liberty*, edited by Kenneth Grasso and Robert Hunt, 115–34. Lanham, MD: Rowman & Littlefield, 2006.
Kraemer, Hendrik. *From Missionfield to Independent Church: Report on a Decisive Decade in the Growth of Indigenous Churches in Indonesia*. World Mission Studies. London: SCM, 1958.
Kromminga, D. H. *The Christian Reformed Tradition*. Grand Rapids: Eerdmans, 1943.
Kvam, Kristen E., et al. *Eve & Adam: Jewish, Christian, and Muslim Readings on Genesis and Gender*. Bloomington: Indiana University Press, 1999.
Lane, Anthony N. S. *John Calvin: Student of the Church Fathers*. Grand Rapids: Baker, 1999.
Laven, Mary. "Encountering the Counter-Reformation." *Renaissance Quarterly* 59 (2006) 706–26.
Lee, Howoo. "Disputes on the Doctrine of Scripture during the 1930s and Establishment of a Theological Paradigm." *Illip Review* 6 (2000) 79–106 [in Korean]
Lee, Sangkyu. "Significance of Dr. Hyungryong Park in Korean Ecclesiastical History." *Papers of Historical Theology* 9 (2005) 186–209. [in Korean]
Lee, Sangsup. "A Comparative Study of the Doctrine of Scripture between Calvin and the Korean Presbyterian church." PhD diss., Jangshin University, 1981. [in Korean]
Leehan, James. *Pastoral Care for Survivors of Family Abuse*. Louisville: Westminster John Knox, 1989.
Lenin, Vladimir I. *The State and Revolution: Marxist Teaching on the State and the Task of the Proletariat in the Revolution*. London: Allen & Unwin, 1919.
Lerner, Gerda. *The Creation of Patriarchy*. Women and History 1. New York: Oxford, 1986.
Ludwig, Ulrike. *Philippismus und orthodoxes Luthertum an der Universität Wittenberg. Die Rolle Jakob Andreäs im lutherischen Konfessionalisierungsprozeß Kursachsens (1576–1580)*. Reformationsgeschichtliche Studien und Texte 153. Münster: Aschendorff, 2009.
Luria, Keith P. *Sacred Boundaries: Religious Coexistence and Conflict in Early Modern France*. Washington, DC: Catholic University of America Press, 2005.
MacPherson, C. B. *The Political Theory of Possessive Individualism: Hobbes to Locke*. Oxford: Oxford University Press, 1962.
Magee, Malcolm D. *What the World Should Be: Woodrow Wilson and the Crafting of a Faith-Based Foreign Policy*. Waco, TX: Baylor University Press, 2008.
Mager, Inge. "Aufnahme und Ablehnung des Konkordienbuches in Nord-, Mittel- und Ostdeutschland." In *Bekenntnis und Einheit der Kirche. Studien zum Konkordienbuch*, edited by Martin Brecht und Reinhard Schwarz, 271–302. Stuttgart: Calwer, 1980.
Malcolm, Norman. *Wittgenstein: A Religious Point of View?* Edited with a response by Peter Winch. London: Routledge, 1993.
Mannhardt, Hermann Gottlieb. *Die Danziger Mennonitengemeinde. Nachdr. der Ausg. Danzig 1919*. Rara zum deutschen Kulturerbe des Ostens. Hildesheim: Olms, 2007.

Bibliography

Maritain, Jacques. *Man and the State.* Charles R. Walgreen Foundation Lectures. Chicago: University of Chicago Press, 1951.

———. *The Person and the Common Good.* Translated by John J. Fitzgerald. Notre Dame Books. Notre Dame: University of Notre Dame Press, 1966.

Marsden, George M. *Jonathan Edwards: A Life.* New Haven: Yale University Press, 2003.

Marshall, Paul A. *God and the Constitution: Christianity and American Politics.* Lanham, Maryland: Rowman & Littlefield, 2002.

———*Their Blood Cries Out: The Untold Story of Persecution against Christians in the Modern World.* Dallas: Word, 1997.

Marx, Karl, and Friedrich Engels. *Manifesto of the Communist Party.* 1848.

Maxwell, William D. *A History of Worship in the Church of Scotland.* London: Oxford University Press, 1955.

McDermott, Gerald R. *One Holy and Happy Society: The Public Theology of Jonathan Edwards.* University Park: Pennsylvania State University Press, 1992.

McGinn, Marie. *Routledge Philosophy Guidebook to Wittgenstein and the "Philosophical Investigations."* Routledge Philosophy Guidebooks. London: Routledge, 1997.

McGrath, Alister E. *A Life of John Calvin: A Study in the Shaping of Western Culture.* Oxford: Blackwell, 1990.

McKee, Elsie A. "Calvin and Praying for 'All People Who Dwell on Earth.'" *Interpretation* 63 (2009) 130–40.

Meeter, H. Henry. *The Basic Ideas of Calvinism.* 6th ed. Revised by Paul A. Marshall. Grand Rapids: Baker, 1990.

Mentzer, Raymond A. "Les débats sur les bancs dans les églises réformées de France." *Bulletin de la Société de l'Histoire du Protestantisme Français* 152 (2006) 393–406.

———. "'Disciplina Nervus Ecclesiae': The Calvinist Reform of Morals at Nîmes." *Sixteenth Century Journal* (1987) 89–115.

———. "Ecclesiastical Discipline and Communal Reorganization among the Protestants of Southern France." *European History Quarterly* 21 (1991) 163–84.

———. "Marking the Taboo: Excommunication in French Reformed Churches." In *Sin and the Calvinists: Morals Control and the Consistory in Reformed Tradition,* edited by Raymond Mentzer, 97–128. Kirksville, MO: Sixteenth Century Journal Publishers, 1994.

———. "Morals and Moral Regulation in Protestant France." *Journal of Interdisciplinary History* 31 (2000) 1–20.

———. "Organizational Endeavour and Charitable Impulse in Sixteenth-Century France: The Case of Protestant Nîmes." *French History* 5 (1991) 1–29.

———, editor. *Sin and the Calvinists. Morals Control and the Consistory in Reformed Tradition.* Kirksville, MO: Sixteenth Century Journal Publishers, 1994.

———. "Sociability and Culpability: Conventions of Mediation and Reconciliation within the Sixteenth-Century Huguenot Community." In *Memory and Identity: The Huguenots in France and the Atlantic Diaspora,* edited by Bertrand van Ruymbeke and Randy J. Sparks, 45–57. The Carolina Lowcountry and the Atlantic World. Columbia: University of South Carolina Press, 2003.

Millar, Patrick. *Four Centuries of Scottish Psalmody.* London: Oxford University Press, 1949.

Monk, Ray. *Ludwig Wittgenstein: The Duty of Genius.* New York: Penguin, 1991.

Bibliography

Monter, E. William. "The Consistory of Geneva, 1559-1569." In *Renaissance, Reformation, Resurgence*, edited by Peter De Klerk, 467-84. Grand Rapids: Calvin Theological Seminary, 1976.

———. "Women in Calvinist Geneva (1550-1800)." *Signs* 6 (1980) 189-209.

Morse, Christopher. "Raising God's Eyebrows: Some Further Thoughts on the Concept of the *Analogia Fidei*." *Union Seminary Quarterly Review* 37 (1981-1982) 39-49.

Müller, Michael G. "Unionsstaat und Region in der Konfessionalisierung: Polen-Litauen und die großen Städte des Königlichen Preußen." In *Konfessionalisierung in Ostmitteleuropa. Wirkungen des religiösen Wandels im 16. und 17. Jahrhunderts in Staat, Gesellschaft und Kultur*, edited by Joachim Bahlke and Arno Strohmeyer, 123-37. Forschungen zur Geschichte und Kultur des östlichen Mitteleuropa 7. Stuttgart: Steiner, 1999.

———. *Zweite Reformation und städtische Autonomie im Königlichen Preußen. Danzig, Elbing und Thorn in der Epoche der Konfessionalisierung (1557-1660)*. Publikationen der Historischen Kommission zu Berlin. Berlin: Akademie, 1997.

Muller, Richard A. "*Ordo docendi*: Melanchthon and the Organization of Calvin's *Institutes*, 1536-1543." In *Melanchthon in Europe: His Work and Influence beyond Wittenberg*, edited by Karin Maag, 123-40. Grand Rapids, MI: Baker Academic, 1999.

———. *The Unaccommodated Calvin: Studies in the Formation of a Theological Tradition*. Oxford Studies in Historical Theology. New York: Oxford University Press, 2000.

Murdock, Graeme. "Calvin, Clothing and the Body in Reformed Geneva." *Proceedings of the Huguenot Society* 28 (2006) 481-94.

———. "Church Building and Discipline in Early Seventeenth-Century Hungary and Transylvania." In *The Reformation in Eastern and Central Europe*, edited by Karin Maag, 136-54. St. Andrews Studies in Reformation History. Aldershot, UK: Scolar, 1997.

———. "Dressed to Repress?: Protestant Clergy Dress and the Regulation of Morality in Early Modern Europe." *Fashion Theory: The Journal of Dress, Body and Culture* 4 (2000) 179-99.

Nagtegaal, Luc. *Riding the Dutch Tiger: The Dutch East Indies Company and the Northern Coast of Java 1680-1743*. Translated by Beverly Jackson. Verhandelingen van het Koninklik Instituut voor Tal-, Land- en Volkenkunde 171. Leiden: KITLV Press, 1996.

Naphy, William G. "Baptisms, Church Riots, and Social Unrest in Calvin's Geneva." *Sixteenth Century Journal* 26 (1995) 87-97.

———. "Calvin and Geneva." In *The Reformation World*, edited by Andrew Pettegree, 309-22. New York: Routledge, 2000.

———. *Calvin and the Consolidation of the Genevan Reformation*. Manchester: Manchester University Press, 1994.

Neumeyer, Heinz. "Danzig." In *TRE*, 8:354. Berlin: de Gruyter, 1977-2004.

Niebuhr, H. Richard. *Christ and Culture*. New York: Harper, 1951.

Nieuw Nederlandsch Biografisch Woordenboek. Leiden: Sijthof 1912.

Nobles, Melissa. *The Politics of Official Apologies*. New York: Cambridge University Press, 2008.

Noske, Frits, editor. *Psalm Preludes: For Organ or Harpsichord*, by Henderick Speuy. Amsterdam: Heuwekemeijer, 1963.

Bibliography

Nugent, Donald. *Ecumenism in the Age of the Reformation: The Colloquy of Poissy.* Harvard Historical Studies 89. Cambridge: Harvard University Press, 1974.
Oort, Johannes van. "John Calvin and the Church Fathers." In *The Reception of the Church Fathers in the West,* edited by Irena Backus, 2:661-700. 2 vols. Leiden: Brill, 1997.
Parales, Heidi Bright. *Hidden Voices: Biblical Women and Our Christian Heritage.* Macon, GA: Smyth & Helwys, 1998.
Parenti, Michael. *History as Mystery.* San Francisco: City Lights, 1999.
Park, Hyungryong. *Works of Hyungryong Park.* 14 vols. Seoul: Reformed Practice Association, 2002. [in Korean]
Park, Jongshin. "Hyungryong Park, Theologian as Seen in the Intellectual History of Korea." In *Revisiting Reformed Theology of Hyungryong Park,* 48-66. Seoul: Society of Korean Reformed Theology, 2007. [in Korean]
Park, Yong Kyu, editor. *The Life and Thought of Dr. Hyung Nong Park.* Seoul: Chongshin University Press, 1996. [in Korean]
Park, Yooshin. *Is Korean Presbyterian Doctrine of Scripture Calvinist?* Seoul: Handol, 2008. [in Korean]
Parker, Charles H. *Faith on the Margins: Catholics and Catholicism in the Dutch Golden Age.* Cambridge: Harvard University Press, 2008.
———. "The Rituals of Reconciliation: Admonition, Confession, and Community in the Dutch Reformed Church." in *Penitence in the Age of Reformations,* edited by Katherine Jackson Lualdi and Anne T. Thayer, 101-15. St. Andrews Studies in Reformation History. Aldershot, UK: Ashgate, 2000.
Parker, T. H. L. *John Calvin: A Biography.* Philadelphia: Westminster, 1975.
Partee, Charles. *The Theology of John Calvin.* Louisville: Westminster John Knox, 2008.
Partonadi, Sutarman. *Sadrach's Community and Its Contextual Roots: A Nineteenth Century Javanese Expression of Christianity.* Currents of Encounter 3. Amsterdam: Rodopi, 1990.
Peter, Rodolphe, and J.-F. Gilmont, editors. *Bibliotheca Calviniana.* 3 vols. Geneva: Droz, 1994.
Philipse, C., and Johannes C. de Groene. *Wemeldinge. Zoals het was 4.* Zierikzee: Steengracht, 1972.
Phillips, D. Z., and Mario von de Ruhr, editors. *Religion and Wittgenstein's Legacy.* Ashgate Wittgensteinian Studies. Aldershot, UK: Ashgate, 2005.
Pippin, Robert B. *Modernism as a Philosophical Problem: On the Dissatisfactions of European High Culture.* 2nd ed. Malden, MA: Blackwell, 1999.
Pollman, Judith. "Off the Record: Problems in the Quantification of Calvinist Church Discipline." *Sixteenth Century Journal* 33 (2002) 423-38.
Rankka, Kristine M. *Women and the Value of Suffering: An Aw(e)ful Rowing toward God.* Collegeville, MN: Liturgical, 1998.
Reitsma, Johannes. *Geschiedenis van de Hervorming en de Hervormde Kerk der Nederlanden.* Groningen: Wolters, 1899.
Reuther, Rosemary Radford. *Introducing Redemption in Christian Feminism.* Introductions in Feminist Theology 1. Sheffield, UK: Sheffield Academic, 1998.
———. *Sexism and God-Talk: Toward a Feminist Theology.* 10th anniversary edition. Boston: Beacon, 1993.
———. *Women and Redemption: A Theological History.* Minneapolis: Fortress, 1998.

Bibliography

Rhees, Rush, editor. *Ludwig Wittgenstein: Personal Recollections.* Oxford: Blackwell, 1981.

Roche, Daniel. *The Culture of Clothing: Dress and Fashion in the* Ancien Regime. Translated by Jean Birrell. Past and Present Publications. Cambridge: Cambridge University Press, 1994.

Romane-Musculus, P. "Histoire de la robe pastorale et du rabat." *Bulletin de la Société de l'Histoire du Protestantisme Français* 115 (1969) 307–38.

Roobol, Marianne. "Landszaken. De godsdienstgesprekken tussen gereformeerde predikanten en D.V. Coornhert onder leiding van de Staten van Holland (1577–1583)." PhD diss., Universiteit Amsterdam, 2005.

Rorem, Paul. "Calvin and Bullinger on the Lord's Supper." *Lutheran Quarterly* 2 (1988) 155–84, 357–89.

Rorty, Richard. *Contingency, Irony, and Solidarity.* Cambridge: Cambridge University Press, 1989.

———. *Objectivity, Relativism, and Truth.* Philosophical Papers 1. Cambridge: Cambridge University Press, 1991.

Ruff, Otto. "A Viewpoint from Migrant Churches on 'Two Hundred Years of Mission.'" *International Review of Mission* 87 (1998) 265–67.

Runner, H. Evan. *Scriptural Religion and Political Task.* 2nd, unrev. ed. Toronto: Wedge Publishing Foundation, 1974.

Sabbe, Maurits. *Brabant in't verweer. Bijdrage tot de studie der Zuid-Nederlandsche Strijdliteratuur in de eerste helft der 17e eeuw.* Antwerp: Resseler, 1933.

Sapalski, A. *Przewodnik dla organistow.* Cracow, 1880.

Schering, Arnold. *Die niederländische Orgelmesse im Zeitalter des Josquin, eine stilkritische Untersuchung.* Leipzig: Breitkopf & Härtel, 1912.

Schilling, Heinz. "Calvinism and the Making of the Modern Mind." In *Civic Calvinism in Northwestern Germany and the Netherlands: Sixteenth to Nineteenth Centuries,* by Heinz Schilling, 40–68. Sixteenth Century Essays & Studies 17. Kirksville, MO: Sixteenth Century Journal Publishers, 1991.

Schreiner, Klaus. "Toleranz." In *Geschichtliche Grundbegriffe*, edited by Otto Brunner et al., 6:528–31. 8 vols. in 9. Stuttgart: Klett-Cotta, 1990.

Schweitzer, Ivy. "Puritan Legacies of Masculinity: John Berryman's Homage to Mistress Bradstreet." In *The Calvinist Roots of the Modern Era,* edited by Aliki Barnstone, et al., 125–41. Hanover, NH: University Press of New England, 1997.

Seo, Jungmin. "Reflection of Dr. Jaejoon Kim," 4–9. [in Korean]

Sewell, William Hamilton, Jr. *Logics of History: Social Theory and Social Transformation.* Chicago Studies in Practices of Meaning. Chicago: University of Chicago Press, 2005.

Shim, Ilsop. "A Study of Theological Thought of Janggong Jaejoon Kim's Historical Engagement." In *Papers of Humanities* 1:7–30. Kangnam University, 1996. [in Korean]

Simon, Yves René Marie. *A General Theory of Authority.* Notre Dame: University of Notre Dame Press, 1962.

———. *Philosophy of Democratic Government.* Charles R. Walgreen Foundation Lectures. Chicago: University of Chicago Press, 1951.

Skillen, James W. *In Pursuit of Justice: Christian-Democratic Explorations.* Lanham, MD: Rowman & Littlefield, 2004.

———. *The Scattered Voice: Christians at Odds in the Public Square.* Grand Rapids: Zondervan, 1990.

Skinner, Quentin. "Meaning and Understanding in the History of Ideas." *History and Theory* 8 (1969) 3–53.

Smith, C. S., and W. Dineen. "Recent Work on Music in the Renaissance." *Modern Philology* 42 (1944) 41–58.

Soleiman, Yusak. "The Propagation of Dutch Reformed Protestantism on Java in the Eighteenth and Early Nineteenth Century c. 1753–1835: A Study of Religion and Society in Two Colonial Towns (Batavia and Semarang) and Its Perception by Early Nineteenth-Century Missionaries." PhD diss., University of Leiden, 2007.

Spicer, Andrew. *Calvinist Churches in Early Modern Europe.* Studies in Early Modern European History. Manchester: Manchester University Press, 2007.

———. "'So Many Painted Jezebels.' Stained Glass Windows and the Formation of an Urban Identity in the Dutch Republic." In *Public Opinion and Changing Identities in the Early Modern Netherlands: Essays in Honour of Alastair Duke,* edited by Judith Pollmann and Andrew Spicer, 249–76. Studies in Medieval and Reformation Traditions 121. Leiden: Brill, 2007.

Spierling, Karen E. "Father, Son, and Pious Christian: Concepts of Masculinity in Reformation Geneva." In *Masculinity in the Reformation Era,* edited by Scott H. Hendrix and Susan C. Karant-Nunn, 95–119. Sixteenth Century Essays & Studies 83. Kirksville, MO: Truman State University Press, 2008.

———. *Infant Baptism in Reformation Geneva: The Shaping of a Community, 1536 – 1564.* St. Andrews Studies in Reformation History. Aldershot, UK: Ashgate, 2005.

Spijker, Willem van 't. "Calvin's Friendship with Martin Bucer: Did It Make Calvin a Calvinist?" In *Calvin and Spirituality: Papers Presented at the 10th Colloquium of the Calvin Studies Society, May 18–20, 1995, Calvin Theological Seminary. Calvin and His Contemporaries: Colleagues, Friends and Conflicts: Papers Presented at the 11th Colloquium of the Calvin Studies Society, April 24–26, 1997, Louisville Theological Seminary,* edited by David Foxgrover, 169–86. Grand Rapids: CRC Product Services, published for the Calvin Studies Society, 1998.

Steinmetz, David C. *Calvin in Context.* New York: Oxford University Press, 1995.

Stone, Martin. "Wittgenstein on Deconstruction." In *The New Wittgenstein,* edited by Alice M. Crary and Rupert J. Read, 83–117. London: Routledge, 2000.

Stone, Merlin. *When God Was a Woman.* New York: Harcourt Brace Jovanovich, 1976.

Strauss, Leo. "What Is Political Philosophy?" In *What Is Political Philosophy? and Other Studies,* by Leo Strauss, 9–55. Glencoe, IL: Free Press, 1959.

Strohm, Christoph. *Johannes Calvin: Leben und Werk des Reformators.* Beck'sche Reihe 2469. Munich: Beck, 2009.

Sunshine, Glen S. "French Protestantism on the Eve of St.-Bartholomew: The Ecclesiastical Discipline of the French Reformed Churches, 1571–1572." *French History* 4 (1990) 340–77.

Swigchem, C. A. van, et al. *Een huis voor het Woord. Het protestantse kerkinterieur in Nederland tot 1900.* Zeist: Rijksdienst voor de Monumentenzorg, 1984.

Tavuchis, Nicholas. *Mea Culpa: A Sociology of Apology and Reconciliation.* Stanford: Stanford University Press, 1991.

Tawney, R. H. *Religion and the Rise of Capitalism.* New York: Harcourt, Brace, 1926.

Bibliography

Tel, Martin. "Gebruyck of Ongebruyck: A Brief Overview of Historic Trends in the Use of the Organ in the Calvinist Churches of the Netherlands." *Princeton Seminary Bulletin* 24 (2003) 313–27.

Thompson, John L. *John Calvin and the Daughters of Sarah: Women in Regular and Exceptional Roles in the Exegesis of Calvin, His Predecessors and His Contemporaries.* Travaux d'Humanisme et Renaissance 259. Geneva: Droz, 1992.

———. "John Calvin's Understanding of What Is Essential in Christianity." *Nanjing Theological Review* 57 (2003) 104–18.

———. "Patriarchs, Polygamy, and Private Resistance: John Calvin and Others on Breaking God's Rules." *Sixteenth Century Journal* 25 (1994) 3–27.

———. "Patriarchy and Prophetesses: Tradition and Innovation in Vermigli's Doctrine of Woman." In *Peter Martyr Vermigli and the European Reformations: Semper Reformanda*, edited by Frank A. James III, 139–58. Studies in the History of Christian Traditions 115. Leiden: Brill, 2004.

———. "Rules Proved by Exceptions: The Exegesis of Paul and Women in the Sixteenth Century." In *A Companion to Paul in the Reformation*, edited by R. Ward Holder, 501–40. Brill's Companions to the Christian Tradition 15. Leiden: Brill, 2009.

———. *Writing the Wrongs: Women of the Old Testament among Biblical Commentators from Philo through the Reformation.* Oxford Studies in Historical Theology. Oxford: Oxford, 2001.

Todd, Margo. *The Culture of Protestantism in Early Modern Scotland.* New Haven: Yale University Press, 2002.

———. "Profane Pastimes and the Reformed Community: The Persistence of Popular Festivities in Early Modern Scotland." *Journal of British Studies* 39 (2000) 123–56.

Torrance, Thomas F. "Knowledge of God and Speech about Him according to John Calvin." In *Theology in Reconstruction*, 76–98. Grand Rapids, Eerdmans, 1966.

Tuck, Patrick, editor. *The East India Company, 1600–1858.* 6 vols. London: Routledge, 1998.

Tucker, Ruth A., and Walter L. Liefeld. *Daughters of the Church: Women and Ministry from New Testament Times to the Present.* Grand Rapids: Academie, 1987.

Tugendhat, Ernst. *Self-Consciousness and Self-Determination.* Translated by Paul Stern. Studies in Contemporary German Social Thought. Cambridge: MIT Press, 1986.

Tulchin, Allan. "The Michelade in Nimes, 1567." *French Historical Studies* 29 (2006) 1–35.

Valeri, Mark. "Calvin and the Social Order in Early America: Moral Ideals and Transatlantic Empire." In *John Calvin's American Legacy*, edited by Thomas J. Davis, 19–41. New York: Oxford University Press, 2010.

Van Biema, David. "Ten Ideas Changing the World Right Now." Time.com, March 12, 2009. Online: http://www.time.com/time/specials/packages/article/0,28804,1884779_1884782_1884760,00.html/.

Van den Borren, Charles. *Les origines de la musique de clavier dans les Pays-Bas (nord et sud) jusque vers 1630.* Brussels: Breitkopf et Haertel, 1914

Van Huyssteen, Wentzel. *Alone in the World? Human Uniqueness in Science and Theology.* Grand Rapids: Eerdmans, 2006.

Van Loon, Hendrik Willem. *The Golden Book of the Dutch Navigators.* New York: Century Co., 1916.

Veen, Mirjam van. *Een nieuwe tijd, een nieuwe kerk. De opkomst van het 'calvinisme' in de Lage Landen.* Zoetermeer: Meinema, 2009.

―――. *"Verschooninghe van de roomsche afgoderye": De polemiek van Calvijn met nicodemieten, in het bijzonder met Coornhert*. Bibliotheca Huamnistica & Reformatorica 60. 't Goy-Houten: HES en De Graaf, 2001.
Venema, Cornelis P. *Heinrich Bullinger and the Doctrine of Predestination: Author of "the Other Reformed Tradition"?* Texts and Studies in Reformation and Post-Reformation Thought. Grand Rapids: Baker Academic, 2002.
Vermaseren, Bernard Antoon. *De katholieke Nederlandse geschiedschrijving in de 16e en 17e eeuw over de Opstand*. Nederlandse Herdrukken 2. Leeuwarden: Dykstra, 1981.
Vision Forum Ministries. "Calvin and Knox on the Doctrine of Male Headship." Online: http://www.visionforumministries.org/issues/family/calvin_and_knox_on_male_headsh.aspx/.
―――. "John Calvin on Women Rejoicing in their Role as Homemakers." No pages. Online: http://www.visionforumministries.org/issues/family/john_calvin_on_woman_rejoicing.aspx/.
―――. "The Tenets of Biblical Patriarchy." No pages. Online: http://www.visionforumministries.org/home/about/biblical_patriarchy.aspx/.
Vogler, Bernard, and Jeanine Estèbe. "La genèse d'une société protestante: Étude comparée de quelques registres consistoriaux Languedociens et Palatins vers 1600." *Annales* 31 (1976) 362–88.
Walker, Williston. *John Calvin; The Organiser of Reformed Protestantism (1509–1564)*. Heroes of the Reformation 9. New York: Putnam, 1909.
Wandel, Lee Palmer. *The Eucharist in the Reformation: Incarnation and Liturgy*. Cambridge: Cambridge University Press, 2006.
Watt, Jeffrey R. "Women and the Consistory in Calvin's Geneva." *Sixteenth Century Journal* 24 (1993) 429–39.
Weber, Max. *The Protestant Ethic and the Spirit of Capitalism*. Translated by Talcott Parsons and Anthony Giddens. London: Unwin Hyman, 1930.
Wendel, François. *Calvin: The Origins and Development of His Religious Thought*. Translated by Philip Mairet. New York: Harper & Row, 1963.
Wessel, Jan Hendrik. *De leerstellige strijd tusschen Nederlandsche Gereformeerden en Doopsgezinden in de zestiende eeuw*. Assen: Van Gorcum, 1945.
Widiasih, Ester Pudjo. "A Survey of Reformed Worship in Indonesia." In *Christian Worship in Reformed Churches Past and Present*, edited by Lukas Vischer, 175–94. The Calvin Institute of Christian Worship Liturgical Studies Series. Grand Rapids: Eerdmans, 2003.
Winch, Peter. "The Expression of Belief." *Proceedings and Addresses of the American Philosophical Association* 70 (1996) 7–23.
―――. "Wittgenstein: Picture and Representation." In *Trying to Make Sense*, 64–80. Oxford: Blackwell, 1987.
Winkelen, C. van. *Wemeldinge in oude ansichten*. Zaltbommel: Europese Bibliotheek, 1976.
Wittgenstein, Ludwig. *Culture and Value*. Edited by G. H. von Wright. Translated by Peter Winch. Chicago: University of Chicago Press, 1980.
―――. *Philosophical Investigations*. Translated by G. E. M. Anscombe. 3rd ed. New York: Macmillan, 1958.
―――. "Philosophy." In *Philosophical Occasions, 1912–1951*. Edited by James Carl Klagge and Alfred Nordmann, 158–99. Indianapolis: Hackett, 1993.

Bibliography

Wolin, *Politics and Vision: Continuity and Innovation in Western Political Thought.* Princeton: Princeton University Press, 2004.

Wolterstorff, Nicholas. *Until Justice and Peace Embrace.* Grand Rapids: Eerdmans, 1983.

Yeon, Kyuhong. "A Study of Calvinist Theology of the Korean Presbyterian Church: for the unity of the Korean Presbyterian Church." PhD diss., Hansin University, 1995. [in Korean]

Yuille, Stephen J. *The Inner Sanctum of Puritan Piety: John Flavels' Doctrine of Mystical Union with Christ.* Grand Rapids: Reformation Heritage, 2007.

Zachman, Randall C. *Image and Word in the Theology of John Calvin.* Notre Dame: University of Notre Dame Press, 2007.

———, editor. *John Calvin and Roman Catholicism: Critique and Engagement, Then and Now.* Grand Rapids: Baker Academic, 2008.

———. *John Calvin as Teacher, Pastor, and Theologian.* Grand Rapids: Baker Academic, 2006.

———. "Restoring Access to the Fountain: Melanchthon and Calvin on the Task of Evangelical Theology." In *Calvin and Spirituality: Papers Presented at the 10th Colloquium of the Calvin Studies Society, May 18-20, 1995, Calvin Theological Seminary. Calvin and His Contemporaries: Colleagues, Friends and Conflicts: Papers Presented at the 11th Colloquium of the Calvin Studies Society, April 24-26, 1997, Louisville Theological Seminary,* edited by David Foxgrover, 205-28. Grand Rapids: CRC Product Services, published for the Calvin Studies Society, 1998.

Zijlstra, Samme. *Om de ware gemeente en de oude gronden. Geschiedenis van de dopersen in de Nederlanden 1531-1675.* FA 908. Hilversum: Verloren, 2000.

Zwart, Jan. "Hendrik Joosten Speuy, een tijdgenoot van Sweelinck." *Het Orgel* 54 (1958) 97-98, 129-32.

Zylstra, Bernard. *From Pluralism to Collectivism: The Development of Harold Laski's Political Thought.* Assen: Van Gorcum, 1970.

Index of Persons, Places, and Subjects

Adiaphora, 47, 49, 50, 51, 52, 122, 124
Africa, 206
Alesius, Alexander, 28
Althusius, Johannes, xv, 197–98, 199
Ambrosiaster, 26, 27
Anabaptists, xv, 126–29, 131–38, 157, 196, 203
Andreae, Jacob, 145
Antwerp, 129, 130
Aquinas, Thomas, 7, 11, 39, 204
Arianism, 130, 158
Aristotelianism, 4, 6
Arminians, xv, 126–37
Arminius, Jacob, 11
Asia, 206
Augsburg Confession, 139, 146, 147, 148, 152, 154, 155, 159, 160
Augsburg Interim, 141, 144
August, Elector of Saxony, 145, 150
Augustine, 26–27, 30, 33, 39, 204, 206
Avignon, 81

Baptism, 97–99, 100, 106
Barth, Karl, 17, 39, 211, 216
Batavia, 92, 97, 100, 102, 103, 104
    Church Order of, 93, 95, 96–104, 106
    see also Java
Bathory, Stephan, king of Poland, 148
Belgic Confession, 92–93, 196
    see also Dutch Confession
Berkouwer, G. C., 17

Beza, Theodore, 8, 17, 145, 149, 151, 152, 156
Bolsec, Jerome, 130
Book of Concord, 145, 148, 153
Bora, Katherine von, 135
Borromeo, Carlo, 63–64
Bremen, 152
British East India Company, 104
Brunner, Emil, 211
Bucer, Martin, 7, 9, 10, 12, 17
Bugenhagen, Johannes, 29
Bullinger, Heinrich, 7, 8, 9, 10, 11, 12, 13, 17, 28, 45, 101, 149, 151, 152

Cajetan, Thomas de Vio, Cardinal, 29
Calckman, Jan Jansz., 111–12, 113, 117
Calvin, John, 5, 26, 60, 130, 132, 135–36, 142, 149, 151, 152, 156, 171–72, 193, 203, 205, 206, 217
    as commentator, 8, 11–12, 17, 30–31, 32, 109
    compared with Wittgenstein, 165–66, 182–88
    correspondence of, 9–10, 41–42, 44, 45
    evaluation of, xiii–xiv, 37, 38–43, 124
    influence of, 8–9, 194, 196, 198
    modern characterizations of the work of, 4–6, 16–17
    on baptism, 98–99
    on catechization, 103
    on Christology, 14

249

Index of Persons, Places, and Subjects

Calvin, John (*continued*)
  on church discipline, 55–56, 57, 62, 64
  on church polity, 49–52, 94
  on governmental authority, 191, 195–97
  on knowledge of God and self, 168–70, 175
  on language, 170–71
  on music in worship, 108–9, 115, 125
  on prayer, xiv, 19, 20–25, 28, 30–36, 49
  on predestination, 10–11, 15–16
  on the covenant, 13
  on the Fall, 39
  on the Lord's Supper, 100
  on the sacrament of penance, 62–63
  on women, xiv–xv, 37, 39–52, 70–72
  retiring personality of, 3
  sermons of, 20, 30, 31–32, 35, 45, 46, 71
  training of, 6–7
Calvinism/Calvinist church, xiii–xiv, xv, 38, 55, 57, 61, 62, 91, 92, 94, 95, 104, 106, 108, 114, 116, 119, 122, 125, 129, 131, 136, 139–52, 159–61, 194, 202, 205, 215
  See also Reformed Church
Calvinists, 5, 6, 46, 93, 118, 121, 125, 126–27, 131–37, 140, 146, 149, 150, 151, 152, 154, 155, 157, 158, 160
  See also Reformed
Cameron, John, 13
Candidius, Georgius, 95
Catechisms, 127, 133, 158
  See also Genevan Catechism; Heidelberg Catechism; Wittenberg Catechism
Catechization, 99–100
Catholics, 29, 42, 43, 44, 63, 72, 74, 75, 79, 81, 93, 98, 119, 126–32, 134–37, 146
  see also Roman Catholicism
Charles V, Emperor, 49
Chemnitz, Martin, 147
Christology, 14–15, 143, 145, 146, 156–57, 158
Chrysostom, John, 26, 27, 32, 33, 34
Church discipline, 53–66
Church fathers, 7, 136
Church office, 96–97, 106
Chytraeus, Daid, 144–45
Communion, 10, 53, 54, 59, 60, 74, 76, 84, 85, 86, 87, 100
  see also Lord's Supper
Confucianism, 210
Consensus Tigurinus, 149
Consistory, Reformed, 61, 64, 78, 82, 124, 137
  in Geneva, xv, 43, 44, 53, 54, 56–61, 63, 73, 98
  in Nîmes, xv, 74, 76–88
Coornhert, Dirck Volckertsz, 128, 134–35, 137
Coster, Franciscus, 130, 136
Covenant theology, 13–14
Cranmer, Thomas, 9
Cruciger, Caspar, 28, 141
Cruciger, Caspar the Younger, 152
Crypto-Calvinism, 143, 145, 147, 148, 150, 151, 160
  See also Philippism
Curaeus, Joachim, 150

Dancing, 80–81
Danckaerts, Sebastian, 95, 96, 104
Danzig, 143, 144, 147, 148, 150, 155
De Carpantier, Pieter, 96
De Ries, Hans, 135
De Sales, François, 72–73
De Witt, Emanuel, 118
Delft, 122, 136–37, 138
Doctrine of Scripture, 208, 211, 212–24
Dooyeweerd, Herman, 205–6
Dordt (Dordrecht), 123
  church order of the synod of, 95, 96–97, 99–100, 106
  synods of, 93, 96–97, 114, 123, 124, 129
Dress
  Ministers', 127
  women's, 29, 71–74, 77–88

Index of Persons, Places, and Subjects

Dubbeldrijk, Jacob, 103
Dutch Confession, 129, 133
  see also Belgic Confession
Dutch Republic, 126, 127, 136
  see also Netherlands
Dutch Revolt, 129, 130-31, 133

East Indies, xvi, 91, 92, 93, 94, 96, 101, 102, 104, 105, 106
Edinburgh, 65
Edwards, Jonathan, 202
Emden, 65
England, 61, 194
Erasmus, 15, 27-28, 30, 31, 32
European Union, 204

Fabritius, Jacob, 148
Fenner, Dudley, 13
Flacius Illyricus, Matthias, 142
Formula of Concord, 145, 146, 153
Fosdick, Harry Emerson, 217
France, 61, 73, 75, 82, 143, 146
Frankfurt, 146
Free will, 8, 15
  see also predestination
Fundamentalism, 203, 211, 215, 222, 223

Galilei, Galileo, 65
Geneva, 7, 32, 43, 44, 54, 57, 65, 73, 97-98, 100, 101-102, 105, 108, 113, 132, 161
  Ecclesiastical Ordinances of, 56, 95, 97, 98, 100, 101
Genevan Catechism, 36
Genevan Psalter, 115, 116, 117, 118, 124
Godparents, 98-99, 106
Gramsci, Antonio, 194
Groen van Prinster, Guillaume, 199-200
Grotius, Hugo, xv, 196

Hardenburg, Albert, 9, 152
Harnack, Adolf von, 216
Heidelberg Catechism, 14, 95, 96-97, 104, 106, 129, 133, 137
Heshusius, Tilemann, 143, 157
Heurnius, Justus, 95, 104

Hobbes, Thomas, 199
Hodge, A. A., 217
Hodge, Charles, 17, 217, 219
Holy Roman Empire, 139, 142, 146, 148, 150, 153, 159-60
Hopkins, Richard, 63
Hugh of St. Cher, 26, 27
Hyperius, Andreas, 8

Iconoclasm, 115, 125, 128, 159
Idolatry, 189, 190
Images, 166, 172, 175, 183, 186, 187, 189-90
Imperialism, Japanese, 209, 214
Inquisition, 132, 137
Institutes of the Christian Religion
  1536 edition, 19, 20-22, 23, 31, 32, 33, 36, 50
  1539 edition, 23, 31, 32, 33, 34, 36, 50
  1543 edition, 49, 50
  1559 edition or unspecified, 5, 7, 8, 11, 14, 15, 18, 20, 24-25, 31, 33, 35, 36, 50, 55, 109, 130, 169, 172, 185, 191, 195-96, 221
Interpretation vs. understanding, 174-75

Japan, 210, 211
Java, 91, 92, 93, 94, 97, 100, 102, 104, 105, 106
  see also Batavia
Jena, 142, 145
Jerome, 48
Jesuits, 140
Jewel, John, 7
Johann Casimir, Elector of the Palatinate, 146
Judex, Matthaeus, 142

Karlstadt, Andreas Bodenstein von, 142
Kim, Jaejoon, xv, 207-15, 217-23
Knox, John, 39, 45
Königsberg, 143, 145, 147, 150, 153
Korea, 207-12, 214-15, 222-23
Korean War, 209, 210, 214
Kuyper, Abraham, xv, 200-202, 205

Index of Persons, Places, and Subjects

Lambert, François, 48
Language, 167–68, 170–71, 180–83, 186, 187, 189
Languedoc, 73, 74, 79, 86, 87
Laski, Jan, 9, 10
League of Nations, 202
Leeuwarden, 137, 138
Lefèvre d'Étaples, Jacques, 48
Liberal theology, 209–11
"Lining-out", 116–17
Locke, John, 192, 193, 194
Lombard, Peter, 7
Lord's Supper, 9, 10, 99, 100, 103, 106, 144, 145, 146, 147, 149, 150, 151–52, 153, 154, 156–57, 160
  see also communion
Loyseleur de Villiers, Pierre, 146, 153, 154
Lust, 70–71
Luther, Martin, 7, 15, 29–30, 32, 36, 38, 39, 48, 51, 135, 141, 142, 144, 146, 151–52, 155, 156, 157, 158, 159, 160, 217
Lutheranism/Lutheran Church, 141, 143, 144, 146, 147, 158–59, 160
Lutherans, xv, 14, 28, 29, 31, 115, 145, 147, 149, 150, 152, 153, 154, 155, 156, 159, 160

Magdeburg Centuries, 142
Major, John, 7
Manicheism, 130
Marlorat, Augustin, 11
Marx, Karl, 193
Mayer, John, 11
Melanchthon, Philipp, 7, 8, 9, 10, 12, 28, 141, 142, 144, 145, 147, 148, 151–52, 160
Middle East, 206
Midwives, 98
Mihelade massacre, 75
Mind/body distinction, 166–68, 180–81
Miracles, 209
Missionaries, 211, 214, 215, 222–23
Mörlin, Joachim, 147
Molina, Luis, 11
Moller, Heinrich, 152

Moore's paradox, 178–80, 185
Münster, Sebastian, 12
Musculus, Wolfgang, 7, 8, 12, 13, 15–16
music, xv

Netherlands, xv, 61, 91, 92, 93, 95, 96, 101, 102, 105, 106, 108, 118, 143, 194, 199
  see also Dutch Republic
Neo-calvinism, 205
Neo-orthodoxy, 216, 221
Neutralists, xv, 127–28, 130–34, 136–37
Nicodemism, 128
Niebuhr, H. Richard, 205
Nietzsche, Friedrich, 192, 193
Nîmes, xv, 65, 73–79, 82–83, 86, 87, 88, 89, 90

Ockham, William, 7
Oecolampadius, Johannes, 142
Olevian, Caspar, 13, 17
Orange, 82
organ, xv, 107–14, 116, 118–25
  cases for, 110–11, 121–22
  construction, 120–21

Pacification of Ghent, 131
Park, Hyungryong, xv, 207–12, 214–23
Patriarchy, 38–40, 45–46, 48, 52
Peace of Augsburg, 139–40, 160
Pellican, Conrad, 29
Penance, sacrament of, 62–64
Perkins, William, 13
Peucer, Caspar, 152
Pezel, Christoph, 144, 145, 152
Philippism, 143, 145, 147, 160
  see also Crypto-Calvinism
Picture theory of propositions, 173–74, 181, 189
Pighius, Albert, 15
Poissy, Colloquy of, 156
Polanus von Polansdorf, Amandus, 7
Polemic, 128–30, 141, 148–49, 160
Polygamy, 40
Pomesania, 141, 143, 151
Poole, Matthew, 12
Portuguese, 91, 92, 93, 98, 99

Index of Persons, Places, and Subjects

Praetorius, Peter, 148
Prayers, 19, 20–36, 49
  in the mass, 26–27, 29
  private, 19–22, 25, 28–29, 32–33, 34–36
Predestination, xiii, 9, 10–11, 38, 106, 128, 134–35
  see also free will
Princeton Seminary, 210, 211, 217
Prussia, 141, 143, 147, 150
Psalms, 95, 101, 103, 105, 106, 107, 115, 116, 117, 120, 121, 122, 125
Purgatory, 135
Puritans, 28, 46

Reconciliation, 53–55, 57, 59–60, 62, 64–66
Reformed, 7, 8, 11, 12, 14, 15, 17, 28, 56, 60, 64, 72, 75, 80, 109, 112, 113, 115, 121, 123, 125, 127–38
Reformed Church, xiii,-xvi, 5, 6, 16, 54, 57, 59, 61, 73, 74, 76, 77, 78, 82, 85, 87, 88, 89, 90, 91–106, 116, 118, 119, 122, 124, 130, 146, 195
Revius, Jacobius, 121
Richard of St. Victor, 7
Ritschl, Albrecht, 216
Rivetus, Andreas, 7
Rollock, Robert, 13
Roman Catholicism/Roman Catholic Church, 35, 49, 55, 62, 64, 65, 70, 73, 91, 89, 98, 99, 107, 108, 109–10, 111, 113, 115, 139, 140, 203, 204
  see also Catholics
Rostock, 142
Rousseau, Jean-Jacques, 192, 193, 198
Ruyl, Albert, 104

Sacramentarians, 142, 143, 149, 155, 156, 157, 158, 159
Saenredam, Pieter, 118
Samland, 141, 143
Saxony, electoral, 143, 145, 147, 150, 151, 153, 155, 160
Schleiermacher, Friedrich, 17, 216
Schleitheim Confession, 203

Schmalkaldic War, 141, 144
Schoolteachers, 102–3, 116
Scotland, 61, 116, 117, 194
Scotus, John Duns, 7
Scultetus, Abraham, 7
Self-knowledge, 166–69, 176–78, 181
Sermons, 28, 58, 59, 81, 87, 97–98, 101, 102, 103, 104, 115–16, 127
Seroyen, Michael, 96
Servetus, Michael, xiii, 38, 41, 132
Slavery, 65
Spaniards, 91, 92, 93, 98, 99
Speuij, Henderick Joostensz, 123–24
Sphere sovereignty, 20–202
Suarez, Francisco, 11
Sumptuary laws, 73
Switzerland, 194
Synod, 153–54, 155
  Catholic, 110
  Reformed, 73–74, 75, 78, 79, 86, 87, 95, 122

Theophylactus, 26
Tocqueville, Alexis de, 194
Tolerance, religious, 132–33, 140, 197
Traheron, Bartholomew, 10
Trent, Council of, 63, 110

United East-India Company (VOC), 92, 94, 95, 96
United States, 194, 196, 202, 211
  Constitution of the, 204
Ursinus, Zacharias, 13, 17

Van Ceulen, Peter, 133, 134, 135
Van Hasel, Jan, 104
Venatorius, Thomas, 29
Verhoeven, Abraham, 129
Vermigli, Peter Martyr, 8, 9, 10, 11, 12, 15–16, 17, 48, 51
Vernacular, 103–5, 115, 140, 149
Violence, domestic, 41–43
Virgin birth, 209
Vincent of Lérins, 185
Visitation of the sick, 100–102, 106
Voetius, Gisbertus, 109, 112
Vrancx, Cornelis, 135

Index of Persons, Places, and Subjects

Warfield, B. B., 217
Weber, Max, xiv, 194
Wemeldinge, 107–8
Westminster Confession, 196
Westphal, Joachim, 156
Wigand, Johannes, xv, 141–60
William of Orange, 146
Wilson, Woodrow, 202
Wiltens, Caspar, 104, 105
Winterthur, 113
Wittenberg, 141, 143, 144, 145, 150, 152
Wittenberg Catechism, 144, 145
Wittgenstein, Ludwig, xv, 165–66, 172–78, 180–90
   Philosophical Investigations, 172, 173
   Tractatus Logico-Philosophicus, 173
Women
   as preachers, 47–48, 50–51
   images of, 70–71, 89

Zanchi, Jerome, 17
Zeeland, 107, 118
Zurich, 28
Zwingli, Ulrich, 13, 17, 28, 33, 142, 156
Zwinglians, 149, 151, 152

Index of Scripture

OLD TESTAMENT

Genesis
3	40, 157

Exodus
14:15	34

1 Samuel
1:13	20, 33–36

Job
19:25	214
26:7	217

Psalms
135:7	217

Ecclesiastes
1:7	217

Isaiah
40:22	217

Daniel
13	69

NEW TESTAMENT

John
1:12	39

Acts
2:42	28
5:29	43

Romans
13	200
13:4, 6	195

1 Corinthians
11:3–16	46
14	22
14:34–35	47
14:34–40	50

1 Thessalonians
5:17	21, 22, 24

1 Timothy
2:1–10	xiv, 19
2:1–2, 8	19, 20–33
2:9	29
2:13–15	45

James
5:16	20

1 Peter
3:1–6	43
3	52

www.ingramcontent.com/pod-product-compliance
Lightning Source LLC
Chambersburg PA
CBHW030822230426
43667CB00008B/1341